INTRODUCING QUALITATIVE METHODS provides a series of volumes which introduce qualitative research to the student and beginning researcher. The approach is interdisciplinary and inter-national. A distinctive feature of these volumes is the helpful student exercises.

One stream of the series provides texts on the key methodologies used in qualitative research. The other stream contains books on qualitative research for different disciplines or occupations. Both streams cover the basic literature in a clear and accessible style, but also cover the 'cutting edge' issues in the area.

SERIES EDITOR
David Silverman (Goldsmiths College)

TITLES IN SERIES

Doing Conversational Analysis
Paul ten Have

Focus Groups in Social Research
Michael Bloor, Jane Frankland, Michelle Thomas, Kate Robson

Using Foucault's Methods
Gavin Kendall and Gary Wickham

Qualitative Research Through Case Studies
Max Travers

The Quality of Qualitative Research
Clive Seale

Researching the Visual
Michael Emmison and Philip Smith

Qualitative Evaluation
Ian Shaw

Methods of critical Discourse Analysis
Ruth Wodak and Michael Meyer

Researching Life Stories and Family Histories
Robert L. Miller

Qualitative Research in Social Work
Ian Shaw and Nick Gould

Categories in Text and Talk
Georgia Lepper

Qualitative Research in Information System
Michael D. Myers and David Avison

Qualitative Research in Education
Peter Freebody

Documents in Social Research
Lindsay Prior

Using Documents in Social Research

Lindsay Prior

Los Angeles | London | New Delhi
Singapore | Washington DC

First published 2003
Reprinted 2009, 2010, 2011, 2012

SAGE Publications Ltd
1 Oliver's Yard
55 City Road
London EC1Y 1SP

SAGE Publications Inc.
2455 Teller Road
Thousand Oaks, California 91320

SAGE Publications India Pvt Ltd
B 1/I 1, Mohan Cooperative Industrial Area
Mathura Road
New Delhi 110 044

SAGE Publications Asia-Pacific Pte Ltd
3 Church Street
#10-04 Samsung Hub
Singapore 049483

British Library Cataloguing in Publication data

A catalogue record for this book is available
from the British Library

ISBN 978 0 7619 5746 1
    978 0 7619 5747 8 (pbk)

Library of Congress Control Number 2002104873

Typeset by C&M Digitals (P) Ltd., Chennai, India
Printed in Great Britain by the MPG Books Group

Contents

List of Figures

List of Tables

Preface

The basic idea for this book arose from my dealings with postgraduate social science students during the mid to late 1990s. Such students, when following, say, a taught postgraduate course, are commonly required to complete a dissertation in addition to other course work. The dissertation provides an opportunity for them to demonstrate their competence as social researchers, and to display their knowledge of some substantive topic or other. In most cases candidates are required to describe and openly reflect on aspects of methodology, as well as on specific techniques that they have adopted to execute their research study. That is, they are required to describe the strengths and weaknesses of the method or methods that they have used to approach the topic, and to justify their methodological stance – often by making reference to available published research.

When faced with a demand to execute a piece of empirically based research the preference of the research novice is usually to think in terms of speech and interview, rather than of writing and documentation. Thus, data collection procedures are very often considered in terms of what is called 'survey' research. Such a survey is commonly assumed to involve the design of a questionnaire and the administration of the instrument in an interpersonal interview. The consequent data analysis is usually undertaken by means of a statistical package. Should students opt for this route they have a wide range of well-designed and thoughtful textbooks and manuals to draw upon, and to refer to in the design and execution of their projects. Good manuals and textbooks are also readily available for those who wish to undertake qualitative research – of various genres – and, at any one time, there are numerous first-class texts on the market available to the novice field researcher and interviewer.

Although many texts suggest strategies for collecting and analysing qualitative data of various kinds, the emphasis is, as I have just hinted, more often than not on the spoken word. For those students who wish to centre their work on the study of documents – or, even, to take account of documents in their research work – there are very few pronouncements on methodology available. Indeed, the scarcity of manuals that deal with research into documents is, itself, a rather puzzling phenomenon. Perhaps, it has something to do with the fact that qualitative work, especially within the anthropological tradition, was developed in the course of examining life in non-literate societies – societies in which documents seemingly played a minor role. Perhaps, however, it is also to do with the fact that, as the modern French philosopher Jacques Derrida has persistently argued, in the metaphysics of the western world, speech has always been privileged over writing. What is written is therefore always to be recognized as secondary, marginal and subsidiary. Yet, despite such antipathy it is clearly the case that writing plays a major role in the

social life of modern societies. It is all the more surprising therefore that social
scientific texts outlining systematic and rigorous methods for dealing with the
written word are, more or less, absent. In fact, it seems fair to say that the world of
writing as a subject of study has been surrendered to the realm of the literary theorist. This is not, of course, the place to speculate on the reasons for such bias. My
aim is merely to alter – at least in small measure – the apparent imbalance.

As anyone who has used documents in social scientific research will know, their
study demands of researchers that they adopt a variety of strategies in both the
planning and the execution of the research. Indeed, almost any study of documentation will serve to contradict the notion that there is a hard and fast line to be drawn
between qualitative and quantitative research. Consequently, rigorous research work
on documents demands a passing knowledge, at least, of a wide variety of social
scientific strategies. Interestingly, many students tend to shy away from research into
documents on the grounds that whilst they might have a good topic for research,
they will not have a suitable 'method' to refer to in the appropriate section of their
dissertation. I hope that this book will go some considerable way to disabusing students of that notion. For, as I shall show, a document, and especially a document in
use, can be considered as a site or field of research in itself. The investigation of that
field requires the adoption of both appropriate research techniques and a suitable
methodological stance, and I hope to outline what those are in the chapters that
follow.

With both postgraduate and undergraduate students in mind, I have attempted
to do a number of things. First, to alert them to the wide range of possibilities
which exist in relation to conducting social scientific research involving documents. Secondly, to outline the various kinds of strategies and debates that need to
be considered whenever it is intended to integrate the study of documents into the
research programme. Thirdly and finally, to outline a distinctive (non-humanist)
position in terms of which documents may be approached and analysed, and
thereby provide a basis for that elusive 'methodological stance' that is said to be
wanting in the study of documents. Throughout the book my focus will be on the
analysis of documents in use. Because of my own particular background in the
sociology of health and illness, many (though not all) of the examples that I have
elected to examine and analyse are drawn from that specific area of interest.
I would sincerely hope, however, that readers from across the social sciences will
be able to see – without too much effort – the applicability of my analyses to documents relating to any and all fields of interest. In every one of the above respects,
of course, a book of this kind can do little more than provide an itinerary of
possibilities. Only the researcher can cover the routes in detail.

Before moving on to matters of substance, I would like to record some debts
that I have incurred in the writing of this book. As I have already suggested, postgraduate students have been to the forefront in offering ideas and insights. Two
such students in particular deserve mention. The first is Jon Banks, whose work on
chronic fatigue syndrome set me to thinking about the importance of documents
in clinical work. The second is Jon Brassey, for allowing me to call upon his network data – as used in Chapter 9 – and for forcing me to think about some of the

concepts that are commonly used in what is called actor – network theory. Colleagues that I have worked with in the medical school have also acted (usually unwittingly) as sources of inspiration. Of these I must record my debt to Jonathan Gray in genetics, Shoumi Deb in neuropsychiatry and Adrian Edwards and Roisin Pill in primary care. I am especially grateful to Dr Edwards for permission to reproduce Figure 8.2. My thanks are also due to Fiona Wood for gathering much of the data referred to in the section on risk and genetics in Chapter 4, as well as for reading the manuscript. Paul Morris provided the impetus for some of the work reported on in Chapter 8. In addition, a good deal of the research that I allude to throughout the book as 'mine' was only made possible by grant aid from a number of sources. I would list among the latter *The Joseph Rowntree Foundation*, for some of the work referred to in Chapters 3 and 5; *The National Assembly for Wales, Office of Research and Development* (WORD), for some of the work referred to in Chapters 4, 5, 8 and 9 (Grant references: R98/1/023; R00/1/050; SG98/134); and *The Economic and Social Research Council* (grant reference L218252046), for underpinning work reported on in Chapter 4. I should add that in all cases, the finance was for purposes other than writing a book, but the writing was nevertheless dependent on the doing. My thanks are due also to the publishers and to the series editor, David Silverman, for waiting patiently for the long-overdue manuscript. Finally, I should note that permission to reproduce Figure 1.1 was kindly given by the *Nuffield Foundation*.

Lindsay Prior
Kilbride, Co. Antrim

1

Basic Themes: Use, Production and Content

What is a document?

In 1917 Marcel Duchamp (1887–1968) adorned a common urinal bowl with the signature of 'R.Mutt', placed it on a pedestal, and presented it as a work of art to an exhibition arranged by the New York Society of Independent Artists. The selection committee rejected it as being 'by no definition a work of art' (de Duve, 1993) and consequently Duchamp resigned from the Society. The 'Fountain', as the artist had entitled the urinal, was just one of many 'ready-mades' that he presented to the world in the form of objets d'art. The latter included bank notes – signed by Duchamp himself – and a copy of the Mona Lisa defaced with a goatee beard and a moustache (a caricature much imitated in later years). The reasoning behind such apparently ridiculous acts and pre-sentations was to challenge the very notion of an independent and singular work of art. For where, Duchamp asked, was the boundary between art and non-art? Indeed, was it possible for anyone to produce works that were not works of art?

Although such questions may seem rather distant from the ones that concern us, they, in fact, go right to the heart of our problem. For it is no easier to specify what a document is than it is to specify, in abstraction, what is and what is not a work of art. Nevertheless, by dwelling on Duchamp's questions we can gain insight into some of the essentially social processes that are involved in acts of definition. Consider the following.

In 1995, the Royal Academy (London) presented an exhibition of works under the title 'Africa: The Art of a Continent'. Among other things, the display included a collection of gold weights from West African societies. Such gold weights took the form of animals and humans in various poses, and as anyone may see from the exhibition catalogue (Phillips, 1995), they are objects of considerable beauty. Yet, when the objects were originally made they were fashioned with rather immediate practical purposes in mind – the weighing of gold. This is not to exclude the possibility that they were also designed with a view to being aesthetically pleasing, but they were certainly not made by 'artists', nor were they made by people who would have considered themselves in any way as 'Africans'. Nevertheless, they were presented to us, in the late twentieth century, as examples of art made in somewhere called Africa during earlier centuries. So what is it that has turned gold weights into African art?

Any answer to such a question must surely lie in the web of activities that surround the objects rather than the things in themselves. That is to say, with the actions of museum curators, critics, and cataloguers who regard the objects as fit for display in an 'art gallery', and the viewers and visitors who are willing to pay to see such tools as very fine vehicles for the expression of human aesthetic sensibilities. This, not to mention the existence of the art gallery itself, which offers a platform or 'frame' for the exhibition of such works. The objects as such cannot contain the answer for they are here defined as weights and there defined as art. Nor would appeal to the original intentions of the creators of such objects settle the matter, for their involvement with things was (necessarily) ephemeral. Indeed, whichever way you look at it, the 'artness' of the art ain't in the things.

In attempting to define the nature of a document one is, of course, presented with very similar problems to those posed by the attempt to define art. Thus, paintings, tapesteries, monuments, diaries, shopping lists, stage plays, adverts, rail tickets, film, photographs, videos, engineering drawings, the content of human tissue archives and World Wide Web (WWW) pages can all stand as documents in one frame or another. Yet, as with the gold weights, their status as documents depends not so much on features intrinsic to their existence, nor on the intentions of their makers, but on factors and processes that lay beyond their boundaries. Indeed, we shall note throughout this book that if we are to get to grips with the nature of documents then we have to move away from a consideration of them as stable, static and pre-defined artefacts. Instead we must consider them in terms of fields, frames and networks of action. In fact, the status of things as 'documents' depends precisely on the ways in which such objects are integrated into fields of action, and documents can only be defined in terms of such fields.

Fields or networks of action, of course, engage and involve creators (agents, writers, publishers, publicists and so on), users (readers, or receivers) and settings. All three realms are implicated in the emergence of documentation. As for the producers and users, they invariably operate on the documents in terms of specific projects and systems of relevance (Schutz, 1962) – say, the study of fine art, or the study of archaeology, or the study of African history. Indeed, borrowing Schutzian terms, we might say that the social world is made up of the 'multiple realities' of its creators. And the objects that interest us are inevitably 'situated' in terms of such systems of reality. That is partly (but only partly) why one and the same physical artefact (gold weights) can appear in different guises (as African art here and as functional implements there).

For Schutz and other humanistic social scientists (such as, say, G.H. Mead, 1934) the most obvious point to enter into the study of fields of action is, of course, through the world of human agents. In fact, for most of anthropology and sociology 'the field' is commonly defined so as to focus specifically on the array of activities that human actors engage in – making gold weights, art, promises, families or whatever. Yet we should remain alert to the fact that there is far more in heaven and earth than human agency. Indeed, human agents only ever appear as one component of a field, for it is quite clear that human beings necessarily live and act and work in a field of things as well as of people. And there is forever a dynamic to 'the field' in such a way that things, such as documents and the information that they contain, can influence and structure human agents every bit as effectively as the agents influence the things. In that respect, there is always a ghost of the sorcerer's apprentice present in the existence of documents and other artefacts.[1] In this book, that dynamic will be central, and in many of the examples provided herein we shall be looking at and analysing the different ways in which documents function in action.

The emphasis that social scientists commonly place on human actors manifests itself most clearly in the attention that they give to what such actors say and think and believe and opine. And should we wish to study human actors in a rigorous social scientific manner there are many manuals available to instruct us as to how we should proceed with our research. Most of these texts focus on ways to capture and analyse speech and thought and behaviour. However, few social science research manuals concentrate on the written word and, more specifically, on documents that contain words. Indeed, when documents are put forward for consideration they are usually approached in terms of their content rather than their status as 'things'. That is, the focus is usually on the language contained in the document as a medium of thought and action. Yet it is quite clear that each and every document stands in a dual relation to fields of action. First, it enters the field as a receptacle (of instructions, commands, wishes, reports, etc.). Secondly, it enters the field as an agent in its own right. And as an agent a document is open to manipulation by others: as an ally, as a resource for further action, as an enemy to be destroyed, or suppressed. (We should not forget that people burn and ban texts as well as read them.) It is the examination of this dual role that forms the intellectual backbone of the current volume.

As I have just stated, in so far as documents have been dealt with as a resource for the social scientific researcher they have hitherto been considered almost exclusively as containers of content. Now, as we shall see, document content is important. We should not, however, let the presence of content bedazzle us to the exclusion of other qualities. For, above all, a document is a product. It is a work – often an expression of a technology. And, in the ordinary way of things, products are produced – they are produced by humankind in socially organized circumstances. Consequently, one set of questions that may quite justifiably be asked by the social scientific researcher concern the processes and circumstances in terms of which document 'X' has been manufactured. It is a theme that recurs throughout the book, and one that is specifically addressed in Chapter 2.

Naturally, documents are not just manufactured, they are consumed. Further, as with all tools, they are manipulated in organized settings for many different ends, and they also function in different ways – irrespective of human manipulations. In short, documents have effects. So a further route of analysis for the researcher is to ask questions about how documents function in specific circumstances. Questions of functioning will be dealt with mainly in Chapters 3–5. Naturally, the way in which a document functions is often affected by its content, but content is not always determinant. (Indeed, at the risk of jumping the starting gun, I should point out that the content of a document is never fixed and static, not least because documents have always to be read, and reading implies that the content of a document will be situated rather than fixed.) In any event, the analysis of content (dealt with in Chapters 6–8), production and use form three of the corner points around which this book is built.

Our focus, then, will be on the study of documents in their social setting – more specifically on how documents are manufactured and how they function rather than simply on what they contain.[2] Of the three dimensions, however, the most fundamental is undoubtedly that which relates to matters of function or use. For, by asking how things function we can move away from a strategy that views documents solely as resources to be scoured for evidence and data, and into the high plains of social scientific research.[3] In most social scientific work, of course, documents are placed at the margins of consideration. They are viewed as mere props for the real (human) action that takes place in and through talk and behaviour. Once one has read Derrida (1976), of course, one sees that such a position is entirely consistent with a long and inbred tradition within western philosophical thought. That tradition, according to Derrida, has persistently valued speech over writing and relegated the latter to a marginal and subsidiary role.[4] Writing thereby appears as an alienating force in the world. Yet, we are aware that the modern world is made through writing and documentation, a point that was emphasized, above all, in Max Weber's perceptive analysis of 'bureaucracy'.[5] It is somewhat telling that the lesson has seemingly been forgotten. Indeed, given the role and significance that written documentation plays in most human societies it is strange to note just how little attention has been paid to it by social researchers. In this book, of course, we can hopefully move documents 'up front', and seek to mark them out as a legitimate field of social scientific enquiry in their own right. How that is to be done will be evident in the remainder of the text. For now we shall merely concentrate on a few preliminaries: first, to consider how documents as a category of 'things' can encompass a wide variety of media; secondly, to assess the significance of text in documentation.[6] Both of these tasks can be achieved by consideration of a few early examples.

Diversity in documentation

We normally think of documents in somewhat uni-dimensional forms – as fixed and static texts. And it is certainly the case that in this book, text will figure prominently. Yet, documents are not coterminous with text. Indeed, it is clear that contemporary documents often express their contents – ideas, arguments, narratives or whatever – in multi-modal forms. That is to say documents frequently contain pictures, diagrams, emblems and the like, as well as words. What is more, an electronic document can also add sound to the multiple dimensions in terms of which it may ordinarily be composed. In some ways, therefore, it is quite artificial to restrict analysis of documents to text (see, for example, Bauer and Gaskell, 2000). Nevertheless, for ease of analysis, it often makes sense to focus on documents in which written words serve as the mastercode (Kress, et al., 1997), and that is what we shall do. One implication of this book, then, is that the analysis of the scribbled word can serve as a paradigm for the analysis of documents in their entirety. In order to emphasize the significance of non-textual features of documents, and to illustrate something of their potential complexity, however, it will prove useful to consider just a few examples of things that do not necessarily involve text, but which may, nevertheless, be used as documents. We will begin with a consideration of sculpture and paintings. I shall offer here an example of how such objects can function as documents in fields of activity, and suggest some ways in which they may be approached as a field for social scientific enquiry.

At the risk of seeming overly gloomy at such an early stage of the book, I would like to consider something about the representation of human attitudes towards death in the western world during the last couple of centuries – in particular with respect to sculpture. I am not so much thinking of the grand and rather eloquent sculptures that may be found in palaces, abbeys and cathedrals – though the tombs of the grand and powerful have much to tell. Instead I am thinking of everyday, routine, funerary sculpture as might be found in almost any of the older cemeteries in the English-speaking world. Such sculpture may, of course, vary from work that is nothing more than rough shaped stone, to rather elaborate representations of angels, cherubs and the like. Outside of the aforementioned cathedrals and abbeys, however, it is unlikely that one could find any form of 'modern' funerary sculpture dating before the mid point of the seventeenth century. It is an absence that can be used to reveal a great deal about western attitudes to death.

One might be tempted to think that the absence of personal gravestones dating from before the latter half of the seventeenth century is something to do with the ravages of time. Perhaps all of the older graveyards have been destroyed, lost or overgrown. It is not so. Very simply (and as far as the western world is concerned) it is only in the seventeenth century that resting places of ordinary men, women and children were individualized and marked. That is to say, before this period the lot of the common person at death was to be dispatched to the common funeral pit, whereas after the seventeenth century and in the world of Protestant Christianity at least, it came to be regarded as more appropriate for 'decent' people to rest in their own private (family) plot. The cemetery nearest to my own home, for example, has its earliest stones and slates dated to the 1720s, even though the area has been inhabited for some 4,000 years or more. (I should add that it is an area that fell beyond the borders of the western Roman Empire – an empire in which personal funerary monuments were extensively used.) In that respect, we have to suspect that the very presence of a cemetery with personalized graves 'documents' a long-term change in social sensibility and social behaviour in relation to death. I leave aside, of course, the fact that large numbers of poor and institutionalized people, as well as stillborn infants, were buried in common plots right into the twentieth century, not to mention the fact that by the first half of that century cremation, as well as burial, came to be regarded as a legitimate form of disposal.

Further, were we to look in more detail at our traditional cemetery we would undoubtedly note other changes. Thus, the sentiments and images on the gravestones would, for example, appear to have altered from one century to another. Skulls, crossbones and hourglasses would probably be present on the earlier seventeenth- and eighteenth-century stones, whilst urns, truncated pillars and angels on a human scale would appear on some of the later, nineteenth-century, graves. Equally, we might note that the seventeenth- and eighteenth-century inscriptions gave a quite heavy emphasis to the body, as in the frequent use of the inscription 'here lies the body of XYZ'. This would stand in contrast to nineteenth- and twentieth-century sentiments that are more likely to ignore, and therefore to elide, the body/soul distinction that earlier peoples took to be central. Again, as we move through the twentieth-century cemetery we would probably see a far greater uniformity of expression on gravestones – often noting standardized heights, spacing and sizes of the stones, fewer elaborate figures, and a marked secularization of expressed feeling and sentiment. In such ways we might consider the shape and size of cemeteries, their internal arrangements, the sentiments expressed on the stones, and the very stones themselves as documenting changes in both western attitudes towards death and features of common social relations, the growing individualization of the dead being, perhaps, the most powerful example of the latter. In fact, by examining the spatial organization of the cemetery we can see how the document acts back on its creators. It achieves this in part by emphasizing the significance of individuals and intimate (as opposed to, say, organizational) relationships, and by emphasizing the significance of a durable personal marker in the face of a transient life (Bauman, 1992). Indeed, it provides one means by which we modern humans attempt to colonize the future.

The use of a cemetery as a document to changing human sensibilities was most powerfully exercised by the French social historian of death, Phillipe Ariès, in his broad review of the Western tradition – *The Hour of Our Death* (1981). More limited and restricted overviews of the cemetery as a social document have been produced by others, such as for example Prior (1989) and Stannard (1977). Archaeologists, of course, use ancient cemeteries as documents in a routine manner and their work, more than any, gives credence to the observation that the arrangement of things – spaces, stones, boundaries – can serve as documents every bit as much as the inscription of text.

In a similar manner we can also use other (non-textual) forms of documentation to plot changing sentiments and behaviours of all kinds, including those at the moment of death. I shall cite only one example. In the Museé des Beaux Arts in Bayonne (south-west France), there is a painting by J.-E. Fragonnard (1732–1806) of the final moments of the Duc de Berry. The Duke is in his large and spacious bed – as one might expect – attended by a priest, but surrounded with a room full of people behaving rather as if the Duke's death were something of a spectacle. I cannot pretend to convey every detail of the artist's eye to you as a reader. However, it is clear that whatever was going on in the Duke's chamber, the assembled collection of worthies suggests to us the fact that, during the late eighteenth century, death was not to be considered a lonely and isolated business. Instead, it appears as a social and religious event of considerable importance – perhaps, even, a communal event. And this theme of a public death is represented many times over in many different paintings of both lesser and greater figures during the seventeenth, eighteenth and nineteenth centuries. (In his *Images of Man and Death* (1985), Ariès provides a selection of similar images relating to European and American people of all social stations.) Only in the twentieth century does death truly appear as a private and isolated affair, and only then are dying people secreted away in hospital wards and hospices to die in seclusion. This move from the public to the private sphere – a process sometimes referred to as the sequestration of death (Seale, 1998; Giddens, 1991) – is, of course, only one of many changes that is represented in European and American painting. It is also only one of thousands of ways in which paintings and visual images of all kinds might be called upon as documentary evidence of fundamental alterations in our sensibilities to that infinite array of human activity that we call 'social'. In this respect we might say that paintings, gravestones, cemeteries, wills and endless other items can often be used to reveal something of the different ways in terms of which death and dying have been 'performed'.[7]

Naturally, it is possible to study representations of death and dying by using written records alone. That is, by the use of documents in the narrow sense of the term. Thus Richard Cobb (1978), for example, trawled through the dossiers of those who died violent deaths in Thermidorian (revolutionary) Paris by examining in considerable detail the records of the Basse-Geole de la Seine. The results of his work throw light on the minute detail of the everyday lives of ordinary Parisians (such as features of dress and occupation), as well as on the detail of the nature of suicide and homicide in Paris between 1795 and 1801. In fact, as Cobb's interest in the wardrobes of his suicides suggests, we should not become beguiled by text. People think with things as well as words, and, very often, the arrangement of things is as significant as the arrangement of words. Human activity finds expression through many media and the shape of things can be regarded as every bit as important as the flow of text. Just to emphasize that point, I shall end this section by looking at how architectural plans (which report on the arrangement of spaces) can be appropriated as documents in a social scientific frame.

By providing visible statements about the ways in which constructed spaces are to be divided and sub-divided, architectural plans inevitably express elements of the discourses in terms of which they are conceived. A society that lived in circular domestic spaces, for example, is more than likely to have different ideas about the 'place' of things and people than a society that lives in square or rectangular spaces (Bourdieu, 1977). And this notion that a study of the manner in which we organize space can reveal basic rules about how daily living is to be managed and arranged can be carried over to the study of more detailed areas of social life. The arrangements of desks in a classroom, the arrangement of classrooms in a school, the positioning of a school, or prison, or psychiatric hospital, or a factory can all be used to reveal evidence about how a society orders social relationships. In some previous work I described how the changing nature of hospital plans can be used to reveal changes in such things as our attitudes and behaviour to mental illness, infectious diseases and infancy (Prior, 1988; 1992). It would be inappropriate for me to review the details of the arguments here. Instead I shall offer you just one plan of a hospital ward (Figure 1.1). It is a plan for a children's ward *circa* 1963. As I have stated elsewhere (Prior, 1992), the very development of hospital wards for children serves to mark out, in large part, the image of childhood as a separate stage of development in western society. The plan in Figure 1.1, however, displays interesting developments over and above those that are apparent in hospital plans that emerged between 1880 and the 1950s. In particular, we may note how rooms have been designed to incorporate mothers as well as children – in homage to the significance of the maternal bond that had been much discussed in post-war 'child psychology'. The open area for play and lessons is also remarkable. In terms of play, it is notable for the way in which such activity has been moved in an open space – to facilitate good observation by the nursing staff. In terms of lessons it is notable as early recognition of the sick child's 'need' for a learning environment. The generally open design of the ward is also intentional, and reflects increasing professional concern with surveillance of children in hospital. (The apotheosis of this concern appears in the late twentieth-century

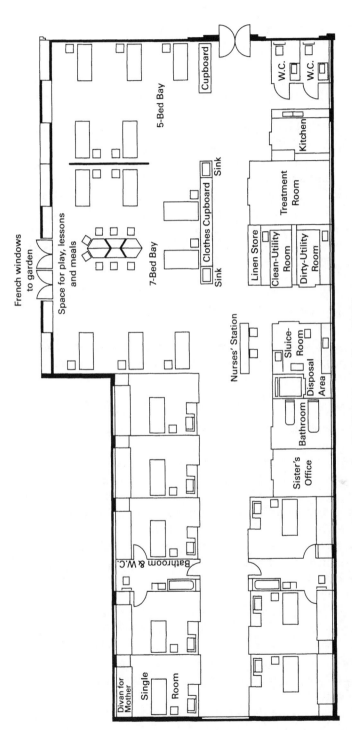

FIGURE 1.1 Spatial organization as documentation (Nuffield Foundation, 1963)

use of two-way mirrors through which parents could be secretly observed interacting with their offspring.) Beyond that the general design of the ward reflects a whole series of ideas about the nature of childhood health and illness and the role of social contact in sickness.

Architectural plans and paintings, then, offer us clear examples of documents in which text plays only a minor role, whilst the cemetery offers us a clear example of a document that represents and reflects through a mixed array of physical and cultural dimensions. Their status as documents (rather than, say, as art) is, of course, dependent on the frame in terms of which they are 'situated', and henceforth appropriated. In our case, that frame has been a social scientific one. As we shall note shortly, social scientific documents can themselves be appropriated, in turn, by other actors and agents and metamorphosed into legal, political or religious documents, or they may be used for the establishment of personal identity or to create new facts and new things. Before we consider such issues, however, it would be as well for us to look at how documents come into the world in the first place. That is, to examine how they are created.

Documents: production and function

In the Gospel of Saint John (I, i) we encounter a truly majestic claim, namely that, 'In the beginning was the word.' The German author Goethe was later to play with this phrase in the first part of his *Faust*. Goethe's Faust is one of those figures that has little compunction in forming a contract with the Devil in order to achieve his worldly ends, and so it is not perhaps surprising that he inverts the Gospel claim so as to assert that, 'In the beginning was the deed.' (See von Goethe, 1986.)

The two sentences point to a rather beguiling opposition between word and deed that, fortunately, we need only approach in a social scientific manner. In that light it seems safe to assert that documents are created in the context of socially organized projects in such a way that word and deed belong together. One plausible line of social research that remains open to all investigators, therefore, is to follow a document through its social trajectory – to examine how it is manufactured or produced in specific contexts of thought and deed. Naturally, the production of documents is a complex business, and, in practice, it is often bound up with processes of consumption – recall that the aforementioned gold weights needed museum visitors and curators as well as craftsmen to turn them into art. For the sake of clarity, however, we will maintain, in this chapter, an analytical division between the production and the consumption of documents, always keeping in mind that it is the active, dynamic assimilation of 'things' into fields of action that is the key to understanding the process of fabrication.

Possibly, the first point that needs to be made is that the birth and life of documents rests on the foundations of a collective rather than individual action. In western societies, of course, we are usually keen to think in terms of individual authors as the makers of documents. And individual authors are, indeed, important figures, but as I will illustrate with the following examples, the author as subject is only one side of a many-sided phenomenon. Indeed, following Foucault (1979), we are far better off thinking in terms of an 'author-function', rather than an author as subject. That is to say, to consider the concept of an author as a tool that can be recruited so as to bypass a consideration of complex social referents. (Indeed in modern scientific and medical journals the concept of authorship is being forsaken in favour of the concept of 'contributor' – see, for example, Smith, 1997a; 1997b). To illustrate the broader issues, however, let us consider some famous texts in this light. I will begin with a look at Homer's *The Odyssey*.

The Odyssey gets an early mention in Aristotle's *Poetics* (fourth century BCE). Aristotle summed up the epic poem of about 12,000 lines in three or four sentences.

> A certain man has been abroad for many years; he is alone and the god Poseidon keeps a hostile eye on him. At home the situation is that suitors for his wife's hand are draining his resources and plotting to kill his son. Then, after suffering storm and shipwreck, he comes home, makes himself known, attacks the suitors: he survives and they are destroyed. (Aristotle, 1995: 17)

The Odyssey, then, is a narrative. The poem itself is estimated to be about 2,700 years old. Whatever its age, it is a masterful piece of literature. As a printed text, however, it can be traced back only to 1488. Before that date it must have existed merely as a handwritten document – presumably contained, at one stage, on papyrus rolls. What is interesting from our (social scientific) viewpoint is that the poem as it presently exists is still attributed to a single poet called Homer – who, it is claimed, wrote it. This is somewhat odd, because, for various reasons, it is clear that the Odyssey epic was created in an oral rather than a literary tradition. For example, not one person in the story is described as being able to read or write. Moreover, in the peasant society of the day, poetry was something more likely to be 'performed' than written (Knox, 1996). Yet, whether it was written or spoken, it certainly seems plausible to argue that the poem was both created and embellished over the 27 centuries by a large number of people – speakers/performers, listeners, scribes, editors, publishers, translators. For example, whoever the originator of the poem may have been, he, she or they produced the narrative and the plot of the Odyssey with an audience in mind – a plot that only resolves itself in the final moments of the text. Indeed, the narrative would have been consciously designed to resonate with audience expectations and experience, and as such one might say that the audience would have had a role in authorship. Thus, we can assume that over 2,000 years performers of the epic would have found bits of the narrative that 'worked' better than others, and that too would have impacted on the poem. In modern times, translators of the epic will have imposed their rhetorical style on the poem, and so forth. In other words, it is not unreasonable to suggest that it is a collective rather than an individual genius that is involved in the poem's rather lengthy production. (Indeed, the eighteenth-century Neapolitan philosopher Giambattista Vico considered the works of Homer to be a product of the Greek people rather than of any individual within the culture.) Naturally, such collective acts have, at different times, been guided by various kinds of rules – concerning the structure of the text, the nature of reading, the art of translation and so on (see Knox, 1990). For example, there were clearly rules that determined the style and flow of the ancient Greek composition, one of which involved the use of the hexameter (six metrical units). There were also rules governing the various epithets that could be attached to people and things (the dawn of Odysseus is always 'rosy fingered', for example, and clouds always 'scud' across the sky). Above and beyond that, the poem expresses rules – about such things as honour, fidelity, justice, and the relationships between gods and mortals – and in that sense reveals to us significant aspects of everyday life in the ancient world (Finley, 1977).

What is of interest here is that the impact of these clear traces of collective action are routinely effaced and then subsumed under the author-function – so that the 'author' functions as the creator. Naturally, it is not for us to decide on the historical issues concerning *The Odyssey* one way or another. Our interest in the example is almost entirely in the fact that western literary tradition rests on the illusion of an identifiable author as a unifying force for textual materials. And we seem to hold to the belief even when we are aware that the existence of a text depends on broad social and organizational processes of production, rather than simple acts of personal genius and inspiration. In this light, it is useful to consider (though only briefly) one of the key texts of twentieth-century linguistics – Saussure's *Course on General Linguistics*. The latter was published after Saussure's death in 1915 (see Saussure, 1983), and was compiled in large part from the lecture notes of his students. Although the text is referred to as Saussure's and quoted and cited as such, there is a sense in which the 'author-subject' had relatively little to do with the final production. (Indeed, the full reference for the book, provided in our bibliography, is of some interest in this light.) And this use of the author-subject (that is, a named person) to endow a sense of unity and order to a document is common to most (though not all) forms of written and published discourse.[8] In fact it is of interest to note which kinds of documents are normally expected to be associated with identifiable author-subjects (books, plays, poems, scientific papers), and which do not (acts of legislation, committee reports, theatre tickets, tax forms, modern maps, train tickets and so on). In a parallel manner it is of interest to note which kinds of documents require signatures and which do not. (It is also instructive to ask what a signature supposedly adds to a document – a rather interesting question taken up by Derrida (1977) and some of his critics.)

What our ancient Greek Odyssey tells us, then, is that documents are essentially social products. They are constructed in accordance with rules, they express a structure, they are nestled within a specific discourse,[9] and their presence in the world depends on collective, organized, action. The same lessons are evident in the study of almost any text, but let us take yet another notable document, merely to emphasize the issues.

The Bible is a text that reports on the word of God, and without questioning the truth of that claim in any way, we can still recognize it as a text that has been mediated in different ways through human intervention and production. For example, in the contemporary world there are many different English translations of The Bible. There is a so-called authorized or King James Bible (1611), an American Revised Standard Version (1952), a Modern English Version (1966), a New International Version (1972), and many others. Each text differs, one from the other, subtly but noticeably in the words and emphases that it contains, as well as in the order of the various books and verses. Differences of order and content are perhaps not surprising since all versions are dependent on translations of Hebrew and Greek texts – texts and fragments of text that were later translated into Latin and used as the Vulgate or common version of the Bible. English language versions, of course, emerge out of a specific Protestant tradition. And among the earliest and most beautiful of English language Bibles was that produced by Tyndale during the 1530s. It was his text that formed the basis for the later King James (1611) Version. And it is from Tyndale's work that we have borrowed many of the best-known English phrases – 'the salt of the earth', 'the powers that be', 'eat, drink and be merry', and 'a law unto themselves' are all Tyndale's phrases (Daniell, 1989). The acceptability and convenience of such phrases is of course a direct product of the translator's art. They are also phrases to which few, if any, would take exception, but taken in its entirety, Tyndale's Bible was objected to – so much so that he was strangled and burned to death for having produced it.

Clearly, were we to become interested in the fine detail of biblical language, and concerned with nuances of meaning and matters of emphases, we would need to take the history of the relevant production and translation processes into account. In particular, we would need to examine the various twists and turns by means of which a biblical text and the manner of its division into chapters and verse came into our hands. In so doing we would come to recognize the fact that documents not only are produced in accordance with rule-governed procedures, but always exist as resources in schemes of action. They both express and represent a set of discursive practices. As such they can be recruited as allies in various forms of social, political and cultural struggle. Indeed, we know that people frequently mobilize and use the detail within documents for social, political and, as in our example, religious purposes and projects. In fact, Tyndale was murdered presumably because his translation expressed and represented a discourse of Protestant individualism at a time when the established authorities felt it necessary to assert the power of the one true church and its monopoly on biblical exegesis. After his death, opponents of the 'one true church' recruited, mobilized and assembled both Tyndale and his Bible into a project relating to what we vaguely call the Protestant Reformation. Note that the (Tyndale) Bible, in this sense, is cast into the early modern world as an actor in its own right and was therefore also liable to destruction and suppression at the behest of the authorities.

This Frankenstein-like quality of documents,[10] that is the capacity of humanly created artefacts to serve as active agents and counter-agents in fields of social action, is not to be underestimated. Indeed, even writing – as script – can serve as an agent. Thus, in many cultures, we know that specific forms of script have been monopolized by a socio-political elite so as to underpin particular bases of power and exploitation, and to exclude outsiders such as peasants and foreigners from making an impact on elite cultures. Goody (1968) provides many examples of such practices, and indicates how various social strata have (in the past) recruited script as a powerful political ally, the practices of the Chinese literati being the most telling of these.

This last point serves to emphasize how a study of the use of documents can be as telling as a study of content. In the next example, we can see how matters of content have often become central solely because of the use to which the document can be put. Though just to keep our eyes on the ball, I should emphasize that the value of the example lies in the issue of production rather than of use.

Questions concerning the authenticity of a document often arise in the research arena. Such questions are, of course, essential – and they often shed direct light on important issues concerning the reliability of text as evidence. Indeed, the few studies that have been devoted to the use of documents in social scientific research (see, for example, Scott, 1990) have often concentrated on issues of authenticity to the exclusion of issues of use and function. It is perhaps yet another reflection of the general emphasis that is given to document content rather than use. Yet, establishing authenticity is far from being the only task of the social scientific researcher. Equally as important are questions about how documents are produced and recruited – and the recruitment of documents, as with the recruitment of soldiers, is not always dependent on a fitness test. In this vein a useful example to call upon involves *Anne Frank's Diary*.

During the 1980s, following a series of ill-founded and crude objections relating to the authenticity of the diary, the latter was subjected to extensive forensic examination by the State Forensic Science Laboratory in the Netherlands (Barnouw and Van Der Stroom, 1989). The use of a forensic platform enabled investigators to concentrate, in the main, on such items as the glue, the ink, the paper, and especially the handwriting contained within the documents. All of these confirmed the authenticity of the time and place in terms of which the diary was produced (Amsterdam, 1942–4), together with the approximate age of the writer (mid teens). A few other investigations focused on the routes by means of which the diary came into public view, and in tracing such routes we can see how Anne's diary did in fact undergo a number of important transformations. For example, her father, Otto, originally typed up her handwritten documents and, in the process, exercised a degree of editorial discretion. Indeed, he extracted only what he considered to be the 'essential' detail from her diary – omitting painful observations – and he also altered spellings and punctuation. These difficulties were accentuated by the fact that Anne herself wrote two versions of her 'diary' and, in addition, a further text entitled 'Tales from the Secret Annex'. The earliest English language (1952) edition is a composite of all three sources. Indeed, it is possible to see that there are many Anne Frank diaries – and it was reported during 1998 that some new pages of the diary had been discovered. (Note that a 'diary' – as with a 'poem' or a 'record' – is always a 'situated' product and not something that can be defined according to its intrinsic features.)

Details of the kind relating to the history of Anne's diary are essential and important because, within the rhetoric of social scientific and academic discourse in general, the establishment of a document's authenticity is, as we pointed out above, central to its acceptability as evidence. That is why it is vital that the conditions under which a given document has been produced are made known and made publicly available. In this particular case these have been made evidently transparent. Yet, we have also to ask why anyone would question the authenticity of a teenage girl's 'diary'. Challenges to authenticity, of course, are normally associated with highly valued or politically charged documents. Indeed, as was pointed out above, it is the position that a document holds in a network or web of activity that contains the key to its use and reception. Thus few people would be interested in investigating the precise history of George and Weedon Grossmith's *The Diary of a Nobody* (1999, first published 1892) – an intensely amusing, fictional account of a City of London clerk's daily life, very much in the 'got up, had breakfast, went to work', genre. This is essentially because it is a diary without social and political consequence (though its supposed author, Mr Pooter, would be devastated to read that judgement). *Anne Frank's Diary*, on the other hand, serves as both a witness to and an advert for the wide variability that exists in the application of human moral codes. As an advert for the darker side of such morality, it can and does play a powerful and influential role – certainly influential enough for right-wing parties to seek to suppress it or to denigrate it.

The Bible, *The Odyssey* and *Anne Frank's Diary* each exhibit elements of collective action. The contemporary forms of all three documents emanate from many different sources and the analysis of the routes and actions by means of which the documents come into the world requires close investigation. As we shall see in Chapter 2, the study of the ways in which documents are produced can constitute a topic for social scientific study in itself. As well as illustrating themes such as those mentioned above, such study can also highlight essential features of social action and interaction in general. Above all, when we begin to look at the manner in which, say, official documents (reports, statistical tables and so on) are manufactured, we will also come to recognize the rule-driven procedure that lies behind the production process. It is through the routine application and interpretation of such rules that facts about society and the world in general come to be known and made. Normally, of course, we prefer to gloss over issues relating to the genealogy and manufacture of documents and simply use them as resources for further study and research. Yet, the above examples serve to illustrate just how a study of the ways in which documents are produced (and how they are used or consumed) in socially organized circumstances is every bit as important as a study of content. Naturally, in the empirical world all three features of documentation are interlinked. Indeed, before we move on to consider matters of content we need to consider issues of use and function a little further, and that is the aim of the following section.

Writers and readers – a dynamic relationship

The consumption of documents is as important as their production, though in terms of the dynamic that is created within fields of action the producer/consumer distinction is of heuristic use only. So before we turn to consider the consumption of documents proper, it may be as well to emphasize how those who use and consume documents are not merely passive actors in the communication process, but also active in the production process itself.

The critical role of the consumer as an active agent is, perhaps, most clearly seen in the contemporary world where computerized documents are common. For as we know from our own experience, a reader of a web page, or any screen-based document, can these days easily cut, paste, edit and re-edit text to suit the user's purpose. Yet, even though cutting and pasting has become a visible, traceable process in the electronic world, we should be aware that every reader in every age has cut and edited documents to suit a personal agenda. It is just that the process was previously invisible and non-traceable. Skipping chapters and pages is, after all, a well-established technique for getting from page 1 to page *n*. Indeed, and as de Certeau (1984: xxi) has argued, 'the act of reading has … all the characteristics of a silent production'. More importantly, perhaps, the social scientific researcher needs to be aware that a reader can enter into the creative/productive process long before he or she opens a document. Indeed, the reader can influence a writer at the exact moment when the text is first being inscribed on paper. Consider the following examples.

In a not so distant world, the written letter was a frequently used form of communication. Indeed, it was an essential means of communication both within countries and between countries. So, in the history of the USA, for example, the letter has come to assume a very special role, especially those letters that European emigrants to the USA wrote to their families in the 'old country'. In fact, and as we shall see, they have subsequently formed an important resource for social scientific study. Naturally, and in the everyday run of things, such letters contain details of routine and mundane events, and in that sense provide unremarkable authors' accounts of the writers' activities, wishes, desires and plans. Yet, what is important from our current viewpoint is that such letters were usually written with the interest of readers in mind. In other words, authors had images of what the readers would want to hear about, and what might hold their attention. So, the absent reader sitting in Europe was, in such ways, present in the USA when the letters were first scribbled down, and was able to fashion the letter according to his or her needs and wishes.

The exact same point can be made with respect to other kinds of document. Take, for instance, a diary or autobiography. Now every personal document of that kind is written with some reader or audience in mind. Some diarists, of course, write as though an audience is of no significance. That is, as if the document can be detached from the social fields in which it is created and lodged. *The Diary of Samuel Pepys* (see the 1970 edition) offers one example of the style, for Pepys was always keen to give the impression that his accounts were produced by the day and off the cuff without thought to a reader. Yet, we have good reason to suspect that he consciously fashioned and shaped his diary for future public consumption – and thus for reader/audience approval. We can, of course, only guess at how Pepys saw his receivers. In the case of John Stuart Mill (1989), on the other hand, he tells us on the first page the kind of reader that he has written his *Autobiography* for, and it is easy to see how his image of the receiver shapes the ensuing document. These routes whereby the reader interpolates a presence into the writer's world are, in fact, numerous, and occur across the entire range of documentary material. Thus, in verbatim accounts of interviews and interrogations we see how the questioner can determine the shape of an author-subject's narrative by posing key questions – questions that stimulate the unfurling of the narrative in specific directions. Similarly, in the posed photograph we see a product that has been negotiated between both the creator and the sitter such that it would be difficult to determine who, exactly, the author-subject of the photograph might be. Such acts of interpolation of 'readers' into the world of the author are, however, often seen at their best when considering creative works of a musical or artistic nature. So let us consider yet a further example.

In the world in which the composer Dmitri Shostakovich (1906–75) operated, the function of art was seen in terms of the glorification of the Soviet Union, the Proletariat, the 'Party' and 'socialism'. Music that glorified individuals and individualism was largely frowned upon. That is, unless the individual was someone of the status of a Comrade Stalin – a man who stood as the living embodiment of the Proletariat, the Party and the Soviet Union. When Shostakovich composed his music, therefore, he was obliged to take such constraining factors into account (Fay, 2000). Often, he dealt with the tensions that arose between his creative capacities and the demands of the Party by writing his music in different intellectual keys. That is to say, he would write a piece of music that supposedly bolstered the principles of communist ideology whilst, at the same time, interpolating himself into the composition. One example of this is evident in his String Quartet Number 8 (Opus 110). It is a thoroughly depressing piece of music. It was composed in 1960 just after Shostakovich had visited Dresden. At that stage, Dresden still exhibited the wreckage of war and the results of the carpet bombing to which the city had been subjected by the Royal Air Force. During the same year Shostakovich had agreed, under pressure, to become a member of the Communist Party of the Soviet Union. He dedicated Opus 110 to the 'victims of fascism and war'. This inscription was taken by the Communist Party's apparatchiks as approval for Soviet ideology and the Dresden connection was obviously a welcome one. Interestingly, at the heart of the quartet is a four-note motif. It is a motif derived from Shostakovich's own name (DSCH, or what we know as D, E flat, C, B). It is a trick that Shostakovich had used in some of his other works – to put himself, rather than the Party, at the core of his own music. And there are also other devices and references that DSCH used in Opus 110 that were somewhat ambiguous. For example, in the last movement there is a repetition of some very aggressive chords that sound very much like three dark beats, evidently representing falling bombs. Much later, however, Shostakovich was to admit that he derived the chords from the sounds made when the Soviet secret police pounded apartment doors in the midst of night.

So what we have in Opus 110 is a piece of music made with the Party audience uppermost in mind, whilst the author, and his ideas, appear only by means of subterfuge. In that sense we might say that the Party (and the Soviet secret police) were as influential as Shostakovich was in creating the string quartet. That, perhaps, is to go too far, but we can legitimately claim that audiences (including those comprising secret police) forever interpolate their presence into texts – if for no other reason than texts (documents) always have readers. And this despite the fact that such acts of construction are inherently unstable and tend to alter in line with changing hierarchies of relevance and socio-political context.

Naturally, the most important reader of a musical (or of a theatrical) text is the performer him- or herself. And it is in the gap that exists between the written notation on the page and performance of music on the stage that allows us to sit through the 'same' concert (or stage play) many times without any sense of weary repetition. Performance reinvents the notation (text). This is as true of a Mozart opera or a Beethoven symphony as it is of, say, a rendition of Frank Sinatra's 'My Way'. And given such considerations, we may be tempted to question the very primacy of authors over readers/performers. This is just what the literary critic Roland Barthes (1915–80) did – though mainly with respect to issues of meaning and interpretation. Thus in an article entitled 'Death of the author' (1977), Barthes argued that a text's unity lies not in its origin, 'but in its destination', that is to say, with the reader. So only the reader can provide a sense of unity to a text and it is, consequently, on readers rather than writers that we ought to concentrate. (A similar argument was advanced in S/Z (Barthes, 1990). We need only quarrel with Barthes to the extent that he considers 'reading' as an inner, subjective and personal act, whereas in this book we shall consider reading as performance. The task of the social researcher is therefore to study how readers use and consume text and notation in everyday life (routine performance). To this end, let us consider a final example.

During the closing years of the nineteenth century, when ethnographic research was in the early years of development, a number of English anthropologists studied family trees in the Torres Straits society of the southern Pacific. A.C. Haddon and W.H.R. Rivers had travelled to the Torres Straits in 1888, and they asserted an interest in Torres Straits society as an entirety. They consequently examined family life, economic and political activity, artistic life, religion and so on, as well as taking an interest in the physiology and psychology of the inhabitants (Haddon, 1904). Among other things that they 'recorded' were the family links of the people being studied. Such ways of recording human relationships were quite foreign to the Torres Straits inhabitants and, in retrospect, it seems as if the locals failed to be entirely open with the anthropologists – or perhaps the anthropologists failed to ask the right kinds of questions and thereby ended up with a limited narrative. The misunderstanding arose in relation to the issue of adoption, which is relatively common in the society in question. Thus, in Murray Island, for example, adults can adopt children without any apparent formal declaration. People can also have more than one name, and can often change names, seemingly at will. Haddon was unable to grasp the significance of these points and despite the fact that he lived on Murray Island for some time, he clearly misunderstood the nature of adoption and inheritance patterns. Such misinterpretation is in itself rather interesting not least because it calls into question the extent to which outsiders can gain knowledge of insider procedures, even when they adopt ethnographic methods. More appropriate to our concerns, however, is the fact that although Haddon's genealogies were developed in an anthropological project and from an academic platform of Cambridge University, Torres Straits inhabitants currently use them for quite different purposes – that is, to establish rights to property. In fact, Haddon's genealogies are used to press land claims.

What the Torres Straits example illustrates, then, is that the nature of the consumption process can alter the entire nature of the document. Thus the Cambridge University Reports were intended to be consumed as objective scientific (anthropological) accounts of family and kinship in an exotic (non-western) society. The detail of the family trees, for example, is meant to illustrate patterns of consanguinity and affinity – as expressed through a discourse of scientific anthropology. Later researchers might have used such reports as data for their theories of kinship. Yet the contemporary inhabitants are using the very same documents in an entirely different context and presenting and lodging them in different kinds of platforms. That is to say, they are lodging them as evidence in courts of law concerned with the definition of property rights. In that field of action, users (or consumers) have effectively turned the anthropological documents into legal documents.

One further point: whatever the shortcomings of the anthropological investigations it is at least clear that drawing up a genealogy is not simply a matter of inscribing names on paper. It is something that has implications for social action – action that cannot always be foreseen by the authors. In an entirely different context, Berg (1996) has referred to this kind of implication as 'action at a distance' – the process whereby making inscriptions in one setting necessarily leads to something being done in another setting. In this respect one might view the act of drawing up a will, or completing a marriage certificate, as standing in exactly the same kind of relationship to legal action as the completion of a Torres Straits genealogy by an anthropologist. More importantly, perhaps, we can begin to see, once again, how the documents themselves become 'actors' in the social process. That is to say, documents can enter into systems of action in their own right, and are not just passive items operated upon by human agents. Their very existence, in that sense, can influence the actions of human beings. It is in this respect that one is drawn, yet again, to consider the fable of the sorcerer's apprentice, which certainly resonates with the Torres Straits genealogies. Other examples abound. Indeed, there are circumstances in which a document may be said to be more pertinent to action than a person. This is evidently so in the case of documents of identification, such as passports and birth certificates, where it is possession of the relevant document that can trigger a series of actions – such as admittance into a country or an organisation (whilst the corporeality of the person can count for little in the absence of the documentary substance). It is a point that echoes throughout Nikolai Gogol's *Dead Souls* (see Gogol, 1996), a story constructed around the theme of a man who bought the names of dead serfs (dead souls) from their landowners so that the landowners would not be liable to taxation – a taxation that was levelled on the 'books' rather than the bodies. And that is only one set of circumstances in which one becomes aware of the role of the document as actor. In that light it is, as Atkinson and Coffey (1997) have argued, rather puzzling as to why researchers continue to produce accounts of complex, literate, social worlds 'as if they were entirely without writing'.

Documents and their content

So far I have highlighted aspects of the context in which documents are produced and consumed. Both the framework of consumption and that of production form an important area for study in the social sciences. Such a focus on context, however, leaves us at risk of ignoring content. As I have stated before, most of the available methods texts that deal with research into documents have focused on content almost exclusively. In this section I intend to outline some of the broader issues that have to be confronted by the social scientific researcher when content is integrated into a research programme.

Content analysis can take many forms. In its simplest, empirical, sense it can involve little more than enumerating the frequency with which certain words, items or categories appear in a text. Some of the earliest methodological statements on content analysis appear in Goode and Hatt (1952), wherein they concentrated mainly on the analysis of political speeches and the like. During later decades the methodology of empirical content analysis developed in more quantitatively complex ways. A good overview of the method is provided in Weber (1990).

Naturally, enumeration of words and themes has its place, but only within a well-considered theoretical frame. For whilst simple counting strategies can reveal much about the focus of a document and what its dominant concerns appear to be, they only add up to anything insightful once the function of the document has been identified. In other words, the enumeration process must always rest on an informed analysis concerning the nature of the 'facts' and 'categories' to be counted. Thus a document might function as the carrier of a message, an object to be translated, an impediment to understanding, or, yet, as a prop to interaction. We will look at a few examples in Chapters 6 and 7. Perhaps it could suffice for now to state that if we wish to move beyond the surface content of a document and into its functioning, then deeper and more sophisticated strategies of analysis may be required. But let us consider the possibilities for a relatively straightforward content analysis first.

The content of the immigrant letter

During the period 1918–20 Florian Znaniecki and W.I. Thomas published a multi-volume work entitled *The Polish Peasant in Europe and America* (see Thomas and Znaniecki, 1958). It reported on a study of family and community life among Polish immigrants to the USA during the very earliest part of the twentieth century. In order to gather data on family and community life Thomas and Znaniecki relied very heavily on the analysis of documents. Such documents were of various kinds and included parish records, life histories and letters. In retrospect, the methodological basis of the study looks rather shaky, but the general design of *The Polish Peasant* has much to recommend it. (The authors did, in fact, devote some time and effort to composing a methodological statement on their work, but it strangely lacks detailed connection with the substance of their study.)

The use of immigrant letters as a source of social scientific data was probably not original – even in 1918 – but it was, nevertheless, inventive. Thomas, in particular, was concerned with individual attitudes – towards possessions, the family, social relationships and so forth. The immigrant letter in this respect was seen to function as a repository of attitudes. For example, the very fact that such letters were written at all indicated that Polish immigrants were willing to invest a considerable amount of time and effort in maintaining family links across two continents. On the other hand, the actual content of the letters suggested to Thomas that in many key respects social solidarity was breaking down in the Polish community. For example, the letters were said to reveal a considerable degree of conflict about such matters as marriage partners and social relationships. As with many researchers Thomas and Znaniecki can be accused of finding in the data only what they wished to see, and the theme of social disorganization was already firmly implanted in the sociology of Thomas well before he had ever looked at any letters. It is not surprising, therefore, that social disorganization in the American urban Polish community is what Thomas saw the letters to reveal. As I have already hinted, Thomas and Znaniecki were not all that clear on basic facts about where the letters were obtained from, or how many letters were received and analysed, but their work nevertheless gave a spur to the use of such documents in the study of American history. Oscar Handlin's *The Uprooted* (1953), for example, may be said to have been partly inspired by ideas drawn from *The Polish Peasant*.

Although *The Polish Peasant* exhibits a considerable degree of theoretical complexity for its day, the use of the letters is relatively straightforward. They are used essentially as a data source for content analysis. That is to say, certain themes were identified – social disorganization, patterns of family interaction, individualization, and so forth – and then the researchers attempted to assess how frequently these themes appeared in the letters. On the face of things, that is a perfectly reasonable line of approach. In fact, however, it encourages a considerable adulteration of the data sources. For, by imposing a pre-organized conceptual grid – derived from professional social scientific work – on a data source, it is more than possible that the social detail of the letters themselves was lost. For instance, one could use immigrant letters to examine the way in which, say, 'self' has been conceived among different groups and at different times (see Barton and Hall, 2000). Letters written with references to 'us' and 'we' for example, signify a different orientation to the self and other from letters written in terms of 'I' and 'me'. (The use of paragraphs, punctuation and other matters of style may also indicate changing aspects of everyday culture.) How the language and style of the letter writers (and readers) is to be linked to the conceptual concerns of social scientists is, of course, a problematic issue. We will pick up on some of the relevant themes in Chapters 6 and 7. For now, we need only to note that relatively straightforward enumeration strategies have their place in content analysis and have been used very successfully in the social sciences. Yet, in the sociological tradition, especially, there have been other, much more sophisticated approaches to matters of content and at this introductory stage we need, at the very least, to be aware of them.

The meaning of the Song

In the Old Testament there is a book entitled the Song of Songs. It was originally written in Hebrew with touches of Aramaic, and borrowings from Greek and Persian. Its earthly genealogy is unknown, but it was probably written between the tenth and second century BCE. Depending on the translation, it can appear as a poem of considerable elegance and beauty. It also has a structure of considerable complexity – though that does not concern us here – and it has been variously interpreted. But what is its meaning and where does such meaning reside?

In rabbinical writing, for example, the Song of Songs has been considered as an allegory of God's love for Israel. In Christian commentary it is Christ that is invoked, or God's love for the Church. Underlying these pious interpretations, however, is a poem that clearly touches (I think that I have the correct verb here) on issues of sexual love and carnal knowledge. Thus, there is a great deal of reference to loins and jewels, as well as references to breasts as ripening fruit and so on. In that sense the Song of Songs may be interpreted as an exceptionally sensual poem of erotic secular, rather than theological, interest. It is in any event a poem that has multiple layers of 'meaning' and therefore varied possibilities for interpretation (Bloch and Bloch, 1995).

Issues of meaning and interpretation have been central to social science since the late nineteenth century, though sociologists have been more concerned with the meaning of action rather than the meaning of text. Nevertheless, the problems about what is to be interpreted and how it is to be done are similar to considerations of both action and text. Max Weber (1864–1920), for example, regarded the interpretation of meaningful action as one of the central tasks of sociology. In fact, Weber is a useful example to us because he developed what is probably his most well-known 'thesis' on the basis of textual interpretation. That thesis (often referred to as the Protestant Ethic Thesis) concerned the affinity between the logic of capital accumulation and productive capacity on the one hand, and the belief systems of European Protestants on the other. And in order to establish the credibility of his claims, Weber drew widely on his reading of texts (theological writings, diaries, etc.) of mainly English Puritans. He thereafter felt able to outline what he considered to be a typical worldview of early Protestants (Weber, 1930). Clearly, Weber's selection of textual materials could be scrutinized and criticized as appropriate or inappropriate, and it has been claimed, for example, that he placed an undue emphasis on the writings of ascetic English Puritans in his characterization of the 'Protestant Ethic'. Those problems, however, need be of no concern here, but we can usefully ask questions about how Weber's interpretation of text related to the matters of meaning. Whose meaning was Weber in search of, for example? Was it, perhaps, the authorial intent of people such as Baxter (one of Weber's sources) and Baxter's contemporaries? If so, then how are we to know that Weber interpreted Baxter's intentions accurately? Perhaps Baxter's writings, like the Song of Songs, are open to various and multiple interpretations. Perhaps Baxter himself would have placed significantly different interpretations on the same work at different stages in his own life. Equally, Weber, as a reader of Baxter's *Christian Directory* (1673), at the cusp of the nineteenth and twentieth centuries, would have offered a different interpretation of the work as compared with a late eighteenth-century reader and so on. There can be few doubts that Weber brought a great deal of himself and his learning to his reading. So perhaps we would have to take account of Weberian meanings as well as Puritan intentions when we assess the essays that are collected together under the title of *The Protestant Ethic and the Spirit of Capitalism* (essays that were brought together in book form by Talcott Parsons only in the 1930s).

The lesson here is that words may be conveyed by text, but meaning and interpretation are undertaken by human actors and attempting to access subjective intentions and meanings of actors is a difficult (some might say impossible) task. There are clearly a large number of problems to be addressed in our one example alone. We will elaborate on some of those difficulties in Chapter 6, in particular. It may as well be stated here, however, that in terms of the framework adopted in this book, a search for 'meaning' is akin to a search for pigs that fly. Indeed, we shall note that when we look at the content of documents it is schemes of referencing that need to be analysed rather than systems of meaning. In other words, our emphasis needs to be on the social activities through which texts are appropriated rather than psychological properties of the reader.

The structure of a dictionary

Pick up a dictionary. The dictionary will contain words and definitions of words, and the words are arranged in some kind of order. In the western world that order is alphabetic and runs from a to z; it couldn't be simpler or more natural you may think.[11] Yet dictionaries are not always organized in such a manner. Consider a Chinese dictionary, for example, which clearly cannot be organized in an alphabetic sequence. Instead, the inscriptions are organized in terms of common picture parts or 'radicals'. So one way of organizing words is to group together all those words with the same pictorial root – say the symbol for the Devil or evil – irrespective of exact meaning. The individual words and their meanings are, to say the least, central to the content of a document, but it is also legitimate for us to take into consideration that structure in terms of which the dictionary is held together.

This notion of a structure as a kind of scaffolding out of which individual and specific images or objects are constructed is one borrowed from Saussure (1983). The latter generally distinguished between language and speech, language containing, if you like, a finite and universal structure out of which is generated an infinite number of sentences, spoken in an infinite variety of circumstances. In fact, for Saussure, language was a property of collectives – of humanity as a whole as it were. Speech was something exhibited by individuals and was dependent on language. In later years these basic ideas were extended to many other fields of human endeavour and action. Roland Barthes (1985), for example, attempted to apply the distinction to the study of women's fashion and style. Claude Lévi-Strauss, rather more intelligibly, applied the notion to such things as the study of *Totemism* (1969).

Structuralist thought had a powerful impact on West European social science during the 1960s and 1970s, and the development of that thought saw endless twists and turns and intellectual acrobatics. François Dosse (1997a; 1997b) has traced many of the key developments in his majestic and masterful history of structuralist thought. The detail of the history is far beyond the concerns of this book. One point of common interest in structuralism, however, is that it is a method that often eschews the search for the elusive 'meaning' of a document, and focuses instead on how what is said has been arranged. In this respect Lévi-Strauss's *Totemism* provides a first-class example. It deserves a few moments consideration.

The fact that human beings in non-western societies had been known to associate themselves with various species of flora and fauna was an observation that had fascinated anthropologists from the late nineteenth century onwards. Durkheim, in his *The Elementary Forms of the Religious Life* (1915), for example, had commented on the manner in which aboriginal Australians had inscribed snake and other symbols on stones and wood and henceforth regarded such artefacts as 'sacred'. Other observers had noted how non-western peoples sometimes referred to themselves as birds or bears or whatever and used various species of animal as 'totems'. Until the publication of Lévi-Strauss's *Totemism*, the predominant question asked about such activities concerned their meaning. What does it mean, for example, when human beings claim that twins are like birds? The genius of Lévi-Strauss was to side-step this kind of question entirely. In his view it made no sense to ask for the meaning of such associations but instead to ask how what was said was arranged. What were the logical relations between things in a classificatory scheme? What was the underlying structure based upon? How were one set of objects opposed to another and a further set of objects allied with others? (You will recall that the Chinese dictionary, for example, groups words relating to 'evil' together, imply-ing that words relating to 'goodness' must also be grouped together in another section of the dictionary.) In following through on such questions Lévi-Strauss came to view totemic systems as systems of taxonomy rather than as systems of belief (or religion), and in that respect to be directly comparable with the taxonomies found in western society.

A focus on the arrangement of the words and sentences and things, instead of on meaning, has much to recommend it. In a somewhat different theoreti-cal context it was an idea taken up by Michel Foucault in his *The Archaeology of Knowledge* (1972). This was a work in which Foucault sought to study the nature of what he later referred to as 'discourse'. Things are both represented in discourse and shaped and fashioned through discursive practices. In Foucault's sense of the term a discourse expresses itself through statements and sentences. Yet, what is of interest to social scientists is not the surface feature of statements (about the objects of medicine, or grammar, or botany, or sexuality), but the underlying rules and principles that bind such statements – and their authors – together in a unifying matrix. Foucault saw discourses as having a history – a beginning and an end – and he viewed one of his tasks as tracing the starting and finishing points of specific systems of ideas. More importantly, Foucault linked discourses and 'discursive regimes' to a world beyond the text.[12] Thus, 'A statement must have substance, a support, a place, and a date' (1972: 101).[13] By linking statements to a non-textual world (of people, roles, places, buildings and institutions) Foucault opened up a route for discourse analysis that moved beyond the world of linguistics and textual analysis, and into the world of social practices. It is such a route that will be followed in this book.

Conclusions and key points

Our concerns have been widespread and varied, yet the central arguments of the chapter can be stated quite simply. I list them as follows:

- Documents form a 'field' for research in their own right, and should not be considered as mere props to human action.
- Documents need to be considered as situated products, rather than as fixed and stable 'things' in the world.
- Documents contain text, but text and documentation are not co-extensive.
- Writing is as significant as speech in social action and the medium through which writing is carried should always be attended to. In everyday life, the form, the list and the letter are, for example, as important as the verbal question, the verbal answer and the command.
- Documents are produced in social settings and are always to be regarded as collective (social) products.
- Determining how documents are consumed and used in organized settings – that is, how they function – should form an important part of any social scientific research project.
- Content is not the most important feature of a document.
- In approaching documents as a field for research we should forever keep in mind the dynamic involved in the relationships between production, consumption, and content.

In the next chapter we shall look at some facets of the production process. In Chapters 3–5 we shall examine the use of documents in action. In Chapters 6–8, we shall turn to matters of content and the rhetoric of social research with documents. Chapter 9 will bring the book to a close. It will do so by opening up a further dimension for research into documents – that dimension relates neither to production, nor consumption, nor even content, but rather to the process of exchange.

RESEARCH EXERCISES

Exercise 1.1

Mundane documents such as shopping lists, 'to-do' lists and appointment diaries usually function in a number of ways. For example, they can serve as a form of 'external memory' for an individual, they can pattern the timing and order of future activity, and they can act as simple records of things done. Consider identifying a small sample of people (say, $N = 5$) who draw up lists and/or appointment diaries on a regular basis and question them about how they use such documents. Pay particular attention to the following issues. (1) Who it is that authors the documents. (2) The extent to which the document reflects and structures relationships between the author and the user (and how such structuring is achieved). (3) How the document functions in the everyday life of the user (try to be as exhaustive as possible here). (4) The extent to which the document may be said to act back on its creator – noting, of course, exactly how this is done. Then consider expanding the sample so as to gain coverage of additional kinds of user or to explore elementary hypotheses that may have emerged from working with the initial sample.

Exercise 1.2

As we shall note in Chapter 5, diaries are documents that can be used to function in various ways. For example, they can serve as a record or 'log' of things done. They can also serve as an aide-memoire, as a receptacle of a personal confession, as an aid to dieting (or quitting smoking), as a legal record (as might be the case with someone attempting to document a disability), and as social scientific research tools. Using suitable WWW searches using the terms 'journals + diaries' draw up an extensive list of functions for the diary/journal. On the basis of your findings generate some hypotheses about the relationships between function and content.

Notes

1   The sorcerer's apprentice used his novice spells to get a broom to carry buckets of water. Unfortunately the broom then acted independently of the apprentice's commands – and flooded the sorcerer's house. It is something of a Mickey Mouse tale, the complete version of which can be found in a 1779 German poem by Goethe. See, www.fln.vcu.edu/goethe/zauber.html

2   Lincoln and Gubba (1985) draw a distinction between a document and a record (based on their functioning). It is not a distinction that I intend to adopt herein for a document can function in many ways. It seems somewhat invidious, therefore, to

isolate just one such function. Other commentators try to classify documents according to whether they are 'private' or public' 'primary' or secondary, solicited or unsolicited (see, for example, Burgess, 1984; Finnegan, 1996). However, it is clearly conditions of consumption and use that will determine which of these categories a document will belong to. The active document is usually too slippery a creature to fall neatly into such classificatory traps. As the Torres Straits example (in this chapter) shows, what is primary in one frame is often secondary in another.

3 Dorothy Smith (1990: 121) has also argued, though in a narrower frame than is adopted here, for a move away from a study of the inert to a study of the 'active text'.

4 It is, however, notable that in social scientific research, 'speech' extracts are always mediated through writing – as, for example, in the work of those who undertake conversation analysis.

5 The operation of which he saw as being 'based upon written documents ("the files")'. See Weber (1979: 957).

6 I use the word text to refer to written (or printed) inscription. Consequently, text is to be distinguished from talk. It is a simple point, yet it is one that needs considerable emphasis: first, because in some elementary methods manuals text is often loosely conflated with talk – see, for example, Burgess (1982: 131) and Watson and Seiler (1992); secondly, and more importantly, because in the world of the semioticians (see, for example, Barthes, 1977; Derrida, 1976), any and all things can be regarded as 'text', and subsequently decoded according to the rules of semiotics. Thus, in contemporary cultural studies as, say, exemplified by Hall (1972), images, sounds, talk and writing are often bundled together as 'text' that is subject to encoding and decoding procedures. A key example for Hall would be television discourse. In addition, some writers also refer to social action as text in order to argue that the study of action can be approached in the same manner as one might approach a written text (Ricoeur, 1977). A further position is that adopted by Geertz (1993: 452), who conflates text and culture, arguing that the latter is, essentially, an ensemble of texts.

7 The concept of performance – borrowed from Goffman (1959) – has been more recently adapted by Law (1994) and Mol (1999; 2000) to place emphasis on how things are done. An emphasis on doing encourages us to avoid speculation about private mental operations such as what people are 'thinking' and 'believing' and to concentrate on the visible effects of activity.

8 An alternative way of looking at this problem is to use the concept of 'actant' (Greimas, 1987). Actants may be said to have functions and effects. For example, the concept of author is suggestive of an 'actant' in so far as it gathers up all the processes, activities and actors involved in the production of a text into a single identifiable bundle. That bundle is usually a named person who is then viewed as the executor of all such processes, activities, etc.

9 The concept of discourse is a tricky and complicated one. Van Dijk (1997) provides a good overview of possible meanings of the term, whilst Gill (2000) usefully discusses some meanings of the term 'discourse analysis'. For an indication of the way in which this is to be used in this book see pp. 25–6.

10 Frankenstein created a monster that turned against its human creator, see Mary Shelley's *Frankenstein or the Modern Prometheus* (1996 – first published, 1818).

11 Even within the English language, however, dictionaries exhibit varying forms of structure and classification. So although *The Oxford English Dictionary* lists words alphabetically, the pattern of each entry is determined by chronology of use rather

than by popularity of usage. So an archaic meaning of a word listed in, say, 1646, will always come before a more popular meaning listed as 1990, or whatever.

12   The supposition of a realm beyond text constituted the basis for one of Foucault's criticisms of Derrida's philosophy. The latter had claimed in *Of Grammatology* (1976: 227) that there is nothing beyond the text. The assertion was part of a larger claim to the effect that texts have no external referent against which their truth or validity may be assessed. According to Derrida (1988), one can only assess a text by factors internal to its composition. It is, as we shall note, a problematic position to adopt.

13   Other attempts to link text to action under the umbrella term of discourse have been developed by a number of Marxist theorists such as Ernesto Laclau and Chantal Mouffe. For outlines of the central debates, see Torfing (1999).

2

Producing Facts

From Paris 1748 to Geneva 1998

In the Paris of 1748 a policeman by the name of Joseph d'Hémery set up a series of files. He named them 'Historique des auteurs' (Darnton, 1984). D'Hémery was an early version of what, today, would be called a secret police-man, and his auteurs were what were later to be referred to as intellectuals and ideologues – though neither word existed in 1748. His interest to us is that he faced a set of problems common to all those who seek to report on the nature of the world. For a start, he had to define an 'auteur' – a business no easier then than now (see Foucault, 1979). Was an auteur someone who wrote a book or a play? Or was it anyone who wrote a pamphlet or even a few lines of prose? (In fact some 67 of d'Hémery's auteurs wrote nothing at all). How was he to impose order on his files? What categories was he to use to organize the infor-mation that he collected? Indeed, what information was he to collect as relevant to his purpose, and what to ignore? (D'Hémery, for example, consid-ered the physiognomy of a person as important as their ideas; thus he describes Voltaire as 'Tall, dry and the bearing of satyr' as well as a 'bad subject'.) In gather-ing data on his auteurs, d'Hémery very naturally gave vent to his own modes of expression, and thus helped to create a new genre of document, a new form of literality – the secret police file. In that respect he is an auteur in his own right, and his writings provide invaluable insight into how a loyal state agent viewed the enemies of the *ancien régime* that was pre-Republican France. (For insight into a more recent secret police file see Ash, 1997.)

Categorizing, defining, sorting, ordering, including, excluding and reporting on the world: these are tasks that concern social scientists every bit as much as secret police (see Kwaśnik, 1991). But how, exactly, are such tasks achieved? The processes that underpin the manufacture of documents are rarely made visible or accountable. Those of us who handle published documents as resources for research, for example, see only a finished product, an object ready for use. Yet in order to produce that object various auteurs have had to call upon a complex system of rules, conventions, organizational strategies and conceptual schemes. Writing anything involves one in a system of production. For example, in order to produce a statistical report, someone has to devise a classificatory system, and operate rules that dictate how events and objects are to be assigned to the specific classes – as to how, say, 'bad' and 'good' subjects (and satyrs) are to be recognized and allocated. Someone has to devise rules of precedence to cope with those instances in which an individual or a case has more than one property – say, 'bad subjects' who are satyrs. On top of that, someone has to devise rules about how numbers are to be allocated to objects – how, for example, acts of disloyalty or treason are to be counted. These days, of course, most of our counting is undertaken in terms of well-defined taxonomies and rule-books. In d'Hémery's day it was devised and developed in a some- what more rudimentary fashion. The essential principles of the construction process are, from our standpoint, however, timeless.

As well as attending to classification and order in writing up their reports, auteurs have, necessarily, to attend to other matters. They have to keep an audi- ence in mind and decide on the purpose of their documentation. And so the systems of relevance of users and readers also impinge on the production process. Further, they have to decide how to locate themselves within the document – whether to declare their presence as an 'auteur', or whether to mask their presence behind the name of a committee, or an office of some kind or invisible 'other'. In this last respect it seems as if d'Hémery was not a very successful secret policeman by modern standards – simply because he declared himself to be present in the files. Writing notes and reports as a committee, an office, or as an anonymous functionary would have been far more professional.

In order to get to grips with these issues of authorship, rule-based systems, and the design and production of documents it is often useful to disassemble – comma by full stop – the documents that we use as data sources. That is to say, to investigate each stage of the process by means of which a document has been put together, concentrating on how each component has entered into the production process, and how the parts are eventually fitted together. Indeed, looking at how documents are manufactured invariably provides insight into how we assemble facts about the world in general. For, in many respects, the procedures through which an auteur (such as d'Hémery) assembles a report on the world is not wildly different from the way in which ordinary individuals assemble accounts of everyday and routine interactions. After all, each and every one of us has to devise and apply some kind of classificatory and cate- gorizing system for dealing with and describing the circumstances and the people that we daily encounter. (Harvey Sacks, who studied processes of the latter kind, coined the term 'membership categorization device' (MCD) to assist with the description of the process – see Lepper, 2000; Silverman, 1998).

In this chapter we are going to unzip a number of what we might call quantitative reports, in order to illustrate some key processes involved in their production. We begin by looking at a World Health Organization (WHO) report on health statistics, published in Geneva during 1998. Following that, we shall look at some of the issues that impinged on the production of a report on psychiatric disorder in Great Britain. Our aim is to demonstrate that 'like all knowledge', statistical reports 'must be analysed as a product' and are 'never mere givens' (Hindess, 1973: 12). We shall begin with the observation that, as products, they reflect both conceptual and organizational (technical) features of their production. It is to the investigation of such matters that we now turn.

Death: a progress report

It is something of a paradox that one of the most useful and malleable of quantitative measures that is called upon to assess the 'health' of populations is the death rate – or, more accurately, the mortality rate. Thus, the rate (per thousand born) of babies who die in the first year of life (the infant mortality rate), for example, has long been used by agencies in the advanced industrial societies as a key measure of both the health and quality of life of a population. Health agencies are, of course, also interested in what people die from as well as how many people die at any given age. Thus, WHO publishes, on an annual basis, a manual of world health statistics (WHO, 1998). The manual provides data on both the numbers of people who die in any one country during a given year, and the cause of death of the individuals concerned. In that respect the manual exists as a resource for social scientific or epidemiological study. One can lift it off the library shelf and consult it for facts about mortality, or health, or, if one wishes, transpose and integrate the data into a measure of the 'quality of life' in Nigeria, Canada, the Ukraine or the USA. Furthermore, where required, the facts within the manual can be plotted on graphs, slotted into tables, or correlated one with another to reveal trends and patterns (see Unwin et al. (1997) for a review of possibilities). Yet, as with many reports of this kind, it is often more revealing to look not so much at what can be derived from the document, but at the building blocks of the document itself – at how the report was put together in the first place.

The foundation stones of big reports – such as the WHO report – are often designed and set at some distance from the final product. In the WHO case this is so in both a bureaucratic and a geographical sense. One 'stone' is the death certificate. In most western societies a medical practitioner completes this certificate, and it provides a cause of death for each deceased person. The certificates are then processed through a series of local, regional and national agencies so as to compile a picture of mortality in any given country. It is from such national pictures that the international (WHO) picture is derived. To illustrate key procedures I am going to begin with the concept of a cause of death – and move upward.

We should be aware that deciding on the cause of death of any individual is not a simple task (Bloor, 1991; Prior, 1989). This is partly because people commonly die of many things at one and the same time, and it is not always easy to disentangle one cause from another. A serious infection of the lung, for example, may accompany a growth in the airways, leading to eventual heart failure. A minor wound may encourage the development of septicaemia, or whatever. In addition, we have to be aware that the physiological 'causes' of death are not always easy to determine in the absence of autopsy. For instance, brain tumours are particularly difficult to diagnose at death without an autopsy and it would be impossible to determine the precise nature of a lung infection without recourse to laboratory analysis. Despite this, only a minority of people are ever autopsied. Indeed, in many cases, the physician or coroner or other individual who certifies a death may not consider it worthwhile to find out exactly why a person died. All that is important is to determine whether the individual died 'naturally' or from foul play. Further, and even if one feels able to overlook the aforementioned (technical) obstacles, one is faced with the fact that, in the discourse of western medicine, only some causes of death are regarded as legitimate in the first place. In that context, readers may be delighted to note that one is simply not allowed to die of either 'old age' or 'poverty'. More significantly, the exclusion of such causes suggests that modern western societies have very specific vocabularies of causation as far as matters relating to death are concerned, and a distinct image of what can and cannot cause a death.

So what can one die of? The answer to that question is buried (if that is not an entirely inappropriate metaphor) in another WHO manual. This latter is called *The International Statistical Classification of Diseases and Related Health Problems* (WHO, 1992). It is often referred to in an abbreviated form as the ICD. The current edition of the manual is the 10th, and so the abbreviation is, more accurately, ICD-10. ICD-10 provides a list of all currently accepted causes of death, and they are classified into 'chapters'. Thus, there are chapters relating to diseases and disorders of the respiratory system, the circulatory system, the nervous system and so on. In different decades different diseases and causes of death are added and deleted from the manual. HIV/AIDS is an obvious example of an addition and it appears as a cause of death only in ICD-10, whilst 'old age' as a cause of death was eliminated in ICD-6. In all cases, of course, the conceptual architecture in terms of which death is comprehended is structured around the human body (Foucault, 1973: 3).

As well as containing a long list of medical causes of death, the ICD also contains rules about which causes of death are more important than others. So when a person dies of many conditions, the people responsible for coding the data on which the health statistics depend 'know' which cause to select as *the* cause of death. Thus, diseases of the heart, for example, commonly take precedence over diseases of any other organ, and cancers take precedence over infections and so on. These rules also change from decade to decade. Thus, during the early part of the twentieth century diseases of the liver and lung took precedence over disease of the heart (see Prior, 1989).

In the context in which it is here considered, the ICD-10 is an excellent example of what we might call a generative document – a document that lays down rules as to how other documents should be constructed. It contains both the conceptual structure in terms of which any explanations have to be built, and, in addition, rules for the building process. Generative documents come in various forms. The ICD is, perhaps, one of the most important for getting to grips with professional, 'expert', understandings of physical health and illness and serves, in many ways, as a window into western culture (Bowker and Star, 1999). A related publication – *The Diagnostic and Statistical Manual of Mental Disorders* (American Psychiatric Association, 2000) or DSM – is available for the classification of psychiatric (mental) conditions. One might say that the DSM provides the conceptual architecture in terms of which western culture comprehends disorders of the mind. And once again, if a disorder is not listed in the DSM then it is not regarded – in expert discourse – as a distinct psychiatric condition. Post-traumatic stress disorder is, for example, recognized as a disorder only in DSM-III (first published in 1974). The route by means of which it attained inclusion is, in itself, a matter of some interest (see Young, 1995). As for stress-related disorders, generally, they tend to appear in the ICD only from the 9th edition onward. (In other words, they were not regarded as legitimate medical conditions before their inclusion, and certainly would not have been enumerated by health agencies.)

It is already clear then that the WHO *World Health Statistics Annual* (1998) that was mentioned at the start of this section is a secondary document – its production dependent on the existence of pre-given items. First, there is a conceptual structure, developed over decades and reflecting fundamental assumptions about the nature of disease, death and the human body. It is best encapsulated in the ICD. Next there are national statistics. These latter sum up all the individual details of people who have died from HIV/AIDS, or lung cancer, or pneumonia, or road accidents, or whatever, and form the basis for the published tables. The national statistics, in turn, are produced partly on the basis of the death certificates of individuals, and partly on the basis of the ICD rules and codes. So, producing a report on mortality clearly requires the development and exploitation of a conceptual (theoretical) as well as a technical and organizational structure. Indeed, to understand the fundamentals of the WHO *Annual*, we probably need, once again, to step down a couple of notches. To that end it would be as well for us to focus on a single topic within the WHO publication. Any topic, such as the provision of heart disease statistics, cancer statistics or AIDS statistics, would serve our purpose. Here, however, I intend to focus on a set of numbers that are reported upon at the foot of each of the national tables, namely suicide statistics.

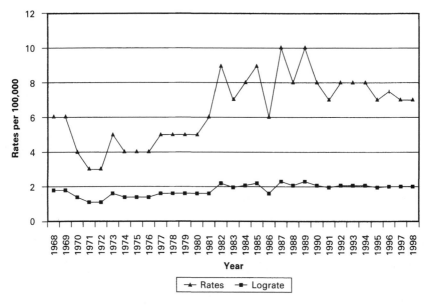

FIGURE 2.1   *Suicide rates for Northern Ireland, 1968–98*

Disassembling Durkheim and other users of statistical data

Suicidal behaviour has fascinated social scientists since the birth of the discipline. Social scientific and mathematical interest in the matter arises from a
number of considerations. Above all, it is clear that although suicide is a
supremely individualistic act, the study of it at a population level seems to
exhibit distinctive social patterns. In fact, the earliest pattern to be noted by
social commentators (mainly early nineteenth-century mathematicians) was
the stability of the rate of suicide in each European society. A rate is normally
measured per hundred, or per thousand, or per ten thousand (the appearance
of rates, though common today, is essentially an invention of nineteenth-
century social science). When one examines rates of suicide, say, per one hundred
thousand in a society such as France or the UK or the USA it is evident that
over some decades, the suicide trace remains reasonably static. Indeed, the
larger the denominator chosen the more stable the rate will appear. Thus
measuring instances of suicide per million or, if possible, per 10 million will
always make it appear as if trends in the phenomena being examined are pre-
dictable and stable. Using raw data, on the other hand, can often make it seem
as if the phenomenon under study is erratic in its occurrence. In Figure 2.1
I have plotted a chart showing the number of suicides in just one small part
of the world – namely, Northern Ireland between 1968 and 1998. There are
two details to note. First, the rate varies over the time period. Secondly, the
trend is rather higher after 1982 compared with the period 1968–82. The

shift is slightly more obvious in the lower of the two traces (the log rate or the rates transposed into logarithmic scores). The transformation of rates into logs and other measures is frequently carried out by quantitative researchers to get good 'fits' of data. Indeed, such manipulations are usually necessary for the manufacture of statistical facts – an issue that, unfortunately, extends beyond the aims of this book. Readers interested in common forms of transformation and something of the reasoning behind them are best referred to Tukey (1977).

It was undoubtedly the apparent stability of data patterns that encouraged many nineteenth-century commentators to suggest that social life is governed by laws every bit as deterministic as are the laws of physics in the natural world. Thus, the English historian Buckle, for example, developed the notion that, in each society, there must be some kind of physical force compelling constant proportions of people to commit suicide year after year (see Hacking, 1990). Such ideas belonged very much to a discourse of what is often called, nineteenth-century positivism, and the French sociologist Durkheim (1855–1917) was very much absorbed in the development of that discourse. Indeed, for him, the study of suicide seemed to offer an excellent occasion for examining the nature and dynamic of a 'social fact', and to elucidate on the nature of the laws that might determine it. As one might guess, the starting point of Durkheim's published analysis of suicide was in the statistical patterns.

A close study of Durkheim's 1897 text (translated into English 1951) always pays a dividend. Even the casual reader cannot fail to note, for example, the manner in which the author uses tables and maps to underpin his general thesis. In fact the use of cartography – to show the distribution of suicide in France between 1878 and 1887 mapped against the distribution of drunkenness, alcoholic insanity, mean family size and so on – provides one of the earliest instances of what was later termed the ecological fallacy. The latter refers to the fallacy of drawing conclusions about individual behaviour from data that refer only to collective behaviour. For example, Durkheim argued that if one studied maps of 'La France' one would note that the regions with high rates of alcohol consumption (say, Normandy and Brittany) did not coincide with areas showing the highest suicide rates (The Paris Basin and the Côte d'Azur). He therefore concluded that the two phenomena were unrelated. Even in terms of a positivist social science, however, such a conclusion is unjustified, since it does not preclude the possibility of the two phenomena being linked, somehow, in the everyday lives of the people who actually committed suicide. (All the suicides in Paris could have been alcohol dependent after all.) Such difficulties do not, of course, prevent people from using maps to undertake social scientific and other forms of reasoning. Maps of mortality, for example, are still plentiful enough in the modern day, though what it is that we are supposed to read off them is never made entirely clear by their authors (see, for example, Burgher, 1997). As well as developing the use of mapping techniques, Durkheim was also among the earliest social scientists to use rates – per million and per thousand – as statistical props to his arguments. Ratios also figured in his thinking, and although he would have been unaware of it, he often provides what these days are called odds ratios on, for example, patterns of male suicides (1951: 199).

We have no need to trouble ourselves too much with these statistical details. We should merely note for the time being that, as far as Durkheim was concerned, the suicide rate exhibited stability and that stability called for explanation. In search of an 'explanation' Durkheim unravelled his empirical data somewhat further, though, once again, we have no cause to delve into the detail of the unravelling. Suffice it to say that his reasoning focused on social variations in the rates. For example, he spotted a variation in the rates of suicide committed by males as against females, married males as against unmarried males, and members of the Catholic faith as against the Protestant faith, and so on. From those observations Durkheim then proceeded to link 'facts' about the lives of the married and the unmarried, of Protestants and Catholics and Jews, to explain the observed variations. (That is, he sought to reason why there should be a higher suicide rate among males than females, among the unmarried than the married, among people associated with Protestant churches than those associated with the Catholic or Jewish faith.) His theorizing is, in so many ways, rather stunning, and the general drift of his empirical claims still stands today as what are commonly regarded to be valid generalizations about the social distribution of suicide (Chauvel, 1997).

We could, of course, usefully disassemble the component parts of Durkheim's analysis of suicide down to the dots and commas, and that would also pay dividends. Some years ago Douglas (1967) more or less did just that in his *The Social Meanings of Suicide*. Indeed, in that book Douglas not only rakes through the Durkheimian theory of suicide with a fine tooth comb, but also traces the influence that Durkheim had on other social factor theories. That is, theories that associated such things as gender and social status with the commission of suicidal acts. Indeed, post-Durkheimian researchers in the positivist mould eventually developed a long list of what would today be called 'risk factors' for suicide on the basis of statistical analyses. One of Douglas's key conclusions, however, was that the manufacture of statistical associations between suicide, and factor 'X' (or 'Y' or 'Z'), more often than not, slid over a consideration of the presence of what he termed situated meanings. That is to say, positivistic social scientists tended to ignore the simple matter that suicide involves a process of judgement and evaluation – judgements that involve, among other things, the attribution of motives to the perpetrator of a suicide. Such attributions are, of course, most commonly made by family members, the police, coroners, or the members of a coroner's jury. And they are necessary to reaching a conclusion as to whether a particular death is a suicide rather than a homicide or an accident. According to Douglas, positivistic researchers not only ignored such meanings, but tended to impose their own (second-order) interpretations onto the statistical data – thus committing, so to speak, a double-strength methodological error.

Situated meanings and the production of data

The claims of J.D. Douglas emanated from a style of social scientific work that revolutionized the study of 'social facts' during the 1960s. The revolution emanated mainly from academics based on the West Coast of the USA. The latter, in particular, sought to take issue with the manner in which social scientists tended to reify the world about them. According to Garfinkel (1967), for instance, acts of reification appeared at every level of conventional social scientific analysis and explanation. Thus, when psychologists or sociologists were asked to explain variations in, say, rates of criminal behaviour or of suicide, they would reify the topic of study (crime, suicide or whatever), the factors that they called upon to explain such variations (socio-economic status, poverty, mental illness and the like), and even the very mechanisms that they used to associate the object of study and the explanatory factors (such as mathematically designed covariances).

A particular *bête noire* of the ethnomethodologists were social scientists who worked in the manner of the Durkheimians. For, to the ethnomethodologists, the kind of work that Durkheim undertook is drenched in serious method-ological flaws. Among such flaws one would have to emphasize his tendency to take 'suicide' as an immediately recognizable and incontrovertible act. For example, Cicourel (1964) – another member of the ethnomethodological camp – had highlighted how terms such as suicide, juvenile delinquency, crime and so on were essentially linguistic categories, and the procedures in terms of which events are assigned to such categories is what sociological study should be all about. In that sense, the Durkheimians appeared to start at stage 2 of the research process – counting and associating events such as suicide with events such as 'alcoholic insanity' – when they should be starting at stage 1 – investi-gating the procedures by means of which happenings in the world are assigned to classes.

According to the ethnomethodologists, then, one major task of the social scientific researcher is to study the manner in which ordinary people recognize and impose order on events as they unfold in the everyday world. That is to say, a study of the ways in which members of society make sense of the situa-tions that they encounter, the ways in which they manage to classify them (and the ways in which they consequently organize them as ongoing accomplish-ments.) One of Cicourel's interests in this respect was the manner in which 'delinquents' and reports about delinquents were manufactured through socially organized and socially sanctioned procedures of arresting officers, desk sergeants and the like (Cicourel, 1976).

Making sense of situations that we encounter is, of course, heavily depen-dent upon pattern recognition. This is as true of our routine, everyday work as it is of social scientific work. So, acts of pattern recognition – of recognizing, say, a greeting situation or a situation for apology – are in many respects similar to those that lay at the heart of social scientific research. In both instances we are required to recognize the 'sameness' of events – such as, say, those instances in an interpersonal exchange when apologies are always appropriate. Such a process of recognizing sameness was referred to by Garfinkel (1967) as the 'documentary method of interpretation' – a given instance of events is seen as 'documenting' the underlying category. The documentary method was said to form the core of the practical or everyday reasoning process. And it is, perhaps, already clear that a documentary method of interpretation comes into play every time that we reach a decision as to whether a sudden death is 'natural' or 'unnatural' – that is, an accident, a suicide or a homicide – or, say, a particular activity is or is not a 'crime'.

Suicide as narrative

Suicide is a sad and depressing business for all of those involved in its discovery. It is rarely clear, however, whether any given death is as a result of personal intent on behalf of the deceased or not. People are found dead. They are found under the wheels of vehicles, and by the side of rail tracks. They are found lying face down in rivers in the late afternoon. They are found in hotel bedrooms with plastic bags over their head. They are found at home, dead in bed, shot through the head, or in fume-filled garages. Yet others are washed up on beaches. But few people leave written or verbal declarations of any intent to kill themselves (and even if they have, such notes must be treated with caution). Consequently, 'suicide' is always something of a problematic category. Indeed, suicidal intent and motives have always to be read into the circumstances and events in question. So suicidal motives are always imputed – that is, imputed to the deceased by others.

Now one of the key insights of the ethnomethodologists was to focus on the process whereby such imputations occurred, and a sudden death is translated into a suicide. In most societies it is a complex process. And the process whereby relatives and friends, police investigators and coroners put together a feasible narrative of death is not an easy one to research. A number of sociologists, however, variously attempted to trace the procedures, and in so doing their work has generated some fascinating conclusions. Thus, J.M. Atkinson (1978) focused on the reasoning processes of English coroners with respect to suicide. Taylor (1982) investigated the organizational processing of deaths of people who had 'jumped' in front of London's trains. Instead of summarizing those works, however, I am going to present some of my own data – derived from a coroner's office – to illustrate the essential points of the construction process. Some of the personal details have been altered so as to disguise the identities of the deceased and I have added a few details (in square brackets) to assist with the reading. The summaries are transcripts of the coroner's 'findings'.

Case 2.1

Married male. Age 28. Unemployed.
Cause of death: Poisoning by alcohol, Valium and Dalmane.

In 1989 the deceased had been attacked and had received head injuries. After that he suffered from headaches for which he took tablets. He spent the night of June 9th alone, in his sister's house. When the deceased failed to return home, his brother-in-law went to the house where the deceased had stayed, and forced an entry. He found the deceased lying dead on the floor of the sitting room. There were 367 mg of alcohol per 100 ml in his blood. Its effects had been increased by the use of the drugs Valium and Dalmane.

Case 2.2

Married Female. Age 58. No occupation.
Cause of death: Poisoning by Maprotiline.

The deceased suffered from depression for 5 years for which she had received hospital outpatient treatment. On 20th June 1990 her husband was admitted to hospital with a chest complaint and she visited him there on June 23rd. Later that day she was visited at home by her grandson. The next day she failed to pay her customary visit to her daughter. Consequently her daughter called at her mother's house and asked the police to force an entry to the house at about 16.00. She found her mother dead in bed with several empty packets of Ludiomil [an anti-depressant] nearby.

Case 2.3

Single Female. Age 20. Student.
Cause of death: Trichloroethane poisoning.

On the 13th November the deceased was living in 32, Apple Street with 4 other girls. She was known to be involved in substance abuse, and had been advised to desist by her friends. On the evening of the 13th, a friend called to see her in her room at about 18.00, and about 19.00 she began to sniff 'Zoff' – a liquid used for removing plaster. Around about 19.15 she began twitching and shouting and the 'Zoff' was taken from her. Some moments later she collapsed on the floor. An ambulance was called, and she was taken to the hospital. She was declared DOA at 20.00.

Case 2.4

Married Male. Age 40. Salesman.
Cause of death: Alcohol and chloral hydrate poisoning.

The deceased had a 10 year history of depression. He had recently received [psychiatric] hospital treatment for his condition. At hospital he had been prescribed 'Noctec' [the source of the chloral hydrate] to help him sleep. In the past he had often taken overdoses of pre- scribed drugs when in a low and confused state. He had also been reckless in taking pills with alcohol. On the 17th of May he returned home after drinking, but was not drunk. He went to bed at 21.00 and took 4 'Noctec' tablets. He was found dead the following morning.

These four narratives of death were written by coroners – the words within square brackets are mine. The narratives are of considerable interest in them- selves, not least for the manner in which they seek to describe the salient history of an event and thereby single out some issues for mention whilst ignoring others. For example, psychiatric histories, dates and times are men- tioned, and so too are family relationships. On the other hand the financial background of the individuals or, say, their religious beliefs are not mentioned. (The use and application of terms such as 'history of depression', 'substance abuse', 'reckless in taking pills' and so on forms potentially useful examples of Sacks' MCDs – mentioned in the opening section of this chapter.)

In each of these narratives there is supposed to be sufficient information in the narrative to enable any reasonable observer to form a judgement as to whether the deceased intended to kill him- or herself, or whether death was accidental. In that sense, such narratives function as what we might call meaning- making devices.

Only one of the above deaths was coded as a suicide. The remaining three were coded as accidental deaths. It would be natural to think that these deci- sions were arrived at by detailed and considerable deliberation of a jury or some such, and that the narratives provided above are only summary statements that emerged from more complex analyses carried on elsewhere. However, it was not so. The only information that the person coding the data had on these events was as above. So the coder had to read into descriptions such as these his or her own personal images of what a suicidal person might or might not do. It would, of course, be useful if the coder had used simple rules about the decision-making process – such as, for example, any mention of a psychiatric history to be taken as being suggestive of a suicide. Once again, however, it was not so. The decision-making process was, and remains, a messy and often inco- herent one. Indeed, some time ago, Garfinkel (1967) had indicated that no matter how rule bound a coding system may be, the rules have always and in every case to be interpreted by the coder. Such a process was referred to as 'ad hocing' – interpreting the information at hand in a manner that enabled the coder to finish his or her task. The study of ad hocing procedures forms a potentially rich terrain for research into the construction of documents. (See, for example, Benson and Hughes, 1983; Reiner, 1996.) For, we do know that when we ask people (such as coders) to explain their reasoning they can and do point towards rule-based systems. For example, they may call upon a rule to the effect that 'several empty packets of a drug' is suggestive of suicidal intent. Usually, however, such reasoning is *post hoc* and constructed for the benefit of the listener.[1]

The significance of these detailed and somewhat concentrated deliberations is that the suicide statistics that were referred to near the opening of this chapter are, ultimately, assembled on the basis of such procedures. Indeed, the examples that I have drawn upon are taken from work conducted in Belfast, and it is on the basis of such narratives that the official statistics for the town and the associated region are constructed. It is, however, important to realize that suicide decisions have not always been executed in this manner. In fact, during the period 1968–82 there were a series of major changes in the law concerning who could and could not bring in a verdict of 'suicide' (Prior, 1989). After 1982 verdicts of suicide, accident and homicide were abolished and so, in the strict legal sense, there are no suicide verdicts in Northern Ireland at all. Deaths are categorized as suicide for the sole purpose of providing mortality statistics (and this could be connected with the upward shift of the log rate in Figure 2.1).

A number of important lessons concerning the production of statistical reports can now be derived from our deliberations. First, the procedures through which events in the world are enumerated constitute an important 'topic' for research in their own right. Most social scientists, of course, prefer to gloss over these considerations and use social and economic statistics as a 'resource' – as if they reflected facts in the world unmediated by organizational processes. (On the distinction between 'topic' and 'resource', see Zimmerman and Pollner, 1971). We have seen that there are good reasons for refuting such an argument. In fact, the claims that we have made above could be applied with equal force and fervour to the construction of crime statistics, cost of living statistics, birth statistics, marriage statistics, business statistics and any other realm of enumeration that one might care to consider.[2] Secondly, we have to be aware that a consideration of the ways in which point prevalence rates (the rate at which something occurs during a point in time) are constructed can be extended to a consideration of the ways in which statistical trends are constructed. Thus in looking at the suicide rate we have seen how the production of a graph – showing deaths over time – lulls both researcher and reader into thinking that 'the same' facts are being reported upon. As we have briefly noted, however, with respect to Northern Ireland statistics the agents who construct those facts have changed markedly over time (they were coroners variously with and without juries until 1982 and then only coders). Different agents call

TABLE 2.1 *Prevalence of psychiatric disorders in private households by gender. Rates per thousand of population in past week, GB 1995*

Nature of disorder	Females	Males
Mixed anxiety and depressive disorder (MADD)	99	54
Generalized anxiety disorder (GAD)	34	28
Depressive episode	25	17
All phobias	14	7
Obsessive–compulsive disorder (OCD)	15	9
Panic disorder	9	8
Functional psychoses*	4	4
Alcohol dependence*	21	75
Drug dependence*	15	29

*Rates per thousand of population in past 12 months.
Source: Meltzer et al. (1995)

upon different reasoning processes and different MCDs in the deliberations and therefore we can justifiably argue that the graph in Figure 2.1 provides a false sense of unity to the phenomena we refer to as suicide rates. Durkheim's tables did likewise. Finally, we have noted how the day-to-day activities of those who manufacture documents work within well-established frameworks of relevance and order: they use generative documents – documents that provide the conceptual framework in terms of which the world is reported upon. In the above cases that framework was encoded in the ICD. In the following section we turn to another framework – that of the DSM. Whatever the framework, however, it is essential to underline the fact that our original document – the WHO *World Health Statistics Annual* – is akin to a rather large Chinese box. Open the lid and we find other boxes within – boxes containing conceptual frames, boxes that contain operational rules, and boxes that contain situated organizational decisions. The WHO *Annual* in that respect serves as little more than a wrapper. It provides an image of a unified and independent object (document), whilst, in fact, hiding a vast machinery of manufacture. The WHO *Annual* is not alone in this respect and one essential (though rarely executed) task of the social researcher bent on collecting 'facts about society' should, therefore, involve removing the dust jackets of the documentary material that he or she encounters, and to ask two very simple questions. How exactly, and by whom, was this document assembled?

Enumerating neurotics

I am looking at a table of research results (Table 2.1). It tells us about the community prevalence rates in Great Britain of certain types of what are sometimes called 'neurotic' disorder, together with some estimates for the 'functional psychoses'. The table represents 'facts' about mental illness, and in line with what we have noted above, it can be used, together with others related to it, as a resource for researchers. Thus, we can, for example, refer to Table 2.1 as evidence for our statement that about 16 per cent of people in any one week show symptoms of a neurotic disorder. But how were this and other facts arrived at, and how was the report put together?

As with the manufacture of crime or suicide or any other form of statistics, the production of psychiatric statistics depends on the existence of a conceptual or theoretical scheme, combined with rules and technical instructions for applying the concepts to a set of events and occurrences. As has already been indicated, the conceptual scheme in terms of which mental illness is comprehended is that contained in *The Diagnostic and Statistical Manual* of the American Psychiatric Association (the DSM-IV, 2000). This contains a series of categories relating to the various psychiatric maladies that people might be said to suffer from, and it also contains diagnostic criteria for recognizing the distinct disorders. Some of the disorders are listed in Table 2.1. We will return to the DSM in a moment. For now let us focus on how the figures in Table 2.1 were obtained.

The data in the table are derived from answers to a survey conducted in over 10,000 private households. The Appendix to the research report from which these figures are derived provides the detail of the sample frame that was used (Meltzer et al., 1995). It tells us the rules by means of which households and the adults within them were selected. It also provides the questionnaire or instrument by which mental illness was recognized. In this particular case the instrument was called the Clinical Interview Schedule (Revised) or CIS-R. The CIS-R is one of a variety of 'instruments' that produce clinical and other phenomena (see, for example, Bowling, 1997). In many respects documents such as the CIS-R are like machine tools – tools for producing 'things'. Indeed, phenomena such as 'disability', types of psychiatric illness and 'quality of life' are conditions routinely manufactured by instruments of the kind referred to here. In the case of the CIS-R the tool operates through a system of questions and answers. For example, there are questions about people feeling fatigued or feeling ill. One such question asks, 'During the past month, have you felt that you've been lacking in energy?' Another question asks, 'have you had any sort of ache or pain in the past month?' Respondents are required to answer 'Yes' or 'No'.

In his *Method and Measurement in Sociology*, Cicourel (1964) discussed the status of questions such as these. As one might expect on the basis of what we have already stated, Cicourel raised issues relating to the ways in which the interview process, and the questions and answers provided within the interview, are socially embedded. In particular, he became interested in the process through which the interview – as a social event – can turn conversation into social scientific data, pointing out that the use of instruments (such as, say, the CIS) involved an act of measurement by fiat. That is to say, the instrument imposes a commonality of meaning on questions and answers that are, in all likelihood, variously understood – at different times and by different people (see Houtkoup-Steenstra, 2000). Indeed, the whole matter of measurement in the social sciences is something of a Pandora's box, raising as it does problems concerning whether or not the CIS (or a similar instrument) is valid for measuring such things as depression and anxiety. Rather than concentrate on measurement issues at the level of the interviewing process, however, it would be more useful at this point to turn to an examination of the computer-assisted procedures by means of which psychiatric diagnoses were made. That is to say, to focus on the rule-based procedures by means of which the research managers moved from the 'Yes'/'No' responses on the interview schedule to the categories of 'depressive episode', 'panic attack' and 'obsessive–compulsive disorder' contained in the tables of the report.

The CIS-R depends on the use of 'lay' interviewers. In other words, the people who ask subjects questions about mood and behaviour are not trained psychiatrists. Consequently, it is impossible for them to diagnose the respondents. Instead, on the return of the completed interview schedules to the research team a set of algorithms were put into play. Many of the algorithms involved scoring responses. For example, the questionnaire was divided into sections and points were awarded in each section. On the section relating to anxiety, for example, respondents would score 1 if they had been 'generally anxious or nervous or tense' for four or more days in the past seven days. They would score another 1 if they felt tense, nervous or anxious for more than three hours in total in any one of the past seven days – and so on. As we move through the questionnaire we add the points, and if they total more than 12 then the subject is assumed to display symptoms of a psychiatric disorder. Which disorder it is, is dependent on which sections of the instrument the respondent scores within. So, no mention of the diagnostic conditions is made in the interview schedule and certainly at no point were subjects asked whether they suffered from obsessive–compulsive neuroses or depression or whatever.

Human beings, of course, rarely pick up disorders singly and sequentially and in an easily labelled fashion. More likely they suffer from many things at once – they are both depressed and psychotic, say. They indulge in substance abuse and suffer from anxiety. So given that many individuals suffer from multiple pathologies at one and the same time, the CIS-R provides precedence rules that enable multiple disorders to be placed in a hierarchical sequence. For example, depressive episodes always rank above phobias. In this respect, the report follows the system prescribed by the DSM.

It was by the posing and coding of questions and answers, then, that diagnoses of psychiatric disorder were arrived at. In fact, there is a sense in which one could argue that the data assembling process – using interview schedule and algorithms – manufactured the disorders. So what does this suggest about our concept of psychiatric disorder? And what would happen if the research managers had set the cut-off point on the schedule to 10 or 18 rather than 12?

Such questions are in many ways related. It is possible, for example, to select a different cut-off point. Moving the point to, say, 10 would increase the prevalence of mental illness in the community. Moving the point to 18 would decrease it. So we can have as much or as little mental illness in the community as we want. (It was once said of Poland that it was a country on wheels, seeing how its borders were changed so frequently, and one might be inclined to take the same view about the prevalence of psychiatric disorders.) There are, of course, conventions about where the point should be, but the fact that the point is movable tells us something about a particular type of discourse on mental illness in the late twentieth century. It is a discourse that argues that mental illness is not something that is a qualitatively different category from sanity, but something of the same order, but which differs only in degree. The implication is, then, that states of health and illness can be arranged along a continuum – a continuum that runs from zero to infinity. Whether or not individuals are to be deemed 'ill' depends not on what they think, feel or do, but on the cut-off point that we use for our classification. The level at which the cut-off is set is important, even in research terms, mainly because the impact of such things as genetic or social factors on psychiatric disorder can be amplified or even 'eradicated' by moving the point upward or downward. (See, for example, Brown, 1981.)

This vision of psychiatric disorder as a quantitative variation on normal behaviour expresses only one of a number of possible positions on the subject. It was, for example, a vision that used to be contained within the DSM. However, the contents and the theoretical ideas behind the DSM have changed markedly between the appearance of the 1st (1952) and the 4th (1994) edition. And one consequence of the alteration of the conceptual scheme is that the conditions that we are referring to in the 1990s are not the same conditions as were referred to in the 1952 edition. For example, the word 'depression' occurs in both, but the nature, course and origin of that depression have radically altered (Healy, 1997). Naturally, our table of statistics (Table 2.1) would not highlight this change, but the changes are nevertheless embodied within it. (A table showing trends in the prevalence of 'depression' over the later half of the twentieth century would, however, be affected, in a fundamental way, by these alterations.)

By examining the history of the DSM, then, we can see how it is produced – as with all forms of 'expert' documentation – in a politically structured space. In fact, the DSM is a document that has been produced by a professional or expert faction. Given the significance of the American Psychiatric Association in the global network of expertise that faction has the power to decide what is and what is not a psychiatric disorder and how that disorder is to be defined. Above all, the DSM is (like the ICD) a machine tool – a tool that, when assembled with others of the same ilk, can generate new products. Such generative documents set out the boundaries in terms of which experts think and talk and write. In the manufacture of data about psychiatric disorder, they are not, of course, the only machine tools at hand. The CIS-R, the coding frame, the algorithms to which we have referred, also serve in the workshop. Put together such instruments produce, and how the production process unfolds is forever a matter of legitimate social research.

Conclusions

Structures of literality (de Certeau, 1984) are produced in a political and social space. In this chapter we have made reference to some very different forms of literality – the statistical report, the death certificate, the interview schedule, the expert manual and the secret police file. How these various forms of literality emerged and the social, political and economic contexts of their emergence are themselves legitimate areas for research – though areas that are, perhaps, often more appropriate to the historian than to the social scientist.

Our tack has led us to concentrate upon the enrolment (Pinch and Bijker, 1989) and mobilization of some key generative documents in specific organizational contexts. Generative documents, as I have stated, constitute the machine tools by means of which other documents are produced. In particular they are central to the manufacture of social scientific data. The manner of their recruitment and deployment for the creation of social facts is therefore crucial. During recent decades a large body of work has developed on the role of documentation as tools in laboratory work and so it is clear that we need not restrict ourselves to the manufacture of social scientific data in this respect. Thus Fujimura (1996), for example, has indicated how key laboratory manuals come to figure as important tools in work in genetics, whilst Bowker and Star (1999) have illustrated how the ICD serves as a tool in medical work.

Some years ago Hindess (1973) pointed out that statistical reports were always produced in and through the operationalization of technical and conceptual frames. In this chapter we have indicated the presence of both conceptual and technical procedures in the manufacture of two types of report – a report on the health of nations and a report on the results of a social survey. Our analysis could, in theory, be extended to reports on economic affairs, crime statistics, quality of life statistics, and any other genre of statistical summary that one might care to mention. In that respect, the lessons of this chapter are uncomfortable for those who routinely use statistical reports as sources of factual data. Indeed, had we extended our analysis, we would not only have accumulated yet more examples of how generative documents, forms of literality and social action intertwine to manufacture 'facts' about the world, but also have seen how knowledge and power interact. For the arrangement of knowledge involves, above all, the operation of power. Knowledge/power (the term is derived from Foucault, 1991) defines how things are to be arranged, and what is to be included and excluded in the realm of what is known and what is knowable.[3]

Darnton (1984), with whom we opened this chapter, provides an excellent illustration of the operation of power/knowledge in his consideration of the *Encyclopédie*. The latter, a 17-volume work produced, among others, by Diderot in the dawn of the age of enlightenment, contains on the face of it little more than a series of entries (listed from A to Z) on commonplace concepts, facts and ideas. Treated as an anthropologically strange treatise, however, Darnton sees within it a world-view, an image of reality. Diderot, of course, was one of d'Hémery's suspects, and unable to impose his vision of the world on anyone in particular. Nevertheless, as Darnton points out, the *Encyclopédie* has been referred to as 'machine de guerre', a key item in the armoury of those who opposed the old regime to its intellectual foundations. By the side of the *Encyclopédie* our examples are, perhaps, puny. Nevertheless we can see within them similar acts of classification and of inclusion and exclusion. It demonstrates that in every arrangement – no matter how puny – there is a world-view to be studied and analysed.

Power/knowledge is not only contained and expressed within documents, of course, but also activated in practice – by interviewers, coders, research managers, 'auteurs'. With that in mind, I shall conclude by listing some simple questions that ought to be kept in mind when reports that enumerate (and even those that do not) are scrutinized:

* What generative documents are called upon for the manufacture of the report? (Be sure to examine the origin, design, conceptual architecture and modes of instrumentation of any that are implicated.)
* Who (as Monsieur d'Hémery would ask) are the auteurs reporting and how does the author-function operate in the document's creation?
* What rules – of selection, coding and precedence – are used in the manufacture of facts?
* How are the rules applied in practice? (The answer to this question will, of course, demand a study of situated actions.)

Dismantling documents is not an easy task, but it is a worthwhile one, not least because every document is packed tight with assumptions and concepts and ideas that reflect on the agents who produced the document, and its intended recipients, as much as upon the people and events reported upon. For what is counted and how it is counted are expressive of specific and distinctive ways of thinking, acting and organizing. In that sense, all documents serve as a two-way mirror on aspects of human culture. That is precisely why Monsieur d'Hémery's police files are every bit as instructive as the 17-volume *Encyclopédie* that was produced by his suspects.

RESEARCH EXERCISE

Exercise 2.1

Use the questions listed immediately above to deconstruct – as far as you can – a set of official statistics on crime, poverty or disability. Some useful pointers to UK statistical data in these three areas (and others) are provided in Levitas and Guy (1996). For a next to comprehensive listing of worldwide sources of official statistical data visit: http://www2.auckland.ac.nz/lbr/stats/offstats/OFFSTATSmain.htm

Notes

1   In that sense 'reasons' for action, rather like 'motives', are not secret inner states of private individuals, but rather drawn from culturally sculpted vocabularies (Gerth and Mills, 1953). That is, vocabularies that individuals can call upon and use so as to give satisfactory and plausible accounts to interrogative others. It is, of course, such processes that the ethnomethodologists regarded as forming the focus for their investigations drawing attention to processes such as 'ad hocing', and the reflexivity of accounts (see Garfinkel, 1967, in particular).

2   Bulmer (1980), for example, has argued that the criticisms levelled against official statistics apply only to a narrow range of suicide and crime statistics. That, of course, is fundamentally to misunderstand what the constructionist argument – with respect to statistics – is all about.

3   A much cruder, Marxist, argument about the role of power in the construction of official statistics is provided by Miles and Irvine (1979). See also papers included in the collection edited by Levitas and Guy (1996), as well as the work of Coleman and Moynihan (1996) on crime data.

3

Documents in Action I. Documents in Organizational Settings

An ethnomethodologist in the archive

In the course of developing a research programme concerning the selection of patients for treatment in a Los Angeles psychiatric clinic, the aforementioned Garfinkel (1967) and his colleagues sought to extract data from a set of clinic folders. The latter were designed so as to contain information on key features of the clients and their interactions with the clinic. So, for example, any one folder might contain data on such things as the age, sex, religion, place of birth, income and other features of the client, as well as the names of the clinic personnel with whom the client came in contact. Space was also allocated for the recording of psychiatric diagnosis, previous psychiatric 'experience' and so on. On examining folder contents, however, Garfinkel noted that many items of routine data that should have been contained in the folders were missing. Thus, age was absent from the folders in 5.5 per cent of cases, occupation was missing in over half of the folders, and place of birth was missing entirely. In a similar way, reasons for the non-acceptance of patients was missing in 20 per cent of the folders, whilst the names of the staff members in charge of the intake conference were missing in just over 50 per cent of cases. Clearly these were 'bad' records, and Garfinkel turned to asking why such incomplete records existed.

One part of the answer to his puzzlement related to what Garfinkel called 'normal, natural troubles'. For example, filling in questionnaires is a time-consuming business for clinic staff. It is therefore not so surprising perhaps that such staff avoided completing those parts of the questionnaire that they considered too costly in terms of time and effort, or that they considered irrelevant to the everyday work of the clinic. Such strategies are fully understandable to anyone who has to complete such routine tasks. Yet, these 'normal natural troubles' constitute only one part of Garfinkel's story. The other part concerns reference to what he called contractual issues within the clinical encounter. And it is this second line of analysis that is of concern to us here.

By making reference to the fact that the folder contents implied contractual relationships, Garfinkel was seeking to highlight how the folders were routinely constructed with other than merely actuarial purposes in mind. In fact, suggested Garfinkel, such documents were just as readily being assembled to 'show' or hint at what had happened in the clinical encounter and what might happen to the patient. For example, clinic personnel assembled the folders aware of the possibility that the detail contained within them might be called on at some future stage to demonstrate that patients had always got the treatment they deserved. So clinic folders were, if you like, being constructed in a medico-legal framework such that it could always be shown that the 'right' things were done to the 'right' person at the 'right' time. (Though exactly how the records were to be read, and how the detail within was to be interpreted, were always dependent on a reader's purpose at hand. In that sense the meaning of the records altered according to circumstance.) Such a contractual reading of folder contents explained why it was that basic items of data could be missing from the files on the one hand, whilst marginal notes and corrections and additions to the folder contents could appear on the other. In short, it accounted for why such bad records were, nevertheless, assiduously kept. (For a study of similar themes with respect to the use of medical records in anaesthesia, see Harper et al., 1997).

The title of Garfinkel's essay was '"Good" organizational reasons for "bad" clinical records'. It successfully demonstrated how records originally designed for one set of purposes could be routinely used for quite different ends. In the Los Angeles case, actuarial purposes were supplemented with medico-legal considerations, but that in itself is of relatively little interest to us. More important is the observation that one very important dimension of any document rests in the manner of its use. What the document 'is', is specified by the way in which it is integrated into routine activity. So one key lesson that we can draw from the Garfinkel example is that people who use documents in their research schemes need to look at how documents are picked up and manipulated *in situ*, and not simply to focus on matters of content. Indeed, when one does that, one can begin to see how documents can function to mediate social relationships.

Garfinkel (1967) and his colleagues often called upon the concept of reflexivity to emphasize aspects of use. The notion of reflexivity implies that words or texts not merely represent some aspect of the world, but that they are also involved in making that world. In part, they constitute the world. With that point in mind, I intend, in this chapter, to look at a variety of ways in which documents are used so as to structure social relationships and social identities in organizational settings – how they enter into what we might call the performance of social life. In doing so it will become clear that in contrast to the usual manner of approaching documents in social research, we will have to subordinate a consideration of document content and focus instead on an anthropology of use.

A Thai village *circa* 1968

In 1968 – one year after Garfinkel published his essay on the Los Angeles clinic – the anthropologist S.J. Tambiah published an essay concerned with literacy in a Thai Buddhist village. The world that Tambiah describes is by this stage, no doubt, a lost and distant world. (We need also to keep in mind the possibility that the world as represented was Tambiah's world more than the world of the inhabitants that he sought to describe.) Despite that, the insights that Tambiah (1968) offers us remain instructive – especially in so far as he demonstrates how documents and the script that they contain can serve to structure the settings of everyday interaction and help constitute the social relationships in which they are embedded.

Documents, as we have already noted in Chapter 1, do not have to contain script. However, in the Thai case they do. What is more, and as Tambiah points out, there were at least three separate forms of script in use in the rural villages of north-east Thailand during the 1960s. Sacred or ritual literature was written in Tham script (and so were some traditional medical texts), whilst Lao script was used for secular purposes, along with the modern form of literacy embodied in Thai script.

The different scripts were associated, in Tambiah's day at least, with different social roles and different social activities. For example, those people that we might regard as the traditionally learned used documents written in Tham script. (They also used other forms of script, but seemingly regarded Tham as the most prestigious.) Consequently, the *acham wat* (the lay leader of the Buddhist congregation), the *mau khwan* (or officiant at religious rites), the *mau ya* (physician) and the *mau du* (the astrologer) used all three forms of scripts (with, apparently, varying degrees of competence). The *mau lum* – singers of the folk opera – had also to be able to read texts in all scripts, mainly so as to gain access to the traditional songs and story lines of the opera.

In village life, of course, there are always varying layers of activity and not all forms of it necessarily entail the existence of written discourse. So, for example, knowledge relating to the cult of the spirits apparently took an oral form and did not require literate participants. This latter type of activity was, Tambiah implies, of lesser status. And in between these two poles were literate people who worked almost entirely in forms of modern script, the most important example being that of the village schoolteacher.

As well as marking out social roles and activities, script was more directly used to encode particular types of knowledge. Thus, religious and traditional documents (sacred texts) were, naturally enough, in Tham script. They were deposited in the village temple along with other texts containing stories about the life of the Buddha, texts on the discipline of monks, the nature of sermons and so on. Access to such texts and to the script that encoded them was via the temple – Buddhist traditional script was taught within the temple. Government documents, on the other hand, were written in Thai script, and would have required of their readers a knowledge and use of such script – the script of the village headman and of the schoolteacher.

So what does this résumé of the Tambiah essay suggest? First, it highlights how script can be used to mark out social roles and associated forms of power/knowledge (Foucault, 1991). In rural Thailand, it seems, the various forms of script marked out the roles of monk, teacher and traditional singer/actor. And whilst there is no direct parallel to such a trio in contemporary western society, there nevertheless remains an association between forms of specialized script and specific activities. The professional (classical) musician, for example, needs to be able to read modern musical notation, whilst the professional mathematician and engineer need to read and use modern mathematical and other forms of scientific notation. Access to the specialized scripts provides access to specialized knowledge and the use of such scripts in practice marks out the specialized roles. Similar considerations no doubt arise in relation to the manipulation and use of modern forms of script such as those, for example, involved in computer programming languages. How these various scripts are accessed and disseminated is clearly related to patterns of social structuration (Giddens, 1984), and throughout this chapter we shall follow through on yet other examples of how a specialized script can enter into, and structure, social interchange. Secondly, it is evident from what Tambiah tells us that the actual use of a text can, in itself, serve to constitute social events and relationships. Thus, the use of a prayer book in Tham script can be used to mark out a 'sacred' – rather than a profane – moment, whilst the use of a form in Thai script may be used to mark out a moment when official (state) business is being conducted. The script serves to constitute the scene and mediates the interactions within it.

One final point: we may note from Tambiah's description that knowledge derived from script is often turned into an oral medium (translated) before circulation. All text that is verbalized involves translation. In Tambiah's world one very important medium of translation involved song, dance and chant (the opera). And the importance of song and performance in aspects of daily life is not to be underestimated.[1] The significance of such matters, however, extends way beyond the boundaries of this text, though the importance of translation and of specialized script does not. In that vein, it will prove more interesting to us to examine a translation process that moves in the opposite direction – from talk to text. To that end I intend to zoom in a little closer on the use of specialized script in organizational settings. The following examples are all drawn from studies of medical clinics.

Talk and text in the clinic

In his discussion of a psychiatric record, Hak (1992) provides an example as to how a professional psychiatrist translates items of patient talk and observed behaviour into a written record. In so doing the psychiatrist – as note taker – highlights the essential details of a patient's conversation, codes them into professional language (of delusions, hallucinations, diagnostic terms, etc.) and makes suggestions for future action (entry into a psychiatric unit or whatever). In Figure 3.1 we can see similar processes at work. Figure 3.1 is a facsimile of a page of nursing assessment notes that I came across in a psychiatric hospital in the late 1980s. It is clear from the notes that the members of the nursing staff were concerned to categorize their patients in a variety of ways. The latter included a one-word diagnosis of the patient's condition, an assessment of 'activities of daily living' (ADL) skills, brief notes concerning the level of co-operation and hygiene exhibited by the patient and so forth. These assessments were based on conversations and interchanges between nurses and patients and among nurses alone. It is important to recall that the patients/clients – as with all human beings – commonly indulged in a wide array of activities and behaviours. For example, patients would talk to themselves, watch television, lend each other cigarettes, shout, laugh, go to work in the hospital workshops and so forth. Yet of such arrays of activity only a few are ever highlighted. Thus, in the case of the first-named patient, it is the patient's 'schizophrenia', poor ADL skills, temper tantrums and quarrelsome behaviour that are highlighted. This selectivity of focus would become even more evident were one to examine other kinds of patient records. Thus, in the hospital to which I am currently referring there were also psychiatric records (called 'charts'), and social work records kept on each patient. The former were maintained by the medically trained psychiatrists and contained other kinds of information, such as data on whether the patients exhibited any 'first-rank symptoms' (of schizophrenia), their medication and its effects, their 'history', items about family life, patient delusions and so forth. In fact the psychiatric records looked very much like those alluded to and reported upon by Hak (1992). Social work records were also made up for each of the patients. These paid relatively little attention to medical diagnoses and the effects of medication and referred more often to the stability and maturity of the patient vis-à-vis relationships with others, the nature and level of the patient's state benefits and the like. Considerable reference to the whereabouts, behaviours and opinions of other family members was also made within social work files. Access to such records and the 'right' to make entries in such records were more or less restricted to the members of the individual professional groupings. In that respect the 'script' in each

Patient	Admissions	Diagnosis	Problems/Constraints	Medication	Plans	Assets
Name: Dob 11/12/36 **Admin area:** East **Dr:** Yellow **Ward:** Blue	**No. of adm.** = 1 **Date of last adm.** 17/06/1962	Schizophrenia	Long time in hospital Temper tantrums & bad language Activities of daily living poor Recently quarrelsome with ASB	Gavison tabs bd Trifluoperazine 2 mg bd Vit BPc 1 tab mane	Maintain	ADL skills good
Name: Dob 23/02/53 North **Dr:** Green **Ward:** Blue	**No. of adm.** = 5 **Date of last adm.** 29/09/1987	Paranoid Schizophrenia	Loner. Poor motivation Wishes to stay in hospital Failed RA (stay in residential accommodation) Injury to right hip	Piroxican 30 mg nocte Ranitidine 150 mg nocte Vit BPc am	Move to community	ADL skills good
Name: Dob 3/07/58 West **Dr:** Green **Ward:** Blue	**No. of adm.** = 3 **Date of last adm.** 17/05/1988	Schizophrenia Low IQ	Poverty of thought Withdrawn ADL skills limited Childish and naïve in manner Mother has encouraged dependence over the years but is now opting out Poor road safety	Benxtropine 2 mg mane Thioridizine 75 mg tid Senna 2 tabs nocte	ADL activities	Pleasant & co-operative Hygiene good
Name: Dob 10/08/60 West **Dr:** Green **Ward:** Blue	**No. of adm.** = 6 **Date of last adm.** 10/03/1988	Dependent Personality	Multiple Somatic complaints Resistant to suggestions Poor compliance tends to opt out Poor response to antidepressant therapy Poor attendance at OT unit Poor Hearing	Thyroxine 0.1 mg mane Nifedipine 10 mg bd Thioridizine 50 mg bd	Maintain	ADL good

FIGURE 3.1   *Facsimile of a ward-based nursing assessment record (UK psychiatric hospital, 1989)*

document served, in part, to mark out the realm and expertise of the various parties – in much the same way as did the various forms of script in Tambiah's Thai village. Social work talk belonged in social work records, psychiatric talk belonged in medical records, and nurse talk belonged in nursing records.

Recorded observations on patients/clients are, then, highly selective. In the case of public service agency files, such records often define the human beings that they refer to in specific and particular ways. In so doing they call upon and activate a whole series of what we referred to in Chapter 2 as membership categorization devices (Silverman, 1998). How a particular device comes to be associated with any individual and how that categorization might be used and called upon to account for and explain an individual's behaviour in specific circumstances can form the occasion for important and fundamental sociological research.

In my work on the psychiatric hospital referred to above, I was primarily interested in how patients came to be classified in different ways through routine procedures (see Prior, 1993). Naturally the use of notes and records forms only one support for the identification system that surrounds patients. Everyday conversation and casual interchanges form another, and in any organization there will always be a constant interchange between talk and text. Thus I provided in my 1993 study a short extract of an exchange between nurses in the ward office concerning the issue as to what was wrong with 'X'. Viz.

Nurse 1:   Does anyone know what's supposed to be wrong with X?
            [*Blank looks and silence meet the question.*]
Nurse 2:   Schizophrenia, I suppose.
Nurse 1:   Hmm. I've never seen any sign of it.
Nurse 3:   Well, he's on chlorpromazine, so he must be schizophrenic.

The MCD of 'schizophrenic' recorded in the notes is, then, sustained and underlined in this case by means of a casual conversation – and especially the reference to 'X's' medication. (The use of medication to define a specific psychiatric disorder, rather than the other way round, is not uncommon in psychiatry.) If, however, there were any real doubt about 'what was wrong with X', it would be the notes that would carry the day. So the researcher who wishes to concentrate on the use of documents in action has to be constantly aware as to how the written record is tied into and anchored within other aspects of organizational life such as conversations at the nursing station. Nevertheless, it is only when assessments are written down and can be pointed to that they are used to form a foundation on which routine social actions are built. Thus medical professionals can and do use 'the files' as a warrant for their actions in relation to their patients, showing how what they do to patients is warranted by the information on the record(s). Indeed, in the context of psychiatry Barrett (1996: 107) has underlined how 'clinical writing' not only describes the treatment of patients, but also constitutes the treatment.

In a wider context, Bowker and Star (1999) and Young (1995) have also pointed out how (documented) nomenclatures of disease are routinely tied into the financial accounting mechanisms of hospital life. So, psychiatrists routinely draw down a diagnostic category from the DSM, 'fit' it to a given patient, and then justify what was done for and to the patient/client in the light of the category. (This, in the full knowledge that categories and patients rarely make a 1:1 fit.) Indeed, the naming of diseases and disorders in modern medical systems is often used more for purposes of financial reimbursement (to and from insurance companies), and other accounting and monitoring purposes, than it is for forming accurate descriptions of a given patient's condition.

Arguing along a similar path, Zerubavel (1979: 45) had previously indicated how notes written up by medical and nursing professionals were 'among the main criteria used by their supervisors to evaluate their clinical competence', as well as forming the primary mechanism through which continuous supervision of patients was maintained. In fact Zerubavel's study highlights the centrality of charts, graphs and records of all kinds in underpinning the routine social organization of hospital life. Thus, printed schedules are used to organize the patient/staff day; printouts of various kinds are routinely used to monitor patients; and notes are written so as indicate how the 'hospital' cares for its clients. (In American hospitals, of course, patient records are, as we have already indicated, also used as a hook on which to hang financial costs and transactions.) Above all perhaps, we see in the use of documents to monitor activity an essential component of that self-reflexive capacity that is said by Bauman (1991) to characterize modernity as a whole.

This capacity of medical records to mediate social relationships of all kinds has been further researched by Berg (1996; 1997) who points out how hospital patients are both structured through records and accessed through records. One important feature of patient existence that is emphasized by Berg is the manner in which medical records are used so as to keep the case (and the patient) 'on track'. Such structuring of patient trajectories through records is achieved in numerous ways – planning and monitoring being two of them. In this respect it is of interest to note the column headed 'Plans' in Figure 3.1. In the context of these records the most important plans concerned whether or not the patient was ready for life in the community. (My own hospital study was executed at that rather important cusp where psychiatric patients were being moved out of hospitals and into 'the community'.) In most cases, the patients were to be 'maintained' (kept in the hospital ward). The detail hardly concerns us here. What is important to note is that records of this type always contain some rules for action. Other rules for action are contained in the column relating to medication. Latour (1987) has used the term 'action at a distance' to indicate how decisions written down in one context and setting

---

Part 2: Special Educational Needs.

(Here set out the child's special educational needs, in terms of the child's learning difficulties which call for special educational provision)

'Z' is a pleasant, likeable boy who has a severely delayed/disordered phonological system and a mild delay in his expressive language. His speech is largely unintelligible. Due to the severity of this delay he has difficulty in accessing the curriculum. He was slow to adapt to the social routines of the school day. His attention span is limited without adult support. He does show a high response in one to one situations with a known adult. Interaction with his peers is improving. Assessment of his non-verbal intellectual functioning is at the bottom end of the high average range, however, verbal intelligence falls into the low average range.

This pupil's special educational needs have been identified as follows:

1 severe speech and language delay/disorder
2 poor social/interactive skills

The attached reports contain more detail about 'Z's' specific attainments.

Part 3: Special Educational Provision.

Objectives. (Here specify the objectives which the special educational provision should aim to meet)

The objectives of the special educational provision to be made for this pupil should be:

1 To improve his receptive and expressive language skills
2 To develop early literacy and numeracy skills
3 To improve social/interactive skills.

Educational provision to meet needs and objectives

FIGURE 3.2   *Extracts from a 'Statement of Special Educational Needs', Great Britain, 1999*

can carry implications for action in future settings. And it is indeed the case that records often contain instructions for future organizational activity. On that note I draw attention to Figure 3.2.

The figure contains extracts from a 'special educational needs assessment' of a young boy. A psychologist executed the assessment. Note the categorization devices used in the assessment – such as 'pleasant, likeable boy [with] a severely delayed/disordered phonological system' – and how the concerns of the psychologist structure the identity of the child. Note also that Part 3 of the assessment contains instructions for future action. How such action was to be implemented was the subject of a later section of the report that has not been reproduced here; nevertheless it is clear that the report is designed not simply to categorize the child and his 'problems' but also so as to instigate future action-at-a-distance. (Alternatively the written assessment was open to recruitment by parents, teachers and others so as to demand more resources for the child even in the event of the 'action' failing to take place.)

There is one final point that perhaps needs emphasis. It is clear that people not only maintain records so as to legitimize action or to claim warrant for their actions, or, indeed, to classify events, objects and processes in the everyday world, but also use records to sustain micro interactions. In this respect the following extract is worth studying. It was obtained in a fatigue clinic. The physician (denoted by D) usually had difficulty in telling his patients (denoted by P) that, despite extensive test procedures, no evident physical pathology could be found to account for their fatigue. The alternative explanation was to raise the possibility of their condition being 'psychological' (lines 70–76) – a suggestion that few of the patients welcomed. In this extract the physician is attempting to 'talk to his notes' and thereby use them as a key prop to his consulting strategy. (Incidentally, the patient referred to below was seated in a wheelchair at the time of the interchange.)

57 D [*reading notes containing test results*]:	MRI scan tells us that you haven't got MS ... Blood tests, fine ... antibodies ... fine/
60 P65:	What is it then?
61 D:	Well, we've checked out the central nervous system and there's nothing untoward there. Maybe we ought to check out the peripheral system. [*Returns to his notes, reading apparently to himself whilst the patient talks to her husband.*]
.	
.	
.	
70 D:	You were treated for depression in ...?/
72 P65:	The doctor [i.e. the Primary Care Practitioner], he just kept on saying I
75	was depressed.
76 D:	And were you?
77 P65:	I'm housebound, I can't get out of bed in the mornings ... I have to climb the
80	stairs on my bum ...

I have explored the wider implications of these kinds of conversations in Banks and Prior (2001). Here I am only interested in drawing attention to the use of written documents as an ally in face-to-face interactions. In the above instance the notes were used as a prop to dealing with a sensitive issue. In that vein it might be useful to examine some further examples of documents in use, this time in the context of homicide.

Documents and organizational activity

In *The Concept of Mind* (1990), Gilbert Ryle uses an illustrative example of a visitor to Oxford being shown around some college buildings and then asking, 'But where is the University?' The visitor, Ryle suggested, was making a category mistake – confusing problems that can be posed in terms of 'where' questions with those that cannot. Yet, be that as it may, in common-sense usage, the visitor's question still stands. 'Where', indeed, is the University?

One answer to such a question is that a university (any university) is in its documents rather than in its buildings. In the UK, for example, universities are established by a charter. The charter – together with other documents – names the university, provides warrant to award degrees, legitimizes the officers of the university and so on. Naturally, a university has buildings and equipment and lecturers and students, but none of those things are sufficient for the award of university status. Only the charter can define the organization as a university, and in that sense provide the one necessary condition for its existence. More importantly, it is documentation that invariably forms the basis for what Atkinson and Coffey (1997) refer to as 'documentary realities' – organizational features that are created and sustained almost entirely in and through the documentation.

Universities are not alone in this respect. Indeed, in any organization it can be quickly seen that it is documentation – rather than its artefacts or members – that underpins the organizational presence. (Atkinson and Coffey (1997), for example, cite a financial statement as a representation of an organizational existence.) On a more specific level we might take the post of university lecturer (or accountant, or media relations officer, or research chair). These posts only exist in the written (documented) job descriptions that brought them into existence. That is not to say that human beings always act in accordance with job descriptions and fail to act in any other way than as described, or that work can be reduced to job descriptions. On the contrary, we know that such things are not possible. It is to say, however, that the warrant for the position and the template against which human performance is to be measured are in the writing rather than the doing. Posts, committees, and even organizational structures themselves (such as departmental structures) exist and can be pointed to, only in so far as they are documented. This is, of course, a point well made by Dorothy Smith (1984) in her paper on textually mediated social organization.

In the normal course of events documentation has a relatively low profile in any organizational system. That is not to say that things, events and processes are not documented, only that such documentation is regarded as routine and thereby becomes invisible. At critical points, however (usually when things go 'wrong', or when procedures are subject to an unusual degree of scrutiny or monitoring), documentation comes into its own (Zimmerman, 1969). Thus, Bowker (1994) points out, for example, how the written traces left by the Schlumberger Company in its own archives changed radically in response to the realization of possible forms of legal and political pressure.

In this section I am going to concentrate on what we might call organizational failure. Such failure is usually only traceable and accountable through the written record and therefore (from a research standpoint) crises in organizational life can provide considerable opportunities for investigation. Thus, if someone claims to have a plan of action, then – when things go wrong – they have to produce its written form in order to convince us that it existed. If someone claims to have 'done the right thing in the circumstances' then their case is only watertight if they can show that they acted in accordance with some written protocol or other. If someone claims to have foreseen a disaster and alerted people to it, then their alarm should be evident in the documentation. And if someone wishes to demonstrate that their work and their projects were organized they must, once again, recruit some documentation to demonstrate systematization and orderliness. In all these respects Dianne Vaughan's (1996) study of the *Challenger* disaster provides invaluable examples that require extensive study.[2] In this section, however, I am going to focus on disasters of another kind. They concern homicides in the UK – homicides committed by people who are said to have psychiatric problems. My main point of focus is on how the 'organization' of care only comes into focus through documentation. In following through to that conclusion, however, we will be enticed to consider a series of other significant issues.

Let us establish at the start that people with psychiatric problems rarely commit homicidal acts. Indeed, such individuals are far more likely to be a danger to themselves than to others. Nevertheless, for reasons that do not concern us here, homicidal events involving people with psychiatric problems normally receive a high media profile. In the UK such events are invariably marked by the publication of a Mental Health Inquiry (MHI) Report. Such Reports first appeared during the 1980s. (By the end of the century there were just over 30 MHI Reports in publication.) It is to the nature of such reports that I now wish to turn.

In 1994 the National Health Service Executive (the body responsible for the policy and planning of the UK health service) published a circular (NHS, 1994) stating – among other things – what should be done 'If things go wrong' in the organization of care for those with a serious psychiatric disorder. It stated that in cases of homicide an MHI would always be required. (There is a sense therefore in which the very presence of an MHI Report marks out a space – a crisis area – where something has gone wrong.) And when things go wrong, people always ask penetrating questions.

In most cases, MHI Reports open with a simple narrative of the events leading up to the murder or murders. The narrative links together things, people and events that until that point had not been so linked. Thus, any and all incidents in which the murderer had made verbal threats, or used violence, or had been involved in unusual behaviour previous to any homicide are closely recorded. For example, Sharon Campbell murdered her social worker in

1984. The previous year it was said that she had assaulted her victim and made threatening telephone calls to her. She had also been in possession of a knife in her hospital ward. Christopher Clunis, who stabbed his victim to death in 1992, had previously been involved in minor theft from a shop, abusive behaviour, sexually explicit behaviour and violence. The very recording of such incidents in the MHI Report (Ritchie et al., 1994) serves to implicate them in the homicidal process. In fact, such events are usually recontextualized in the Reports as 'warning signals', and it is subsequently implied or suggested that various professionals should have picked up the signals and acted on them. Indeed, among the many recommendations that the MHI Reports make, time and again, are those that concern the fact that notable incidents be recorded (see Reith, 1998). So Sharon Campbell's possession of a knife 'should have been recorded' in her medical record. The various misdemeanours of Clunis should also have been recorded − by nurses, social workers, the police − and so forth. The absence of a record is in such contexts interpreted as a 'failure'. Indeed, lack of documentation is commonly invoked to demonstrate lack of concern, planning, foresight and organization.

Yet, it is also clear from the MHI Reports that recording, in itself, is usually viewed as an insufficient demonstration of 'organized' care. Thus if we take the case of S.A. Armstrong who raped and murdered 4-year-old Rosie Palmer during the summer of 1994, we see that whilst there were many notes, files and dossiers on the man, none of them were linked. Indeed, Armstrong was only ever considered a single, undifferentiated and identifiable case in retrospect − that is, in the MHI Report (Freeman et al., 1996). (The same, incidentally, was true of Clunis as a 'case'.) So Armstrong, as a client and as a subject, was formally described, accounted for and referred to in various registers − social services registers, probation registers, registers concerning child sexual abuse, police registers, in-patient and out-patient registers and so on. Yet, the exchange of information on Armstrong as a single autonomous subject was limited to the extent that no agency ever 'looked at the totality of the case' (1996: 88). Each criminal and medical episode in his life was therefore investigated and dealt with on an isolated basis (1996: 88), and there was little communication of information between agencies. In other words, the organization of care was not demonstrable in the documentation.

In line with this fragmentation of records, Armstrong had numerous histories − written up by different people working in different agencies. The MIH Report's authors in fact criticized the paucity of history taking in both nursing and social work. They were especially critical of the manner in which hospital nurses had described Armstrong in terms of a specific ('Roper–Logan–Tierney') model that had been designed for use in the hospital as a whole and which was unsuitable for use with psychiatric patients. In other words, nurses had used the wrong template when they recorded his detail. Somewhat interestingly, nursing staff had variously described Armstrong as '(1) pleasant and sociable ... (9) tall with glasses ... (12) wearing Cuban heels ... (13) slimy (14) a story teller' (1996: 74).

Not being in receipt of psychotropic medication, however, Armstrong was not truly considered as a case of mental illness.

So the organization of community care – the 'seamless web' that is supposed to surround psychiatric clients placed in the community – is judged, at times of crisis, not so much in terms of what goes on in a given location or institution, nor by street-level activity, but more in terms of written plans, registers and monitoring procedures. Indeed, the actual organization of care can only be made evident in plans, registers and written protocols. In the absence of relevant documents a systematic and planned approach to professional practice cannot be demonstrated. Indeed, we might say that 'care' is something that is, essentially, 'performed' (Goffman, 1959; Mol, 1999; 2000). One important component of such performance is in the documentation – for the documents specify how the performance is to be executed. Moreover, unlike physical interactions, documents can extend across time and place and can be pointed to and recruited as evidence in a way that transitory actions and talk cannot. That is, perhaps, why 'performance indicators' usually take a documentary form. For action turned into documentary outputs (figures, reports and so forth) can be evaluated long after the physical performances, to which they supposedly refer, have passed.

One final point; it is a point often made in the MHI Reports themselves: namely, that the only time that the lives of the damaged individuals of whom we speak is reported upon in a holistic manner is in an MHI Report. Outside of the Reports such lives and identities remain partial and fragmented. We shall follow through on the relationships between documents and identity in Chapter 5. For now, however, I want to provide just one more example of the ways in which documents can be used to constitute an event. On this occasion the event is an environmental one rather than a personal one. Our focus, as ever, is on how the document functions in the network of concerns that we are about to unravel.

The politics of fog

In December 1952 an anti-cyclone came to rest over the town of London. A combination of warm air from the Gulf Stream and the slow-moving anti-cyclone produced a temperature inversion over the city. The warm air trapped beneath the cloud cover and the cold air above it were ideal conditions for fog. Indeed, it was and is referred to as the Great Fog of 1952. The fog lasted from about 4 December until 8 December. Visibility was reduced astoundingly – theatregoers at Sadler's Wells, for example, were unable to see the stage on which *La Traviata* was being performed. The performances were cancelled. Londoners had difficulty in breathing and the number of people with respiratory problems admitted to hospital increased dramatically over the December period. Indeed, an interim report on the fog suggested that some 12,000 people died as a result of it.[3] Fog, it would seem, has such consequences. The official report on these events, published in 1954 – Ministry of Health *Report on Mortality and Morbidity during the London Fog of December 1952* – later reduced the estimate of the number of casualties to 8,000, simply by using a cut-off point for deaths of 20 December. As we have seen in Chapter 2, quantitative analysts are allowed such tricks. Yet, the deviousness with numbers was, perhaps, the least disturbing thing about these events.

A few years earlier in Donora, Pennsylvania, a similar set of circumstances had arisen.[4] The Donora Smog disaster of October 1948 had claimed 18 to 20 lives. Some 7,000 citizens were hospitalized. The root of such disaster lay in the presence of toxic levels of sulphur dioxide in the air. The poisonous gas had, like the London fog, been trapped in a temperature inversion, on this occasion an inversion in the Monongehela Valley. Unlike the London fog, however, many individuals had an idea that the smog (a word denoting smoke mixed with fog) was far from 'natural'. For, on at least three previous occasions, the American Steel and Wire Company – which owned a zinc plant in the valley – had been cited in damage suits filed in the State Supreme Court for generating noxious fumes 'wilfully, wantonly and maliciously'. In fact, the 1949 state investigation report on the disaster argued that the events were caused neither by smog nor by fog, but by 'air pollution' during unusual weather conditions. Fog is a natural occurrence. Under specific conditions it occurs in valleys and coastal sites. Air pollution, on the other hand, is manufactured. It is, if you like, person-made. The description of the London pollution as 'fog' was, of course, extremely useful to the government of the day. Fog was natural. Nothing could be done to prevent it. (The government had, however, issued flimsy face-masks to the population in order to be seen to be 'doing' something.) But air pollution – the emphasis is on 'pollution' here – demands action. The Donora disaster led to the adoption of state and federal laws to control levels of air pollution. The London disaster resulted in few immediate changes.

Fog was known to be endemic in London. Towards the end of the nineteenth century there had occurred a series of particularly dense fogs. The twentieth century, however, had been relatively free from fog. Apart from Donora, the most renowned case of air pollution had occurred in the Meuse Valley (Belgium) rather than London. The base cause of such fogs lay in the burning of fuels – particularly coal and petrol – and the consequent pollution of the atmosphere with sulphur dioxide and other contaminants. In calm winter weather of the type that affected London in December 1952, the pollutants became trapped below the cloud level and thickened up with each passing day. The 1952 fog was probably exacerbated by the fact that a number of very large coal-burning power stations had been recently opened in and around London, and together with the smoke from other industrial, domestic and traffic outputs the density of pollution was increased. (How and why the technological style of the London power system required the construction and operation of a large number of coal-fired power stations is of considerable interest in itself – see Hughes, 1989.) The official report on the fog, however, side-stepped these issues entirely. 'It is not within the scope of this report', stated the anonymous authors, 'to draw attention to measures necessary for the prevention of atmospheric pollution' (Ministry of Health, 1954: 3).

Instead, what the report concentrated on was deaths and the causes of death during the month of December. There had clearly been an excess of deaths over the average for the previous five years – though the size of that excess, as we have seen, depends on the cut-off point that is used to measure it. People, of course, die naturally. Indeed, claimed the anonymous authors of the 1954 report, the pattern of deaths from respiratory diseases was not all that different in 1952 from what it had been in previous years, but 'the fog hastened the deaths of a number of patients' (1954: 18). Fog was a 'precipitating agent' on a susceptible group of people whose life-expectancy must, in any case, 'have been short' (1954: 1). So there were 'no deaths attributable to fog among those who were previously healthy' (1954: 38), and there was no evidence in anyone of a 'smog lesion' (1954: 25). Finally, the committee responsible for the report concluded that in the present state of knowledge it was impossible to state that any one pollutant was the cause of death.

In restricting itself to a report on the causes of death, the committee thereby confined itself to a focus on the anatomical sites of death. For, as we have seen in Chapter 2, modern western culture understands death solely in terms of anatomical sites and named diseases. In this respect the reference to a 'smog lesion' is particularly instructive. The interpretation of disease as involving the production of a lesion (a visible pathology in the body) has its origins in the development of Paris medicine during the early nineteenth century. Foucault (1973) has already described the significance of Paris medicine for western understandings of disease and death, and there is no need for us to follow his path from this particular junction. We need only add that during the very last quarter of the nineteenth century a further theory of disease (let us call it the 'germ' theory) indicated how lesions could be caused by microbes. Henceforth, there was a belief that for every lesion there was one and only one causative agent. The tuberculosis (TB) lesions were produced by inhalation of the (TB) bacillus. The spiral-shaped bacterium that travelled through the genito-urinary system caused the lesions of the syphilitic – and so forth. So if 'smog' were a cause of disease then, by implication, it too should have a lesion – but there was none. The lesion that was evident upon post-mortem was similar to that caused by the pneumococcus. That is to say, the dead had died from the pneumonias and especially bronchopneumonia. In the medical frame of the age, then, the deaths were caused by things that had no relation to smog or fog. If the fog were significant, then it was significant only as some exacerbating agent – it affected the rate of death not the causes of death.

A similar kind of expert argument was widely used by other authorities during the twentieth century. Cigarette smokers, for example, fell victim to heart disease, lung cancer, respiratory conditions and other things that people died of 'naturally', so it would be foolish to claim that cigarettes caused death. Coal miners and cotton workers as well as those who worked in asbestos factories died similarly. So it would be equally mistaken to blame their deaths on coal dust, or cotton dust, or asbestos dust. A focus on a lesion and its specific cause is clearly a useful mechanism for distributing and redistributing responsibility. Robert Proctor (1995) demonstrates just how useful a mechanism it has been in obscuring our knowledge about carcinogens in the modern world. This is not to suggest sleight of hand on behalf of all authorities that argued in this manner. Those who affirmed the medical frame of the age were unable to integrate things such as cigarette smoke and smog into their causal schemes. People died of diseases and diseases were caused by specific agents – mostly microbes – whose presence was visible in the (dead) human frame. Neither smog nor any of its component elements were known to cause a 'smog disease'.

We can begin to see, then, how the report as a document enters as an actor into a network of actions. It serves as a repository of 'expert' knowledge on a problem. In fact, it defines what the problem is (people are dying of respiratory diseases). It collects evidence in accordance with its definition of that problem. Within its realm of expertise, it hints at possible solutions (people with respiratory diseases should stay indoors during fogs). It functions to provide adequate, expert, accounts and explanations of what has happened (it narrates the biography of a disaster from within a specialist, technical frame). It segments the world into that of which one can speak rationally, and that which lies beyond the realm of expertise (issues relating to atmospheric pollution). It maps out what, if any, political actions may have to flow from the findings. The fact that the authors of the report chose to remain absolutely silent on what many might regard as the single most important thing that was relevant to the events (namely, atmospheric pollution), clearly meant that no decisions had to be made or taken on measures to control air quality. Power, and other industrial facilities could continue to belch out smoke, vehicle emissions required no control, and householders could continue to stoke their coal-burning fires. The expert report could, when required, be appropriately recruited by active parties to support a laissez-faire attitude towards pollution control. The experts had spoken and had failed to identify pollution as of any primary significance.

As we have seen with the MHI Reports, the report on the London fog may be analysed in terms of its content or of its use. These are not mutually exclusive options, but it is truly the active rather than the inert document that should form the field for the social scientific investigator. In that frame what we need to do is to look at how the text is used by social actors in the course of their everyday activities, and how the text itself can become an agent in the various social networks in which it becomes embedded. Who recruits the report as an ally, and who is arraigned against it? What is enrolled within the report and what is excluded? And how does the text (report) itself become an agent in a network of action?

Conclusion: how to do things with documents

In his justly renowned *How to do things with words*, J.L. Austin (1962) refers to performatives. The sentence 'I promise' is an example of a performative. For, in speaking the sentence the speaker also does something (acts). It is an idea that can be usefully transferred to the study of documents, which also 'do' things by the very condition of their existence. For example, the common or garden office memo not only carries (mundane) information, but also gives expression to a set of (power) relations within an organizational setting. Indeed, memos give concrete expression to systems of hierarchy – of superordination and subordination – and certainly serve to define social networks. Further, by containing demands and instructions, the memo becomes engaged in a system of action-at-a-distance. (The memo written in one co-ordinate of time and place triggers activity in another.) The same might be said of summonses, invoices and contracts of all kinds (see, for example, Hughes and Griffiths, 1999). Indeed texts routinely have such 'structuring' effects (Smith, 1984) and are central to the patterning and organizing of everyday activities. So the manner in which documents circulate and are accessed serves to mark off social groupings and organizational positions.

The content of memos, registers, contracts, blackboards and other 'inscription devices' (Latour, 1987) are, then, of considerable significance. Yet, a focus on content to the exclusion of the manner in which a document is used could easily lead the social scientific researcher astray. Thus, a study of legislation (such as was embodied in, say, the Constitution of the old Soviet Union) and the history and manner of its production would provide a thin picture of the legal process unless we also studied how such legislation was used in action. That is, how it was drawn down, referred to, interpreted, recruited by opposing parties in the courts and so forth. And the same might be said of any legal system. Documents as inert matter offer a very different field of study from documents as agents.

It is for such reasons that I have attempted, in this chapter, to focus on documents in organizational settings. I have focused, in particular, on how documents can both mediate and structure episodes of social interaction. Above and beyond that, I have also shown how documents can be recruited into alliances of interests so as to develop and underpin particular visions of the world and the things and events within that world. Thus we have examined, for example, how the identities of 'patients', 'clients' and the criminally insane are structured through documentation; how forms of documentation can be used as warrants for action, or as props in interaction; and how 'organization' is made evident – 'performed' – through the written record. Finally we have seen how an investigative report can both structure a view of events and be enrolled so as to justify political and administrative (in)action with respect to environmental problems. In that light, it is very clear that, ultimately, documents can damage

2 1

your health! If there is one single lesson to be learnt from these diverse examples, however, it is that documents serve to constitute the events of which they form a part. In that respect they deserve parity of esteem with talk and behaviour in the execution of the research process.

So just to summarize the key points:

- People do things with documents.
- The task of the researcher should therefore be to follow a document in use.

Following documents in use requires situated (empirical) studies. In particular, we need to pay attention to the manner in which:

- A document is enrolled into routine activity, who enrols it and who opposes it.
- A document functions, and whether its function alters with context.
- A document serves to constitute an event or phenomenon of which it is itself part.

RESEARCH EXERCISES

Exercise 3.1

Locate an official (local or national, state or federal) government report on a set of events where 'something has gone wrong' – such as a report on an environmental tragedy, an economic or political failure or a failure of personal duty. (1) Examine the limitations and boundaries set by the terms of the report. (2) Try to determine whether any parties attempted to broaden or narrow the scope of the report. (3) Examine any key assumptions contained within the report and their implications for the report's findings. (4) Try to determine the ways in which any results have been used, and by whom. (5) Note particularly the individuals who used the report to establish claims about issues that lay outside of the report's field of concern.

Exercise 3.2

Examine exactly how published crime statistics are used and recruited by members of political parties for various ends. Make a special note of differences of 'reading' with respect to published results. In the UK case, Reiner (1996) provides some useful leads on this issue. See also Coleman and Moynihan (1996).

Exercise 3.3

Using a selection of school reports on individuals, identify an array of characteristic MCDs used in the reports. Examine how the MCDs are used so as to construct an identity for the people being reported upon. Analyse and identify how the reports may implicate others in action-at-a-distance.

Exercise 3.4

Identify and study a small sample of e-mail communications and try to determine how such mailings have been used to demarcate and under-pin a social network.

In executing work for exercises of the type mentioned in 3.3 and 3.4 above, think carefully about the ethical implications of your investiga-tion before undertaking it. In executing work for exercises of the type mentioned in 1 and 2 searches of electronic newspaper databases and WWW pages are indispensable.

Notes

1 For example, in his analysis of the street songs and common conversation of pre-Revolutionary France, Darnton (2000) emphasizes how stories, songs, jokes and pamphlets belong to a dense web of communication that are sometimes used to further important political ends. Thus in the world of pre-Revolutionary France the songs and literature of the street tended to emphasize the scandals of the French court and the sexual life of the king. The *libelles* and the *chroniques scandaleuses* embodied in written documentation echoed in the notes of the *chansonnier* in the cafés. A modern example of translations between talk and text is provided by Jönsson and Linell (1991).

2 For another example of organizational failure involving documentation see Vaughan (1983), and Vaughan (1999).

3 At the time of writing, information on the Great London Smog of 1952 was avail-able on the following web pages: http://www.docm.mmu.ac.uk/aric/eae/Air_Quality/Older/Great_London_Smog.html and http://www.met-office.gov.uk/education/historic/smog.html

4 http://www.dep.state.pa.us/dep/rachel_carson/donora.htm

4

Documents in Action II. Making things visible

The tree of knowledge

People think with things as well as with words (Prior, 1997). How they arrange
and organize things in the world is important, not least because – as was shown
in Chapter 2 – the organization of things provides insight into the most fundamental aspects of human culture. In literate cultures, of course, the organization of things is anchored in writing as well as in three-dimensional space. As
a result the social researcher of such cultures has a wealth of data available for
analysis that is simply not open to researchers in cultures where writing is
absent – though access to other symbolic systems may well be available (see,
for example, Poole, 1969).

For a panoramic view of the ways in which people arrange things in the
world there are few better objects for study than encyclopaedias. Nowadays
encyclopaedias are common enough items, accepting that the weighty tomes
of the past have been replaced by electronic rather than written media. Yet the
world has not always been brimming with encyclopaedias. In fact, it seems fair
to assert that a set of volumes that claim to provide a comprehensive overview
of the world and the contents within is essentially a feature of modern western
culture.

There is probably little point in entering into debates about the first instance
of any one thing. Yet, it seems fair to suggest that one of the earliest of all
encyclopaedias was that published in Paris during the period 1751–72. The editors
of the vast work sought, above all, to provide a map of available 'knowledge'
and of all the by-ways within it. In short, to impose an encyclopaedic order

on the world. In so doing they used a number of simple ordering devices. Foremost among these was the use of an alphabetic sequence – so the entries in the encyclopaedia were arranged in dictionary order.[1] (Indeed, in the one set of volumes we see the emergence of two rather impressive forms of literality – encyclopaedias and dictionaries.) Alphabetic sequence, was not, however, the only ordering device that was used by the encyclopaedia's editors. They also used an ordering metaphor to organize knowledge. That metaphor was of a tree. The image of a tree of knowledge has, as Darnton (1984) points out, a much older pedigree than that of the *Encyclopédie*. It is also of some interest to note that the only image of evolution provided in Darwin's *Origin of Species* is of a tree, and that the image of a branching tree continues to play an important symbolic role in western science generally – see Gould (1989). In the case of Diderot and d'Alembert (the editors of the Paris encyclopaedia) there were really three trees – named, respectively, Memory, Reason and Imagination. Within each tree there were many branches. So, for example, the tree of Memory had branches leading to 'nature' and its many divisions. Within that there were divisions relating to the 'uniformity of nature', and the 'irregularities of nature'. Among the latter, we find in turn articles on monstrous vegetables, unusual meteors, wonders of the earth – and so forth.

Monsters are not to be laughed at, and dividing or segmenting the world into the routine and the monstrous is a serious matter. Above all, it is a form of exercise that provides telling insight into how societies think (see, for example, Douglas, 1966; Ritvo, 1997). Indeed, one might say that the study of taxonomic structure (or forms of classification) is key to the study of any culture precisely because it makes 'thought' visible. That is, in so far as it can reveal a map of concepts and of the links and associations that are made between concepts. With that point in mind it is easy to understand why the authors of the Paris encyclopaedia often referred to their work as a 'Mappemonde'. Yet, whenever things are divided, much more is implicated than human thought and culture. For, associated with each and every classificatory system is a set of practices. And it is truly in the links between human practices and forms of taxonomy that a space for social research opens up.

In fact, if we reconceptualize Diderot's *Encyclopédie* as an information storage and retrieval system – rather than as a mere dictionary – we will be led to pose questions not merely about the content of the system, but also about how the system was accessed and used and modified and challenged. That is, how the system – as a technology – is nested within a web of activities (Bijker et al., 1987). In recent decades, investigations into the nature of information storage systems and their relationship to organizational life have emerged as a distinct subject area in itself (see, for example, Berg, 1997; Bowker and Star, 1999). And as an introduction to just a few of the issues contained within this newly emergent field it would, perhaps, be useful for us to consider yet another encyclopaedia.

Key C Basidiomycotina
(Gill bearing and pore-bearing forms)

1a Hymenium consisting of gills
1b Hymenium consisting of tubes opening by pores

.

.

.

.

24a Cap campanulate or conical
24b Cap not campanulate or conical
25a Cap greasy or viscid, brightly coloured   Hygrocybe
25b Cap not with this combination
26a Smelling distinctly of fish
26b Not smelling of fish

.

.

.

30a On wood   Micromphale
30b On cones   Baeospora, Strobilurus

FIGURE 4.1   *The identification of fungi (adapted from M. Jordan,* the Encyclopaedia of Fungi of Britain and Europe, *1995, London: David and Charles)*

Of fungi and fish

Consider Figure 4.1. It is an extract from a table concerned with the manner in which we classify what, in England, are often referred to as 'toadstools'. The table is to be found in a modern encyclopaedia (Jordan, 1995). It is an encyclopaedia of fungi, and it is designed to enable users to identify specimens found 'in the field'. In an anthropological sense the table facilitates the task of identification in an interesting manner. Thus, one can see that the table is based on a little more than a series of binary divisions. So, either something is, or it is not. For example, the fungi either smell distinctly of fish or they do not. They either have rounded caps or they do not. This manner of operating in binary pairs – sometimes referred to as an Aristotelian system of classification – was regarded by Lévi-Strauss (1969) as fundamental to all human cultures. Indeed, Lévi-Strauss tried to decode myths and totems in terms of such logic, pointing out how we should concentrate on how what is said is ordered, rather than with what it 'means'. (For further comments on the approach see Chapters 1 and 7.)

Now the content of any classificatory system is important – as is this one. Consequently, the order on the page requires analysis. However, what many structuralists in the literary tradition tend to overlook is that order on the page is invariably tied into forms of social order and it is the connection between the two that demands investigation. For example, the use and manipulation of classificatory systems, as tools, invariably serves to mark out the limits of social groupings.

In this light, were we to examine the fungi encyclopaedia a little more closely, it would quickly become evident that the frame within which the classification is embedded marks out a certain kind of user. In fact, it is an encyclopaedia aimed at 'amateurs' (p. 7) – designed for use by the amateur in the field, rather than, say, bench scientists in the laboratory. So, from the outset, it provides the reader with a specific identity for reading (and doing). At a more detailed level we would also be able to determine that the text urges people to act in specific directions. In particular, it encourages people to 'perform' classification in a defined manner. Thus it suggests that readers smell, taste, look, pick and preserve fungi in order to identify and distinguish one from the other using 'a logical and progressive sequence of checks' (p. 7) – such checks as are outlined in Figure 4.1. So as well as providing the reader with the identity of an 'amateur', the system of classification also provides a script for doing. In that sense, the text orders its readers as much as it orders 'things' (fungi) in the world.

In the same way, the alphabetic ordering of entries in the great Paris encyclopaedia also orders its readers as much as it orders the entries – it orders them to search the text by letter order rather than by entry size, or date, or author, or topic link. (It is, of course, an ordering process that would be considered by most people to be one that is both efficient and convenient.) In any event, one of the things that is happening with our fungi encyclopaedia (in use) is that it is acting back on its readers and structuring them as amateur field scientists. There are, of course, other ways of ordering fungi, and other classificatory systems. They, however, would be linked into different technological systems and thereby into different social groupings. Thus, a classification of fungi according to, say, the features of the genetic (DNA) code would require a very different group of readers – with different skills, different ways of working and alternative arrays of technological hardware.

How documents place things, how they make things visible, and how such systems of visibility are tied into social practices are the dominant themes of this chapter. Our aim is to look at various ways in which graphical and similar forms of representation can materialize things (phenomena) that would otherwise remain opaque and diffuse. Naturally, in order to make things visible, human actors and agents have to translate ideas into images and traces. Such processes of translation are various. Indeed as we shall note the 'same' object can be translated (Serres, 1995) into a number of alternative forms. How the forms relate one to the other and how they act back on their creators are, however, always a matter open to empirical research.

Making disease visible

The diseased brain

In his *Art and Artifact in Laboratory Science*, Lynch (1985: 153) points out how, 'Documents are integrally a part of the work of doing science'. Documents serve not simply as a source of ideas and information but also as an integral component of bench work itself (in the form of notes, recipes, instructions and so forth). One type of document that appears prominently in Lynch's study is the pencil and paper diagram. In most cases such diagrams portray structural aspects of a particular part of rats' brains (the hippocampus). Such drawings are themselves based on other images – derived, for example, from laboratory slides of sliced sections of rat brain, and electron microscope enlargements of brain tissue. The preparation of slides, the staining or 'labelling' of tissue and the microscopic enlargements serve to make the hippocampus and its functioning processes visible. In the interaction between organic materials, technical processes and human activity, of course, the possibility arises that some of the things that are visible are not 'natural'. In the language of the lab scientist these latter are referred to as artefacts. For example, it may be that the staining process or the cutting process alluded to above produces marks, blotches, appearances that are a product of the experimental interventions rather than ordinary features of the hippocampus. Exactly how lab scientists distinguished between artefactual and natural effects was one of the issues that Lynch set to examining. This was especially difficult in those cases where the artefact was an absence rather than a presence – that is, in those cases where something that should have appeared on a slide or an enlargement failed to appear. (Note also references in this chapter to Figure 4.2.)

This relationship between organic matter, pencil and paper images, electron microscope images, staining techniques and so forth is central to the production of many kinds of fact. As other science analysts have indicated (Bastide, 1990; Fujimura, 1996; Latour and Woolgar, 1979; Lynch, 1990; Myers, 1990; Rapp, 2000) the world of nature is never immediately visible but has to be made and manufactured in order to be seen – Rapp (2000) refers to 'imagistic knowledge' in this context. Among the procedures for making things visible, photographic imaging techniques have an important place. (Since the completion of Lynch's work, of course, other imaging strategies and technologies have come to the fore, some of which will be mentioned below.) The graphic image thus presents only one of many ways of reading or seeing 'things'. Indeed, as the following example illustrates, the same 'thing' can usually be seen or read in many different ways, some of which are graphical and some of which are, shall we say, numerical, and some of which are behavioural. The relationship between ways of seeing (documenting) things and forms of professional practice constitutes a potentially important field for social scientific research. In the first part of the discussion that follows we shall focus on ways of documenting what is known to be a common form of disease in older people – Alzheimer's.

Alzheimer's disease is a well-known form of dementia. The key features of dementia are memory loss, confusion, mood and behavioural disturbance. In most cases people simply lose ordinary skills of daily living. Dementia is most frequently found in older people (it affects around 20 per cent of people aged 80 years or more), but in rare cases it can occur in people of half that age. In the literature of the UK Alzheimer's Disease Society, the disorder was described as follows during 2001:

> Alzheimer's is a physical disease which attacks brain cells (where we store memory) and brain nerves and transmitters (which carry instructions around the brain). Production of a chemical messenger acetylcholine is disrupted, nerve ends are attacked and cells die. The brain shrinks as gaps develop in the temporal lobe and hippocampus, important for receiving and storing new information. The ability to remember, speak, think and make decisions is disrupted. After death, tangles and plaques made from protein fragments, dying cells and nerve ends are discovered in the brain. This confirms the diagnosis. (http://www.alzheimers.org.uk)

The Alzheimer's Disease Society literature also lists a range of specialists who can be involved in the diagnosis and the management of the disease – these include psychiatrists, neuro-psychiatrists, psychologists, nurses and social workers. The list is in itself instructive because it suggests that what the disease 'is' is likely to differ according to the forms of professional practice that surround it. In particular, it seems likely that different professional groupings have different images of the disease in practice. Note that, according to the passage above, the 'disease' can only be confirmed at autopsy (that is, after death).

Making Alzheimer's visible in living people (as opposed to making it visible in the dead brain) is a difficult process and as with so many things, it can be done in different ways. Thus diagnosing people on what are called clinical grounds is possible and desirable, but clinical diagnosis and diagnosis at autopsy do not always match. Thus it is sometimes said that clinical diagnosis is only up to 80 to 90 per cent 'accurate', a point that serves to highlight how different forms of visibility provide different answers to our problems.

Clinically, the condition is determined by examining how the patient behaves and talks and reacts. In fact, clinicians usually refer to three realms of evidence in the determination of a diagnosis. These are the symptoms that the patient brings to the consultation (say, a report of 'not feeling right'); the signs that the doctor discovers in the patient (such as memory loss and confusion); and evidence available from investigations (such as brain scans). So there is always an ensemble of traces – of visibilities and translations – used to determine whether a person is or is not dementing (Harding and Palfrey, 1997), and in the early stages of the disorder the decision may be far from clear cut. (There is a sense in which the diagnosis is always and forever a matter for negotiation.)[2]

Even were we to concentrate solely on visual data – from brain scans – we would still be faced with alternative pictures of what is apparently the same disease. Thus, there are several types of brain scan available. For example, CT or CAT (computerized axial tomography) scans are a way of taking pictures of the brain using X-rays and a computer. MRI (magnetic resonance imaging) scans also use a computer to create an image of the brain but, instead of X-rays, they use radio signals produced by the body in response to the effects of a very strong magnet contained within the scanner. SPECT (single photon emission computerized tomography) scans look at the blood flow through the brain rather than at its structure, whilst electroencephalography (EEG) traces would provide yet another means of imaging brain dysfunction. Indeed, each type of scan provides different kinds of visibility and evidence for brain 'pathology', though none of them on their own would suffice to provide a diagnosis of Alzheimer's. Indeed more important than the evidence derived from scans would be evidence gathered from an examination of a patient's routine behaviour. All in all, then, and to use a term that we have called upon previously, we can say that there are radically different performances (Mol, 1999; 2000) of Alzheimer's – neurological, psychological and behavioural. How the one form is translated and then meshed into the other is a matter of interest in itself, though here we shall focus simply on the role of documentation in providing translations.

As an adjunct to a doctor looking at and talking to the patient, it is possible for him or her to use a standardized set of questions in the shape of what is usually referred to as an outcome measure. (Note how the very term 'outcome' gives emphasis to the notion of performance.) Outcome measures usually take the form of a series of observations or questions about behaviour, the answers to which can be scored. For example, in looking at dementia, an outcome measure is likely to include questions about whether a person forgets names, and dates, and events; about whether they lose their way around familiar places, or lose things; or whether they have lost ordinary daily skills – of dressing, washing and self-care. To each question there is attached a numerical score. Scores can then be added up. As we saw with the CIS-R in Chapter 2, the results can then be translated in terms of a numerical scale (say, from 0 to 100) so as to form a judgement about the presence or absence of Alzheimer's. (For an example of such a measure see the references to the Mini Mental State Examination on http://www.alzheimers.org.uk)

As just stated, Alzheimer's usually affects older people. In some families, however, it can have what is called an 'early onset'. That is to say, it can appear in people aged from 35 to 60 years. So, for example, there are about 17,000 affected people in this age group within the UK. One group of people who tend to suffer from an early onset of Alzheimer's are those with Down's syndrome. Down's syndrome is a genetic disorder which usually results in people having learning difficulties. In conjunction with the learning difficulties, there is often a characteristic facial appearance. (More often than not, it is the facial appearance that people focus on. One might say that that is how the syndrome is made visible in lay culture.) Naturally, the severity of the learning difficulties and the accentuation of the facial features vary considerably in the Down's population.

Autopsy studies have shown brain changes (neuropathology) similar to that of Alzheimer's disease in almost all adults with Down's syndrome over the age of 40 years. It is an observation that is supported by neuroimaging findings – of the type derived from the scanning procedures noted above. Neuroimaging is a relatively new kind of technology. As a form of documentation it provides us with new translations of what Down's syndrome is. In the absence of neuro-images, however, professionals tend to restrict themselves to looking at the behavioural dimensions of the disorder. Yet, by looking at behaviour, dementia can be diagnosed in only around 9 per cent of adults with Down's syndrome aged 40–49 years, and around 55 per cent of those aged 60–69 years. In short, although one might be able to 'see' the presence of Alzheimer's disease in a human brain (if one had the tools), one cannot easily detect it in daily life.

In a sociological sense therefore we might say that there are at least three different sites in which Alzheimer's can be made visible – namely, in the autopsy room, in the neuroimaging suite and in the clinic. Different forms of text and visual image are associated with the different kinds of setting, and one of the tasks of the social scientific researcher should be to examine how the various forms of documentary evidence available to human actors are woven into specific forms of translation. This is because what the disease 'is' changes according to the availability of the images. Or, to put things another way, the visibility of the disease is dependent on the use of different kinds of inscription device (Latour, 1987) by different kinds of professional.

As we have stated, an important set of such devices are the outcome measures. Yet, there are various kinds of such measures, and they in turn give different images of the disorder. For example, one such instrument is the Mini Mental State Examination (MMSE) (Folstein et al., 1975). Another is the 'Dementia Questionnaire for Mentally Retarded Persons' (DMR) (Evenhuis et al., 1992). Yet a third is the 'Dementia Scale for Down's Syndrome' (DSDS) (Gedye, 1995). In one clinic, where all three measures were applied to a rather mixed group of people, it became evident that of 30 subjects who had an MMSE score of less than 24 (which is taken to be the usual cut-off for the detection of possible dementia), 23 did not have a diagnosis of dementia according to any other criteria. In other words, the instrument produced dementia where it was not otherwise evident – indeed, it seemingly overestimated prevalence by about 75 per cent.

So the upshot of all this is that the outcome measures very often give different answers to the same basic question, 'is this person dementing?' In so far as that is the case, we might say that whether a living person has Alzheimer's or not is often a matter of documentation rather than of biology. It is documents that make the disorder visible, and it is documents that define its severity. In terms of situated social scientific enquiries, of course, it would be crucial to note how the various means for making Alzheimer's visible are called upon and manipulated by different kinds of people. And how those tools are used in different kinds of organizational setting – hospitals, care homes, day centres and so forth. Rather than pursue the Alzheimer's example any further, however, I will turn to a published example in order to illustrate how forms of classification and scaling are linked into professional practice, and how they often serve to define professional boundaries.

Viewing pathology

In an intriguing essay on the classification of the lymphomas (tumours) and leukaemias, Keating and Cambrosio (2000) indicate how classificatory order has changed during the last 30 years and how such changes have been linked into forms of professional activity. For example, until the 1970s the classification of the lymphomas and leukaemias was essentially based on the study of cell morphology (the shape and size of cells). Using microscopes and staining techniques, lymphomas could be seen and differentiated according their gross characteristics. During the 1970s, however, a different form of classification came into operation. It involved a study not so much of cell morphology but of cell function. In particular, the new system depended on the identification of different types of cells called 'T' and 'B' cells, which (at that time) were not distinguishable under the microscope. The new classification led to a new understanding of what lymphoma was. Unfortunately, the classification was a product of (laboratory-based) pathologists and not deemed to be useful to clinicians (the doctors who actually speak to patients). Above all, the latter want to be able to 'see' a disease in the patients that they deal with, and to make predictions about eventual outcome. Clinicians are not particularly interested in new ways of classifying things – especially if this does not help them to deal with patients. So although new ways of seeing had been introduced into the medical world, not all professional groupings were happy to adopt the new vantage points. In fact, as Keating and Cambrosio point out, as far as the classification of lymphomas is concerned there is a constant tension between what can be seen and discovered in the laboratory and what can be used in the clinic.

Such tension can itself be turned to productive use. In terms of the example that we are discussing here, the tension between clinicians and pathologists was in part responsible for further developments in classificatory techniques, for during the 1980s a specific way of seeing 'T' and 'B' cells was developed. The new method involved treating the cells with fluorescent antibodies and then running them through a machine called a flow cytometer.

The arrival of the flow cytometer meant that cells could be counted and quantified in various ways. Clinicians like to quantify things. For, as in the Alzheimer's case, once things can be counted, they can be scored, and once scored they can be used to classify anew. Unfortunately, despite the fact that the flow cytometer technology had found a way of making cells fluorescent and thereby amenable to quantification, the results were still of little direct use to the clinicians. Many clinicians therefore tended to hang on to the old (morphological) ways of seeing the lymphomas and leukaemias. One consequence of all this is that the modern pathology reports that move out of the laboratory and into the clinic contain many visions of the same thing. Thus, pathology reports commonly contain diagrams illustrating gross pathology, flow cytometer counts, and more. Ways of seeing and ways of classifying proliferate.

The pathology reports, then, have to make disease visible in different ways. They have to take account of the fact that clinicians have been trained in different ways and educated into various forms of classification. In that respect such reports might still be thought to serve merely as conduits for the transmission of data between one person and another. What we need to note is that as well as serving as a conduit of information, the reports also mark out spheres and boundaries of professional influence. Indeed, systems of classification can be seen to act as 'boundary objects' (Star, 1989; Star and Griesemer, 1989). In short, the world as ordered on the page (in text) is linked to other forms of order in social practice.[3] In this instance, forms of classification are related to different ways of doing analysis, to different ways of observing the world, and to different sites of professional practice. In this light it is interesting to note the claims of Myers (1990) who compares scientific illustrations in popular and professional scientific journals. In the former case, he suggests, illustrations are tied into a mode of presentation that emphasizes the independence of things (or a narrative of nature as he refers to it). In the latter case the illustrations are tied into what scientists do – to a narrative of science.

In this subsection I have focused almost exclusively on classification and medical practice. However, it is evident from the published work that these same issues arise in other fields of human endeavour – including, for example, business practice (see Desrosieres, 1994). In the following section, however, I intend to stick with medical practice as a source of my examples. This time I am going to consider how risk, rather than disease, is to be made visible. In particular I am going to consider the notion of genetic risk. The clinic that is to be referred to was the site for a research project that sought to discover how 'risk' is assembled by medical professionals.[4]

Making risk visible

Risk looms large in contemporary medical discourse (Gabe, 1995). Indeed, Skolbekken (1995) has spoken of a risk epidemic and has documented the marked rise of risk-related publications during the 1967–91 period (see Chapter 8). It is of considerable interest in itself as to why the language of risk came to dominate medicine in the last quarter of the twentieth century. Whatever the reason or reasons, however, it is quite clear that being-at-risk is now a major focal point for medical research and clinical work. One of the consequences of such a focus is that it draws healthy as well as unhealthy people into the orbit of medical investigation. This is simply because being-at-risk necessarily predates being diseased. The language of risk can therefore be used quite easily to extend the domain of medical knowledge and of medical practice almost without limit. In the world of clinical genetics and genomics, especially, this capacity to be 'at risk' is central to the entire medical enterprise. That is because the clinical emphasis is on the detection and prevention of pathologies rather than on 'cure'.

The new genetics is very much a product of the late twentieth century. In fact, during the mid point of the twentieth century, scientific knowledge of genetic inheritance underwent a revolution (Keller, 2000). Until then, it was recognized that genetic properties were carried in chromosomes, but the interior structure of chromosomes remained a mystery.[5] In 1951, however, Crick and Watson published an important paper on the helical structure of DNA and discussed its chemical components. Bazerman (1988) both reproduces and examines the paper in terms of the scientific rhetoric of the age.

Crick and Watson argued that the long strands of DNA that were contained within chromosomes were composed of four different chemicals. These chemicals are often referred to as C, A, G and T. (There is no need here to specify what these letters represent.) Put very bluntly, these four chemicals combine in various ways to make proteins, and it is out of such proteins that human physiology is structured (Pilnick, 2002). In some people, however, the sequences in terms of which the four chemicals are replicated are abnormal. Perhaps, for example, key sequences of CAGT are missing (truncated), or perhaps they are duplicated a few too many times (repeated). In yet other instances the sequences will be jumbled. When such things occur, there is a possibility that the abnormality indicates a 'mutation', and in many cases mutations are associated with bodily pathology.

For example, the two genes associated with breast cancer (BRCA1 and 2) are located on chromosomes 17q and 13q respectively. If some of the chemicals in the BRCA sequences on those chromosomes appear in abnormal proportions, or are missing altogether, then there is a high probability that the individual concerned will develop a cancer. (More than 300 mutations are currently identified for BRCA1.) Mismatches or mutations are carried in many families and individuals, but whether an individual person may be said to be at 'low', 'medium' or 'high' risk of developing an inherited pathology is always a tricky and awkward business (the mismatches have to be of the right kind). In the UK, finding mismatches of the right kind is a business that involves a considerable amount of documentation. In fact, documents are central to the entire process through which risk assessments are manufactured.

An estimate of being at risk of breast or of any other cancer is commonly calculated as an average lifetime risk (currently around 1 in 12 for female breast cancer). That is to say, risk is calculated in terms of populations. Yet for any individual the risk may be higher or lower than the average. This element of uncertainty about personal risk requires management in many different spheres, some of which belong to the world of lay people and others of which are firmly lodged in the world of professionals.

In order to identify people who are at a potentially high risk of an inherited cancer, geneticists have devised their own rules for distinguishing between people (and families) at different levels of risk. These rules are usually drawn up as a product of expert meetings and discussions, consultation of published research studies and so forth. In an individual clinic they are usually contained in a 'protocol'. A protocol serves to classify the kinds of people that a clinician is most likely to be interested in focusing on. For example, as far as breast cancer is concerned, the protocol for inclusion in the genetics service being referred to here required at least one of the following criteria to be met by a man or woman seeking help. One first-degree female aged under 40 affected by breast cancer; two first-degree relatives (on the same side of the family) affected at 60 years of age or less, three first- or second-degree relatives of any age (on the same side of the family); one first-degree relative with bilateral breast cancer; one first-degree male breast cancer. Different criteria (the Amsterdam criteria) would be used for colorectal cancers, whilst for ovarian cancers the requirement would be for two or more such cancers within the family with at least one first-degree relative affected. In practice, of course, these criteria are open to modification in the light of various factors – some 'social' and others 'scientific' – and it is an intriguing problem in itself to look at how the protocol is applied in everyday clinical work. In what follows clinical professionals are attempting to determine the risk of breast cancer for a specific individual. The extract, in itself, provides intriguing data on how people 'follow' rules in action. You will also note that reference is made in the talk to a computer program called 'Cyrillic'. We will examine the nature of that program shortly.

CG1: So the proband at 39. Mum [cancer of] breast 38. Dad is alive and well. The only other family history which we are trying to find is a mum's sister who allegedly had breast cancer at the age of 49, but she knows very little about her, and hasn't kind of got back to us, but clearly quite young. So the breast was at 38 and the bowel was at 63.

CG2: She is moderate for breast isn't she?

CG3: She is automatically moderate for two under 60. And one is under 40 isn't she?

CG1: Yeah one is 38. Does that make her high with one under 40?

CG3: Well she might end up being a 24 per cent or a 26 per cent.

CG1: On Cyrillic.

CG3: On Cyrillic. Which will switch her from one to t'other. Gut feeling is moderate.

CG2: Mm. She has got a sister here who is ...

CG3: OK.

CG2: And she is fine. And there is nothing else here now. So she is probably moderate. She will fit the moderate criteria.

CG1: She is coming up for 40 [*the age at which mammography is offered for women who are at moderate risk*].

CG2: She is 40 anyway. Yeah.

CG3: Well one under 40 would automatically put her into moderate. So that is why I'm wondering whether we should think high with another one over here. [*Pointing to the maternal aunt.*] The only other thing is because of having a second primary is therefore ... if she was at 27 per cent on Cyrillic and mum had a second primary I would be more inclined to accept that as high risk.

CG1:   So do you want me to run Cyrillic?

CG3:   Yeah.

CG1:   OK. And so therefore if she is above 25 per cent it takes her into high?

CG3:   Yeah.

CG1:   And so below 25 per cent is moderate? Sorry [*CG1 writes in patient's file*] writing it all down.

CG2:   It won't take in the bowel though will it, Cyrillic?

CG3:   No. And I don't think it should either. It's just that we know that if you have got a breast cancer ...

CG1:   So if it's dead on 25 per cent?

CG3:   Come and speak to me. [*Laughs.*]

Clearly age and previous family history are all important in the determination of risk. Family history is gathered by using a questionnaire on the medical history of a person's relatives. The questionnaire seeks information of dates of birth (and death) of blood relatives, dates at which any cancers appeared, types of cancer, patterns of marriage and reproduction and so forth (information that is not always available – as we can deduce from the early stage of the extract above). When this information is put together clinic professionals talk of having a pedigree – of the kind indicated in Figure 4.2.

Producing pedigrees – as with the production of DNA sequences – is a matter of inscription. How that inscription is executed often differs between cultures. Thus, Nukuga (2002), and Nukuga and Cambrosio (1997) offer examples of how medical pedigrees are assembled in Japanese and Canadian contexts. As Nukuga and Cambrosio point out, the results look very different. They look different because pedigrees are not simply transcriptions of how things really are, but in large part cultural representations of human relationships. (We referred to a further example of this representative power of family trees in Chapter 1.)

In the clinic to which I am referring the pedigrees were put together through a complex process of talk, investigation and transcription. Information provided by patients, for example, was often checked and rechecked against various sources. Thus professionals sometimes sought data from a cancer registry in order to complete or to confirm a pedigree. A cancer registry is, of course, yet another information storage and retrieval system – and one worthy of detailed investigation. It registers all cases of cancer morbidity in a given region and is often crucial to the work of geneticists and epidemiologists seeking evidence for familial cancers. Naturally, other blood relatives could also serve as a source of data on family illnesses. But whether from a registry, or a hospital, or from relatives, such information was sifted through talk and technology not only so as to represent a family tree, but also so as to constitute the nature of the family under investigation. This capacity of documentation to constitute the

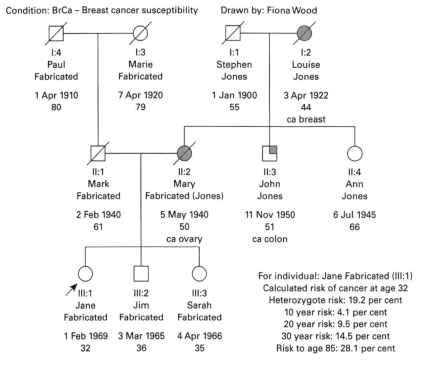

Condition: BrCa – Breast cancer susceptibility   Drawn by: Fiona Wood

FIGURE 4.2   *Cancer in the family: the fabricated family's pedigree*

object of which it is supposedly nothing more than a representation has, of course, appeared in some of the examples drawn upon in earlier chapters.

In large part, the assembling of a pedigree is a matter of paper and pencil technology – and pedigrees are normally stored in paper files within the clinic. To translate the data in the files into a risk assessment, however, requires further productive work. For clinical purposes this is partly achieved through the use of a computer program known as Cyrillic (Chapman, 1997). (You will note that Cyrillic is referred to a number of times in the extract above.)

Cyrillic is a program that draws a family tree and provides a numerical risk estimate for an individual. It is an inscription device (Latour and Woolgar, 1979) par excellence. It makes risk visible. It provides an explicit trace of hereditary influences, and it constitutes objects for medical scrutiny afresh. It is always worth taking inscription devices apart. In the case of Cyrillic the act of disassembling is particularly instructive. For what the program is ultimately dependent upon is a statistical model, and that in turn is linked to surveys concerning the incidence of breast cancers in specific communities. Two of the more widely used models are the Gail model (Spiegelman et al., 1994), and the Claus model (Claus et al., 1991). The role of family history – and of other factors – is somewhat different in each model and so a given woman's risk of cancer is dependent not simply on items drawn from her personal biography, but also on the relative weight that is given to different factors. For example, risk alters according to such things as age, age at menarche, etc. Thus a 50-year-old woman who has not had breast cancer has a lifetime risk of 11 per cent instead of 12 per cent (for she has lived through most of her risk period and been free of cancer). Since the different models allocate different weights to each of the factors they can often produce widely different estimates of risk for the same human being.

Thus, in a recent comparison of risk assessments applied to 200 UK women attending a breast cancer clinic (Tischkowitz et al., 2000), it was noted that the proportion of such women allocated to a high-risk (of hereditary breast cancer) category varied markedly – from 0.27 using one method, as against 0.53 for a second method. A third method allocated only 0.14 to the high-risk category. So there are some women for whom risk is systematically 'underestimated' by the very nature of the models. This is so because the populations on which the risk models are based are themselves biased. For example, they contain only (North American) women; women who predominantly work in the professions; and women with documented family histories. Further, the samples under-represent ethnic groups known to be at high risk – such as women of Ashkenazi Jewish descent.

Such biases in the computerized inscription devices naturally create difficulties for clinicians, and they serve to underline the problems inherent in the primary translation of risk from populations to individuals. As a result, the data from the paper and pencil exercises, the discussions of professionals, the data derived from Cyrillic are always open to expert interpretation. In fact, the documents of which we speak always need to be mobilized as evidence for or against the further investigation of risk. In those instances where a high risk is conferred on an individual (known as the index case or proband), the option to undertake DNA testing arises. And when patients opt to be tested it is, in theory, possible to produce laboratory traces of risk.

As with so many other things in the world of science, there are different ways of making DNA structures visible. Indeed, laboratory scientists routinely manufacture images of mutations through the use of centrifuges, dyes, gels, electrical currents, and ad hoc laboratory techniques, in different combinations. For example, Figure 4.3 provides an image of a DNA sequence (relating the breast cancer gene) that was produced in a dyed gel. Using this technique, DNA is obtained from a blood sample, mixed with a fluorescent tag and inserted into 'wells' in a gel. The mixture is then 'filtered' through the gel by means of electric currents. In this instance the figure contains DNA sequences from a number of samples (samples obtained from individuals). Thus there are samples from person 'B1', 'B6', 'C6', 'D6' and so forth. I have emphasized two such samples with vertical arrows along the top of the image. We can also see that there are a number of bright and not so bright bands running (horizontally) across the diagram. I have attempted to highlight two such bands with horizontal arrows in the left hand margin of the figure.

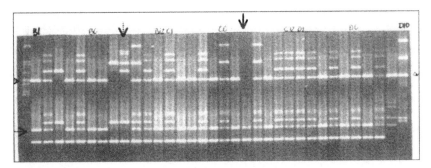

FIGURE 4.3   *Visualizing mutations through gels (UK laboratory, 2000)*

In many ways the appearance of the bright (fluorescent) and dark bands ought to be similar for each individual. We can see, however, that they are not. For example, the pattern of bands for the person highlighted with the first (broken) vertical arrow seems to be somewhat out of sequence with other samples in terms of where the bright bands are occurring, whilst the column highlighted by the rightmost vertical arrow seems to have hardly any bright bands in it at all.

Now, the fact that the columns are different – one from the other – emphasizes the fact of human variability in genetic structure. In short, the gene sequence for individuals can be very different even when we look at what is supposedly the same gene (in this case BRCA1). However, whether such differences are to be regarded as significant or not is a matter for expert interpretation. For example, the expert reading the gel represented in Figure 4.3 has to decide whether a visual difference in a sequence indicates the presence of a mutation or what is called a 'polymorphism'. In the latter case there is said to be an abnormality in a person's gene sequence, but one that is, perhaps, relatively common and therefore assumed to be unimportant. In the former case, the abnormality is assumed to be significant.

In the case of Figure 4.3 all of the variations were considered by the laboratory scientists to indicate the presence of a polymorphism. (The column highlighted by the rightmost vertical arrow represents a technical aberration, a failure – it is, if you like, an artefact of the production process.) Consequently, none of these samples were considered for further laboratory investigation. However, had a mutation been suspected then a further stage of investigation would have been warranted.

Figures 4.4 and 4.5 provide a second means of imaging DNA sequences. Here the graphical representation is presented in four different colours – each colour provides a trace of one of the four key chemicals C, A, G, T. In Figure 4.4 a trace of a normal fragment of BRCA1 is illustrated. To the professional eye it looks smooth and regular, and the sequence as traced between the two arrows is known to correspond to a normal pattern for this particular segment. Figure 4.5 should in many ways look rather similar to 4.4, but it does not.

Between the points marked as 50 and 60 all is well, and then the trace goes haywire. Comparing the two diagrams one can easily see irregularities from the second row onward in Figure 4.5. Colours get mixed and the ambiguities of colour lead to the appearance of the letter 'N' in the sequence. The laboratory scientist explaining this fragment to a social scientist spoke as follows:

LS: This one starts off the same – let me find it – so it goes along it is pretty much the same and then you hit this point [*pointing to the second row of the sequence*] yeah?
SS: Yeah.
LS: And it looks like it's a bloody mess. And the reason is if you have a look at it, it means that the base can either be a T or an A and that one can be a G or an A. That one is an A on its own. That is a T. That is a G or an A. If you write the sequence out, one of them will have a normal sequence in it, and this (Figure 4.5) is a big 40 base pair deletion. So at 40 bases along the other one – it's very difficult to show you without the sequence in front of me, but you can see that. Let's get the file out. This is fragment 1294. It goes AGTGATGAAC, and then it goes nuts. The next one is a G or an A – the normal is a G ... [*Figure 4.5 shows a T.*]

In short, then, the figures are used to demonstrate abnormality. One can 'see' the mutation (if one knows how to read the diagrams). Such traces can be used to make risk visible in any number of contexts – including consultations with the affected person. Indeed, genetic risk is made manifest through various media: talk, machinery and documentation. From the standpoint of the social researcher, however, it is important to look at how these items and elements are worked up in practice, at how the documentation is produced and at how it is mobilized and enrolled by various parties to practical ends (see for example Barley and Bechky, 1994). In clinical genetics (and genomics in general) making things visible is of paramount significance. Luminosity (as we have noted) is central. Often such luminosity is achieved through what are regarded as high-tech fixes. On other occasions, however, it is achieved in remarkably ordinary ways using nothing more than pencil and paper traces. Nevertheless, it is clear from what we have said so far that assessments of genetic risk call upon a complex ensemble of technologies, and in the midst of such technologies it is documentation that makes the world – and the risk within – perceptible and palpable (for further examples see Prior et al., 2002).

Conclusions: making work visible

In *Sorting things out*, Bowker and Star (1999) pay considerable attention to a classificatory system referred to as NIC. NIC stands for Nursing Interventions Classification. Among other things the NIC provides lists of activities that

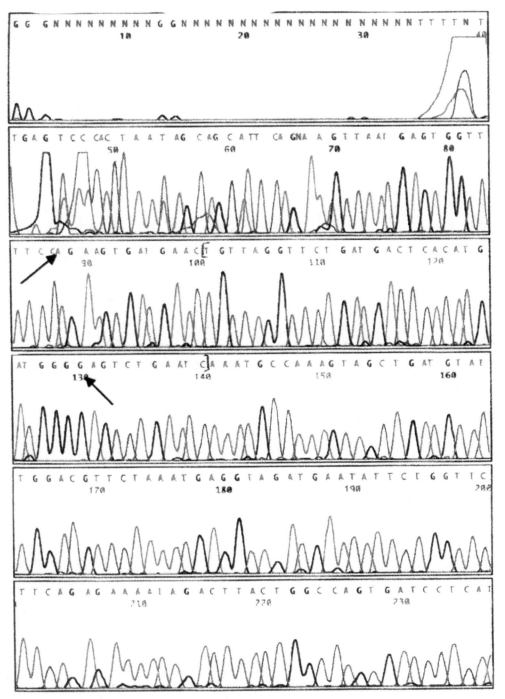

FIGURE 4.4   *A normal DNA sequence (UK laboratory, 2000)*

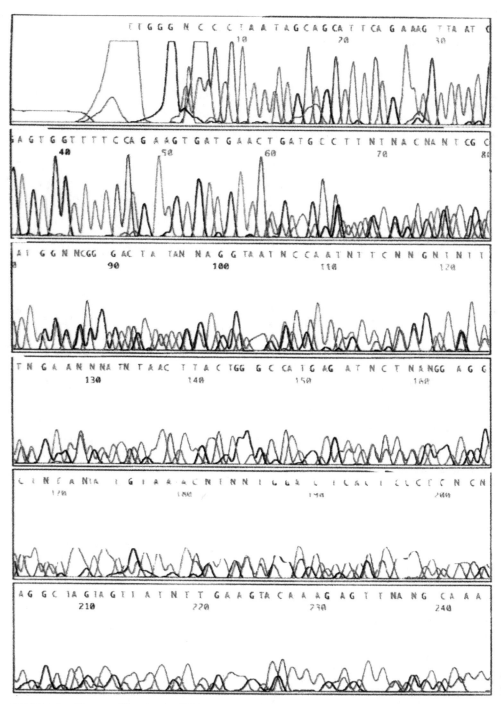

FIGURE 4.5 *Abnormalities in the DNA sequence (UK laboratory, 2000)*

nurses do. For example, nurses help patients with respiratory problems to breathe more easily. So in the NIC there is a section on 'airways management'. Yet again, nurses might also be expected to provide 'spiritual support' for their patients and so the NIC provides a list of spiritual support activities. In like manner, whatever nurses 'do' is documented in the NIC.

There are numerous justifications for developing an instrument such as the NIC. One of the major ones, however, is that it enables nurse work to be made visible and (in a literal sense) accountable. Thus by allocating numerical codes to the kinds of activities just referred to it becomes possible to computerize the billing of nurse time. This, as we have noted before, is especially important in the health care systems of North America. In fact, as the authors of the NIC have argued, once one has developed categories of action one can bill them, time them, control them, monitor them, research them, teach them and manipulate them in endless ways. In that respect many forms of what might first appear to be nothing more than forms of technical documentation can be used to exercise both surveillance and power in organizational life (Foucault, 1991).

In making work and other phenomena visible, documents play a key role. We have noted in this chapter how both diseases (Alzheimer's) and processes (risk assessments) can be made visible through the manipulation of pencil and paper traces. Making things visible is not, of course, simply a process that occurs in medical settings. Thus, Porter (1994) and Desrosieres (1994) have both indicated how the measurement of 'value' and quality in economic settings depends, in the first instance, on the means by which we make such entities visible. And the example of the NIC (above) extends the process of making things visible into new dimensions. In fact, it does so for a number of reasons, not least because it serves to highlight how documents (computerized categories and classifications) can be accessed and used in a multiplicity of ways. This multiplicity of use arises from the fact that documentation of the kind that we have referred to is always embedded in contexts. The prime issues for the social scientific researcher is therefore to investigate how documentation functions in situated contexts, not least because such documentation is invariably used in ways undreamed of by its creators.

Here are some key points from our analysis:

- Documents make 'things' visible and traceable.
- Since the same things are often made visible (translated) in different ways, we need to look at how forms of visibility and forms of documentation are linked.
- Since different agents use different tools for making things visible, we need also to look at how the agents and the tools are linked – how documents function as boundary objects (Star, 1989).
- In any system of translations there will be controversies and disagreements about what is being made visible. How documents are used in such controversies should be central to the social scientific enquirer.
- Never look at documents in organizational settings as isolated tools, but seek to discover how a document is linked into the wider information storage and retrieval system of which it will form a part.

RESEARCH EXERCISES

Exercise 4.1

Ideally, studies of the ways in which 'things' are made visible are best executed through forms of ethnographic investigation. However, it is possible to study images as representations in various ways. Emmison and Smith (2000) provide a series of excellent examples. The following suggestions are merely illustrative of some possibilities.

Classification of 'things' often occurs in space and place as well as on the inert page. Art galleries and museums of all kinds offer two kinds of setting in which things are classified and arranged. By concentrating on just one or, at most, two galleries of exhibited artefacts it should be possible to carry out the following tasks. (1) Make a note of criteria used to classify and organize the items contained in the galleries. (2) Make a note of key concepts that are contained in the written inscriptions connected to the artefacts. (3) Locate the organization of the things studied in the wider classificatory scheme of the museum as a whole, and (4) note how the physical organization of the exhibits structures and guides the experience of the visitor. To assist with analysis of findings the essay by Lidchi (1997), cited in the bibliography, should prove useful.

Exercise 4.2

For those who prefer to save their soles, examine the ways in which social class was made visible in social research during the twentieth century. For a starting point consult D. Rose (1995) 'Social classifications in the UK' at http://www.soc.surrey.ac.uk/sru/Srug.html

Notes

1 In this respect we can see how radically different is an electronic text from an eighteenth-century printed text. In our example, the latter orders by alphabetic sequence. In the former the use of hypertext links allows for nested and web-like arrangement of content.

2 The International Psychogeriatric Association also provides a guide to the diagnosis and assessment of Alzheimer's disease on its web pages. Search for 'International Psychogeriatric Association', and then for 'Alzheimers'.

3 Another suitable example would be that relating to the classification of viruses. See Murphy et al. (1995).

4 The research work was funded by the UK's Economic and Social Research Council under its innovative health technology programme, grant number L218252046. Ethical approval for the work was given by the MREC for Wales.

5 Rapp (2000) describes how chromosomes are, these days, made visible by modern laboratory practice, arguing that chromosomes produced by cell cultures are 'not natural objects but cultural ones' (p. 213).

5

Texts, Authors, Identities

Authors. What use are they?

In 1761 Rousseau's fictional work, *La Nouvelle Héloïse*, appeared. By 1800 more than 70 editions of the book had been published (Darnton, 1984). The book's full title is *'Julie or the New Héloïse. Letters of two lovers, residents of a small town at the foot of the Alps'*. For a twenty-first century reader the novel has little to attract it. As a book, it is overlong, it has no discernible plot, it rambles persistently, and it contains no explicit reference whatsoever to sex or violence. Yet, as Darnton (1984) suggests, and as the single statistic cited above would support, it had considerable audience appeal in its day. Indeed, the book seems to have generated feelings of intimacy towards Rousseau on behalf of the readers and to have resulted in considerable quantities of what, these days, would be called fan mail. In short, readers came to regard the author of 'Julie' as a friend and confidant, and corresponded with him as such.

This brief reference to an eighteenth-century author and his readers is instructive to us on a number of grounds. First, it suggests that the markedly under-researched process of reading documents is as significant as the process of writing (see, for example, Jackson, 2001). Certainly it shows that reading is not quite the personal and individualistic activity that, at first consideration, it appears to be, but rather a task undertaken within, and fashioned by, a certain cultural milieu.[1] (Indeed, in some cultures we know that acts of reading are highly regulated, as is often the case in societies that encompass a guru system.) Secondly, our example suggests that both a text and its author are, to a considerable degree, constituted by readers. (Rousseau, was henceforth viewed as a man of great sensitivity, a 'new Socrates' and an 'apostle of virtue'.) And thirdly, it suggests that the manner in which a document is integrated into a 'lifeworld', or network of everyday action, forms a worthy topic for investigation in itself. In this chapter I intend to pick up on a few of these themes (together with some related issues) and explore them heuristically. Let us start with the author.

In the introductory chapter oblique references were made to the desire on the part of writers such as Barthes (1977; 1990) and Foucault (1979) to de-centre the author. That is to say, a wish to displace onto other agents (such as readers, intellectual associates and publishers) the creative and productive functions that we normally associate with the author (or the author as subject). Questioning the reality of authors is a dangerous business – especially when one is writing a book. Yet, the theme of de-centring does have virtue. This, not least because it encourages us to consider the author-subject as a canopy that is used to cover the background procedures of social interaction on which the production of documents depends. The creative author is in that sense a convenient fiction, a fiction that enables us to abbreviate, or to short-circuit, an examination of the essentially social nature of documents – see Chapters 1 and 2. In the language of Latour (1987) we can refer to the author as a 'black box'. And it is a box that needs to be opened up and closely examined if we wish to reveal anything at all about how documents are assembled, used and function in everyday life.

It may also be as well to note that challenges to authorial magnificence are only a part of a deeper and more general project. The latter is one that seeks to dispossess the active, conscious 'subject' in general – much loved by humanistic sociology, psychology and anthropology – of many of its supposedly private 'inner' capacities. Indeed, some commentators have argued that the image of a social scientific subject is in itself nothing more than a cultural configuration. Thus, suggests Foucault (1970: xxiii), 'Man [is] no more than a kind of rift in the order of things ... a recent invention ... a new wrinkle in our knowledge' – and, we may add, a transitory presence. Indeed, with the encouragement of Foucault, we have every entitlement to view the social scientific 'subject' as a de-centred phenomenon.

The de-centred author and the de-centred subject in general – whose capacities are dispersed to other forms of agency – is an intriguing phenomenon. We have glimpsed, for example, how it is possible to get a much fuller grip on personal motives, intentions, reasons and explanations in the light of such a creature. That is to say, we have seen how it is possible to view what are commonly regarded as properties of a secret, individual and personal consciousness, as collective properties. For example, in Chapter 2 (in the context of suicide) we looked, very briefly, at the manner in which it is possible to speak of vocabularies of motive and vocabularies of causation, pointing out how human beings assemble – in writing and in speech – an account of their actions (and the actions of others) from a range of culturally available 'good' reasons, 'worthy' motives and 'sound and acceptable' explanations. In brief, motives, reasons, impulses and dispositions emerge from a socially sanctioned store of such entities, rather than from an inner store of psychological qualities.

The same might be said of beliefs (see, for example, Prior et al., 2000). Thus what people relate to interviewers and other enquirers (when asked about what they believe in) are not so much secret, inner states of knowing or believing, but socially structured accounts,[2] and statements that they consider will fit the investigator's bill. In a parallel vein one can argue that scientific 'beliefs' are more properly viewed as being contained in scientific documents than inside the heads of scientists. (This is an issue that we will return to in Chapters 6 and 7.) Indeed, in all of these instances, it is plausible to assert that human dispositions and qualities are more likely than not carried along by agents and processes external to any individual, rather than within people's heads.

This is also the case with identities. And one form of media by means of which identities are carried (and dispersed) is that of the written document (in a myriad of forms). In this chapter I hope to demonstrate how documents actually serve in the processes through which subjects, subjectivity and identities are created and stabilized. In fact, and in line with the general tenor of this book, I shall base my analyses on the premise that documents function not merely as simple repositories of facts and detail (about subjects), but actively structure the nature of subjects. Remember: documents are never inert, but enter into projects as independent agents. This, no doubt, sounds a most peculiar claim to those brought up with the notion that only humans can be actors or agents. So perhaps I should point out that it is an idea that I have borrowed from the work of European sociologists such as Callon (1989), Latour (1983) and Law (1994). In fact, writers of the latter kind have developed a mode of analysis that is built around the notion of an actor–network. This is not perhaps the place to expound on the nature or limitations of actor–networks nor of actor network theory – ANT (see, for example, Law, 1994; Law and Hassard, 1999). Nevertheless, it is the case that ANT is suggestive of a number of possibilities that are pertinent to our purpose.

One such possibility concerns a focus on the function that a document, thing or person plays in a network of activities. For example, in his analysis of the attempts of automobile manufacturer Renault, to engineer an electric vehicle, Callon (1989) refers to an ensemble of entities in a network such that it is the linkages between things that form the actor rather than any single item within the ensemble. Thus, in Callon's example, the fuel cell, lead accumulators, the French middle class, city councillors and so forth all entwine so as to comprise an actor. In the framework of our concerns, this manner of viewing things implies that non-human components can serve as active agents in an actor–network. Such agents may, for example, impose restrictions on, or facilitate possibilities for, other agents – that is, structure the action of others. They can also serve as agents in so far as they (as inanimate objects) are open to recruitment by a network as an ally, or even expulsion from it as a traitor. Such a reconceptualization of actors points towards the possibility of regarding documents as agents that can restrict and facilitate, serve as allies or foes, become involved in systems of domination and subjection, make and unmake the nature of the material world. In short, documents can have effects and in so far as they have effects then they can be researched as part of a field – as dynamic rather than inert phenomena.

In what follows I intend to investigate some of the ways in which human subjectivity and human identity are tied up with documentation. I shall begin by looking at the way in which subjectivity and identity might be contained in and structured through records. I shall then move on to examine how personal identity can and has been shaped through the use of biographical technology. Following that I shall consider how identities truly belong to networks of action. I shall end the chapter with a consideration of some of the ways in which identities can be performed through writing.

A dossier manufactures its subject

Sometime during the morning of 3 June, 1835, in the village of la Faucterie, in the district of Calvados (northern France), a young man by the name of Pierre Rivière grabbed a pruning hook and used it to slaughter his mother, his 8-year-old brother and his teenage sister as they busied themselves with their daily affairs. Some five years after these events, at the age of 25, Rivière was found hanged in his cell in the prison at Beaulieu. Over a century later, a team based at the Collège de France assembled the documents surrounding this gruesome case. They were published during the 1970s (Foucault, 1978). The collected documents comprise a dossier. That is to say, a collection of statements drawn from various sources – the courts, medical practitioners, a confession written by Rivière himself, newspaper cuttings and prison receipt books. These statements not only circle the events of murder but also seek to define how the central characters relate to it.

In a stark and very direct way the papers that emerged from the unusual happenings that occurred at la Faucterie mark out, 'a case, an affair, an event, that provided the intersection of discourses that differed in origin, form, organisation, and function' (Foucault, 1978: x). In short, the dossier serves to mirror a number of mid nineteenth-century ideas about sanity and madness, the normal and the abnormal, the reasonable and the unreasonable, and the fathomable and the unfathomable. Indeed, the dossier and the documents within it lay at the cusp of a period in which legal definitions of 'responsibility' and 'insanity' were being refashioned across the western world.

As a mirror on events, the dossier provides us with an outline of other worlds and other ways of thinking. Initially, however, the dossier functioned otherwise. It functioned in a network of forensic actions. For example, much of it was written so as to serve as 'evidence' in a court of law. The Cantonal judge thus took care to describe the scene of the murder on the morning of the 3rd, a description that was intended to stand in place of the physical reality it described. The death certificates of the doctors who examined the bodies were to stand in place of the corpses. The recorded statements of the parish priest, and other character witnesses who spoke about Rivière, were to stand in place of his persona, and so forth. The preliminary and subsequent interrogation of the accused (which contains the record of the questions posed to him and the answers obtained from him) took on a special status. For these recorded statements – that, for example, the accused acted in accordance with God's Providence – are awarded a power and a strength over and above that of any verbal statements that Rivière might have made elsewhere. Indeed, the 'admission' to the murders is lodged in the dossier (there exists a signed confession – the signature somehow confirming a truth that might otherwise be considered provisional[3]). Put together, the documents generate a narrative of the events leading up to the murders, and define them as such (rather than accidents or suicides). One might argue that the dossier as a whole features as an actant,[4] and that the individual records within it function to implicate, accuse, explain and identify a network of human actor/agents involved in the murder.

Now, it is clear that things happened in la Faucterie independent of any documentation – in the same way that billions of things and events occur in the universe independently of human consciousness and reflection. Yet, the documents surrounding the aforementioned murders add something to those happenings. In a sense, they order the events and produce them anew. They thereby give shape to phenomena that were (necessarily) disarranged. We might even say that they translate occurrences into a 'murder'. In addition, they serve to create the persona that was Pierre Rivière, and to define him as a subject of legal action (a murderer and a criminal). This, particularly in so far as they are directed towards the decision as to whether Rivière was sane or insane – whether, indeed, he was, in the language of the day, a 'monomaniac'.

In such a context, it is, perhaps, useful to point to a comparison between the attribution of madness to Rivière and the recognition of mental illness in Dorothy Smith's 'K' (Smith, 1978). In both instances insanity was read, by observers, into quite ordinary and mundane activities that were variously undertaken by these individuals. Rivière, for example, was once seen to attack some cabbages, and to have buried a churning instrument and a Jay in a field. He also liked frightening children. (Not such a bad man, perhaps!) 'K', on the other hand, was observed to swim up and down a pool rather too exuberantly, and to have talked in whispers when there was 'no need'. In all instances it was the incorporation of these events into a series of observer narratives that manufactured abnormality (madness). Naturally, both 'K' and Rivière acted in multifarious ways. They did a thousand things, but of those thousand things only a few that indicate the presence of madness were highlighted and subsequently recorded. On the basis of such selectivity both lay and expert diagnoses were constructed. Indeed, biographical work of that kind is far from being restricted to the manufacture of madness, and is ubiquitous in contemporary societies.

Thus public records in schools, hospitals, courts and welfare agencies can all serve as basic materials for the construction of personal biography (Gubrium et al., 1994), and, indeed, for the construction of identities.

Let us stop, then, to summarize how the documents within the Rivière dossier actually functioned, and how they were integrated into a web of social action. First, the documents comprise a readable space, they mark out the limits of concern and attention for the various agents involved in the happenings of which we have spoken – they mark out the boundaries of events and, to a certain extent, boundaries of professional competence. Many documents, of course, stood in place of events (the report of the Cantonal judge, for example). Others stood in place of bodies (the death certificates). Some served to define the nature of the murderer (the character witness statements). Others stood as a confession (the record of interrogation). Individually and collectively, the documents provided a structured narrative of what happened, albeit a narrative of multiple authorship. The various author-subjects rewrote (fashioned) the events and, at one time, their documents and oral statements functioned as evidence in a court of law (for an interesting comparison, see Jönsson and Linell, 1991). Further, the documents allocate and define responsibility for the acts; they accuse. They also reflect back on their creators so as to define the role of doctor, magistrate, witness – for 'this' is how doctors write and 'this' is what they write about, and this is how magistrates/witnesses/jailers write and so forth. Finally, they define the identity of the perpetrator (a deranged man not driven by malice, nor witchcraft, but by madness). These days, of course the only reality of the murders was, and is, in the documents, and they thereby enter into the world as 'records'. Should anyone ever wish to challenge the facts of Rivière's guilt, they would have to challenge and counter the documentation. Indeed, at this distance all that we have is the documentation, but be that as it may, once written statements are put into the world, they have a solidity – in any culture – that is not easy to overcome nor to ignore. They have, forever, to be accounted for, interrogated, recontextualized (for example, as forgeries, as false statements, as forced confessions or whatever), and subsequently integrated into new schemes of social action. Such is the destiny of any dossier.[5]

We can see then that the identity of Rivière is intimately connected to documentation. Who he 'is' – or was – is to be found as much in the documentation as it ever was in the live person. His human capacities and qualities are dispersed across the written spaces. Indeed, his 'monomania' could only ever be lodged in documentation – it was certainly never in his head – and so too his other attributes. This capacity of documents to structure identities and bestow attributes on human subjects was, of course, also evident in some of our examples contained in Chapter 3. Those examples suggest that identities are commonly dispersed across records held in schools, hospitals, prisons and other organizations. However, it is seldom that such records are ever brought together to provide a unified image of a single person. (Our references to Mental Health

Inquiry Reports in Chapter 3 provided a rare insight into such a practice.) Yet, western culture does have a mechanism for manufacturing coherent and unified identities, and it is to a consideration of such mechanisms that we now turn.

Autobiography as a technology of self

Whilst in prison Rivière wrote a 'Memoir'. It is full of grammatical errors, errors of punctuation, spelling and so forth, and was printed as such in 1835. Indeed, it is interesting to speculate as to why such errors were left in the manuscript by the original printers, and why Foucault (1978) saw fit to 'correct' them at a later date. Was it that in the first case the printed page conveyed an image of an uneducated peasant scribbler (a brute), and in the second case an image of a reasoning being? It is not for us to decide on such issues, but merely to note how the 'I' of Rivière has been instantly mediated through the work of others. Indeed, more relevant from our standpoint is the fact that the Memoir provides an autobiographical account of a peasant life,[6] and the narrative opens by Rivière defining himself in terms of his murderous acts, thus:

> I, Pierre Rivière, having slaughtered my mother, my sister, and my brother, and wishing to make known the motives which led me to this deed, have written down the whole of the life which my father and my mother led together since their marriage. (Foucault, 1978: 54–5)

This use of an autobiographical memoir to unfold the personal history of an 'I' is itself a specialized form of literality (de Certeau, 1984). And it is, perhaps, notable that the 'I' (ego) of the philosopher, the self-portrait of the painter, and the entire genre of biography and autobiography all seem to emerge – albeit gradually – out of a specifically western culture from the sixteenth century onward. These days, of course, everyone is expected to construct some form of autobiography – to indulge in identity creation and to specify who one 'is' through documentation – even if it is only at the level of a curriculum vitae. Indeed, Castells (1997) argues that identity creation and maintenance figure as key strategies in what he refers to as the network society, though it is only in a culture that is conscious of self, subjectivity, and individuality that autobiography has any place and purpose.[7]

The substantive contents of biographies and autobiographies are, naturally, of considerable interest, but what I wish to do here is focus, briefly, on how biography and autobiography function, rather than with what they contain. In order to follow that process let us return to the first line of Rivière's Memoir, above.

We can see at once that the Memoir is, in part, intended to provide a sense of unity to the writer's past (he refers to the 'whole' of a life). It is also designed so as to reveal the workings of a secret, inner self (his motives and dispositions), and executed so as to provide an ordered narrative of events (that led up to the murders). Such narratives usually unfold in terms of a linear sequence – a chronology – though we cannot, of course, deduce that from the initial sentence. However, we can make a reasonable guess that Rivière's tale is highly selective in its focus. The 'I', as ever, is situated so that the author emerges as that person that he elects to write about and nothing more. (He is, from beginning to end, a person that slaughtered his mother, his sister and his brother.)

Clearly, Rivière's Memoir (autobiography) is a work of construction. It involves the exercise of what has been called biographical work so as to ensure the 'storying' of a life (Bruner, 1987). In fact, autobiography is indispensable to the construction of a unitary self (Sacks, 1986: 105). For where else might one find such unity? That question is one that was posed and answered – rhetorically – by Bruner (1993: 38) and Barthes (1977). Such biographical work need not, of course, be as detailed as that undertaken by Rivière. Indeed, it might not stretch far beyond a brief c.v. Or, for actors and singers, a brief career outline in some programme notes, or even a brief verbal account of whom one 'is'.

Verbal accounts of identity are plausible over the shorter term, but to reinvent oneself thoroughly, documentation is essential, whether it be through the production of identity cards, passports, degree certificates, electronic number systems, or whatever. For we know of many cases where a documented identity can take precedence over a lived identity. (For example, in the case of transsexuals where the sex stated on a birth certificate can override the gendered identity of the person in life – or even in death.) 'False' and stolen identities, of course, are almost entirely dependent on documentation.

Providing a sense of unity of self, constructing or reconstructing an identity, situating oneself in an unfolding narrative of events, are only some of the things that can be achieved by an autobiographical account. For autobiography (and even biography), in the modern world, form part of the technology of self (Foucault, 1988), a technology that enables one to unburden oneself of inner conflicts (Rousseau's *Confessions*, 2000); justify one's thoughts and actions (Marshall Zhukov's *Memoirs*, 1971); construct 'identity' anew (Wilkomirski, 1996; Mächler, 2001); or manufacture a philosophy of life (J.S. Mill's *Autobiography*, 1989). Yet, no matter how sophisticated the purpose, it is also the case that identity always depends on the existence of some 'other'. The other for whom an autobiography is written is rarely immediately evident, but nevertheless always present. In the latter sense it is, perhaps, biography rather than autobiography that makes visible the social relations on which human identities are dependent. And biography is certainly more interesting in that respect. For a biography is an account of a life as manufactured through an interactive process between writer and subject. (In some rather nimble cases, of course, the writer explicitly constructs him- or herself in the process of constructing another – as did Boswell (1976) in recording the life of Dr Johnson.) The emergence of an identity through a network of action is something that we will consider in a later section of this chapter. For now we need only note that autobiographical writing is an expression of a cultural rather than a personal process.

The creation of identity through documentation is, of course, something that social science has itself exploited. In that respect, Foucault's recruitment of Rivière's Memoir serves to emphasize a strong trend in twentieth-century social science that has consistently made extensive use of such accounts to further its investigative aims. In fact, the 'life story' as a social scientific resource has appeared in numerous sociological and anthropological contexts.

For example, researchers in the so-called Chicago tradition (or school) of sociology gave voice to many human actors (Platt, 1996), though, as in the Foucault case, 'delinquents' and criminals figured largely in such accounts (see, for example, Shaw, 1931; Sutherland, 1937). Anthropologists on the other hand normally sought out autobiographies of those who had played more traditional roles. Thus Simmons (1942), for example, elected to publish the autobiography of Don Talayesa, a Hopi Indian. And according to Kluckhohn's (1945) review of life history method in anthropology it was fairly typical of the genre – a focus on just one person (usually male and usually over 50 years of age) in just one tribe. Such themes persisted well after the 1940s – as with Casagrande's (1960) omnibus of around 20 anthropological life histories of 'native' life. Unlike the Memoir of Rivière, however, the twentieth-century accounts have often been directly coaxed, encouraged and thereby filtered through the interests of social scientists themselves, which is why the term 'life history' rather than biography is used in anthropology (Langness, 1965). Indeed, in the hands of social scientists autobiographical and biographical sequence is allowed to unfold only through a conceptual grid of the expert observer. Thus a personal reflection is turned into an autobiography of 'a professional thief' (Sutherland, 1937), or of a Hopi Indian (Simmons, 1942), a hermaphrodite (Garfinkel, 1967), a Polish émigré to Chicago (Thomas and Znaniecki, 1958), all of whom become the object of social scientific puzzlement. These 'others' invariably emerge only through the categorizing language of the social scientists – concerned as they are with gender, ethnicity, class or life style (and sometimes through concepts of colonization and oppression). In fact, the identities and selves that fascinate social scientists are routinely filtered through the changing interests, concepts and concerns of the age (see, for example, Smith and Watson, 1992; and Stanley and Morgan, 1993, on gender).

Further, although life reports are normally presented as first-hand and individual accounts of personal experiences, it is clear that (as was pointed out in Chapter 1) such texts are always the product of collective action – of editors, data gatherers, publishers, translators and so forth. In some cases, of course, the researcher as data gatherer is openly aware of the role that he or she has played in creating a life. Thus Crapanzano (1980) in his study of Tuhami points out how he became, 'an active participant in his [Tuhami's] life history, even though I rarely appear directly in his recitations' (p. 11). In other accounts, however, the researcher often claims to be nothing more than the instrument of the biographical subject. In this context, for example, it is interesting to read Burgos-Debray's (1984) claim that, 'I became what I really was: Rigoberta's listener. I allowed her to speak and then became her instrument … by allowing her to make the transition from the spoken to the written word.' (1984: xx). Rigoberta was billed by Burgos-Debray as an 'Indian Woman in Guatemala', and the biographical text is entitled, 'I, Rigoberta Menchú'. Yet, just who that 'I' is, is a matter for some debate – the final text was edited and translated by Burgos-Debray. (On the methodological issues surrounding the Rigoberta Menchú story and how the account can be variously used, see Beverley, 2000.) A similar question about the 'I' of autobiography is also raised by Klockars (1975) in his account of how he obtained textual information from his fence, Vincent.

As with ethnographic reports[8] (see Chapter 7), it is usually of interest to ask questions as to how the reporting subject is structured by the documents through which they speak. For example, in the case of Rivière (and to a lesser extent Rigoberta Menchú) the subject is structured as an isolated and untarnished reporter on self – as an active narrator rather than as a witness or informant. In the case of Tuhami the subject is recognized to be a construction of the subject plus researcher. In social science, of course, one can always find rules and rule-books about how researcher and researched ought to position themselves in their enquiries. And ever since the life story was objectified as a distinct social scientific 'method of enquiry' there has appeared a stream of publications on how the method should be operationalized and used. Many of the issues here discussed were explored in a special issue of *Sociology* (Stanley and Morgan, 1993), and other statements on the method are to be found in Atkinson (1998), Denzin (1989) and Watson and Watson-Franke (1985). Plummer (2001) provides an excellent overview of the history of the method and its source materials.

Sybil. A network of text and action

The examples mentioned above give vent to another important issue in matters of identity. In particular, they point to the possibility of viewing identity as a relational property rather than a personal one. That is, a property that emerges out of the relations between actors rather than one that emerges out of the individual alone. In this section we need to examine that possibility a little more closely. So, in what follows we are set to investigate how a specific identity was brought into the world through a network of action and text (of various kinds).

In 1974 F.R. Schreiber published a book entitled *Sybil*. It concerned a woman who claimed to have 16 personalities. Sybil was not, of course, the first 'case' of multiple personality. Hacking (1995) lists a number of precursors, though probably the best known must be that nice Dr Jekyll, and that rather nasty Mr Hyde (a story first published in 1886).[9] Sybil's notoriety, however, lay in the fact that she was the first person in which the emergence of multiple personality was linked to sexual abuse in childhood (Hacking, 1995).

Sybil was born in the mid-west USA during the 1930s. She had an unusual childhood, but no memory of any form of sexual abuse as 'herself'. When hypnotized by her psychoanalyst – Cornelia Wilbur – however, she recalled episodes of abuse by her mother. During the 11 years and 2,354 psychoanalytic sessions in which Dr Wilbur treated Sybil, some 16 different personalities were revealed – and, eventually, a 17th appeared when all of the previous selves were fused into one and Sybil was 'cured'. The case was written up by Schreiber (1974) and became a best-selling book. It was also turned into a film drama in 1976. Following the Schreiber book a number of others appeared on the theme of multiple personality. The appearance of multiple personality disorder (MPD) as a disorder in DSM-III (see Chapter 2) in 1980 is far from being unconnected with this narrative. (MPD does not, however, appear in DSM-IV, though a condition referred to as dissociative identity disorder does appear.)

So the Schreiber biography not only created an identity – in Sybil – but also gave the concept of identity a new dimension. For previous to the Sybil case, the notion of a multiple identity was rare, and certainly did not figure in the caseloads of most psychoanalysts – as the absence of the condition from the DSM testifies. (Indeed, and even at a common-sense level, one wonders about the meaning of the word 'personality' when it has to share space with some 16 others.) The Sybil case also provided a fillip to those who wished to trace adult psychological problems back to childhood sexual experiences. In the wake of the Sybil case thousands of Americans were diagnosed with MPD. Most of these individuals also managed to 'recover' lost memories of abuse.[10]

One of the analysts who met and treated Sybil – Dr Herbert Spiegel – was, however, not so convinced about the veracity of MPD. Spiegel (1997) has reported that, based on his experiences, he found Sybil (who was at one stage diagnosed as 'schizophrenic') to be highly suggestible – easy to hypnotize and easy to influence. He also reports that Sybil had read a book on a case of multiple personality called *The Three Faces of Eve* (Thigpen and Cleckley, 1957), and had been deeply impressed by it. She had also seen the 1957 (Nunnally Johnson) film of the same name. In fact, states Spiegel, Sybil had already encountered a template of the disorder before she displayed the symptoms of it. In addition, he claims that Sybil's analyst had probably suggested to Sybil that she was a multiple. (At one stage, Sybil wrote a letter to Wilbur refuting the facts of any childhood abuse or of any multiple personality, but Sybil's plea was regarded in true Freudian fashion as 'denial' (Schreiber, 1974: 374)[11].) Indeed, Spiegel argues that, in psychotherapy 'we become engaged in storytelling and we impose our hypothesis on the patient by the way we ask our questions. Highly suggestible people will of course respond in a way that can please the doctors' (1997: 62). So MPD, in his view, was an invention of the psychoanalytic interaction between these two particular individuals, and Spiegel has gone further to argue that patients, generally, have been trained (rather than diagnosed) by their therapists to become multiples. (Hacking (1995) advances a similar argument.)

Whether Spiegel is correct or not, it is clear that what we see here is a process of identity creation. It begins with patient and analyst, and involves them as readers (of various texts including *The Three Faces of Eve,* the DSM, professional journal articles and so on), and, possibly, as moviegoers. In fact, the identity of MPD and of Sybil emerges out of and becomes lodged in a network. Books, films and people are progressively recruited into the network and with each act of recruitment the identity becomes stronger.

We can also see how the circuit of recruitment expands the network so as to incorporate a new book (on Sybil), a new film (Daniel Petrie, 1977) and a new disorder, and that circuit, in turn, provides an impetus for other books and accounts of multiples. Our interest, of course, is truly in the role that documentation plays in the network and circuit. In that light one is inclined to argue that MPD is truly in the documents rather than in any human being. That is where it is created and structured, and it is the documents (books and films and manuals) that provide the template and foundations for the condition. Even the experience of MPD is measured through a document – the dissociative experience scale (Hacking, 1995: 96–112). Like our examples in Chapter 4, the scale is an instrument that makes 'experience' visible. Indeed, the disorder is woven through text in every way. So individual human beings provide only instances (with peculiar variations) of the pathology. 'Subjects' are, in this sense, not to be confused with individuals. The former are manufactured in documents – in text – as cases; individuals (human beings) are subsequently recruited to fit the templates *in situ* – as Sybil was.

It is somewhat paradoxical, then, that having made a claim in the previous section to the effect that autobiographies and biographies unify a sense of self, we have ended with a narrative of many selves in one human being. The Sybil case, however, serves to emphasize how subjects and subjectivity are manufactured through collective processes – including processes of documentation. They emerge out of networks of action. Thus, Sybil's 'personality' was constructed by others, and it was garlanded with features and activities that eventually comprised a 'case'. That case was then open to recruitment and manipulation in various contexts – as is often so in medical practice. This is at its clearest in matters of psychiatry. Indeed, psychiatric and other illness identities and their personal histories are, as we have seen, routinely created in medical notes – Sybil, you will have noted, was once identified 'as a schizophrenic' (Spiegel, 1997: 61).[12]

One final point: we can also begin to see in the Sybil case how an identity is a matter of performance (Goffman, 1959). That is, a matter of following, interpreting and acting out a script. In that sense we might say that Sybil became a person with MPD in much the same way as Becker (1953–4) had suggested that one could 'become' a marijuana user. Naturally, the script for such performances is lodged in various media and not just in writing. In the next section, however, we shall see how a performance can indeed be lodged in script alone.

Identity as performed through writing – and reading

In a paper published in 1993, Miller and Morgan examined the social nature of the academic c.v. In that paper they indicated how such c.v.s can be understood as a form of autobiographical practice – a form of practice that is centrally concerned with the presentation of self in occupational settings. Using Goffman's aforementioned (1959) work they seek to demonstrate how the academic c.v. involves matters of presentation of front and manufacture of self. Above all, however, they point out how the academic c.v. is a matter of performance.

Performances of the kind just referred to are, of course, executed solely through writing. In that respect they are of special concern to us. It is also of interest to note that Miller and Morgan indicate how the construction of a c.v. can itself engage the use of generative documents of the kind mentioned in Chapter 2. In this instance the generative document referred to was the *Guidelines for the Presentation of a Curriculum Vitae* of Manchester University. Rather than look at how human actors can use and manufacture documentation for the presentation of the self, however, I propose in this section to look at how documents can structure their readers. That is, to look at how they might guide readers to perform in specific ways.

In this context it is helpful to note Iser's (1989) claims about how the reader's role in the work of English fiction altered between the eighteenth century and the twentieth. We need not attend to the detail, but simply note examples of the manner in which texts provide the reader (and the writer) with specific scripts for performance. For example, Iser points out how fictional texts have structured the reader as a passive recipient of a narrative or – as with Thackeray's *Vanity Fair* – as an observer of life's variety and display. With Charles Dickens, on the other hand, the reader is almost invariably structured as a judge of moral character. This, nowhere more so, perhaps, than with *Oliver Twist*, a text in which we are inveigled into taking up a moral stance on poverty and exploitation, subservience and domination, whilst the writer remains positioned as a dispassionate teller of a tale. That stance of reader and of writer is, of course, quite different from, say, the one adopted in Dashiel Hammet's *The Maltese Falcon*, a story that features the unforgettably amoral Sam Spade.

Naturally, our concern is not with works of fiction but with routine forms of documentation. In that respect, we have already glimpsed, in Chapter 4, at how a work of non-fiction (the encyclopaedia of fungi) can structure its readers. There we noted how the reader was structured as an amateur and how that amateur was directed to identify fungi in particular ways. But even with everyday documents readers and writers are structured and allocated to specific roles (see, for example, Abelen et al., 1993). To this end I intend to examine, albeit briefly, a form of documentation that is provided to people in the UK when they collect medicines from a pharmacy. In each case where that happens the client should be provided with a Patient Information Leaflet (appropriately abbreviated to PIL). For each form of medication there is also a 'data sheet' for pharmacists. It will serve our purposes to analyse the text for both forms of document. We will do so with respect to leaflets that relate to one and the same drug.

The PIL to which I am going to refer is that for ziduvodine. The latter is commonly prescribed (under a trademarked name) for people who show symptoms of HIV infection and AIDS. The PIL for ziduvodine opens by highlighting the possibility of the taker of the medication having doubts and worries. Should the 'patient' have any doubts it is suggested that he or she consult his or her doctor. And this pattern of the doctor as an expert (with full knowledge, but without doubt and worry) and the consumer as in need of advice is replicated throughout the leaflet. Consequently, the doctor is presented as someone who will assuage doubt and worry, someone who can provide advice on all aspects of medication, and as someone who will give instructions that ought to be followed.

> If you forget to take a dose, don't worry ... If you take a larger dose than prescribed ... you should let your doctor know as soon as possible if this happens ... If someone else takes your medicine by mistake, tell your doctor at once ... You should not stop treatment unless your doctor tells you to. (ABPI 1996)

In line with the structuring of the patient as a non-expert, the leaflet also provides a lay narrative of the manner in which the drug acts on the body. The narrative indicates how the anti-viral agent that is ziduvodine serves to delay the progression of HIV and AIDS but does not provide a 'cure'. Instead it 'fights' against HIV. For, according to the leaflet, HIV – left unchecked – will enter into a group of cells called CD4 cells and turn them into a 'mini factory' for infection. But in the great struggle against HIV, the anti-viral agent also seeks to invade the CD4 cells and stop the factory producing viral agent. (It is, if you like, an heroic narrative.)

In the respective data sheet for pharmacists, however, a somewhat different narrative is provided. There one can read of the fact that ziduvodine is 'phosphorylated to the monophosphate derivative by cellular thymydine kinase', that it is 'catalysed', and that it acts as 'an inhibitor of, and substrate for, the viral reverse transcriptase'. Naturally, one would both hope and expect the data sheet for pharmacists to read somewhat differently from that for patients – so as to provide more complex information, for example. But what is important from our standpoint is that in using this complex lexicon of chemistry, rather than metaphors of mini factories, the texts are also structuring experts and non-experts. And this structuring of expertise is also evident in more direct ways. Thus the pharmacist's data sheet talks, for example, about 'the management of patients', and how patients ought to be cautioned, advised, monitored and so forth. All in all, then, the PIL structures the reader as an individual subject to the direction of others (who are experts), whilst the data sheet structures the reader as an expert in control of patients. None of this tells us, of course, how such information might be used in practice – but that is a topic that lies well beyond the boundaries of this particular chapter.[13]

Conclusions

Some decades ago Harvey Sacks (1984; 1992) referred to the work involved in 'being ordinary'. Being ordinary demands work. For, to be ordinary is to be unexceptional. That in turn demands a detailed knowledge about the routine and the unusual – in forms of behaviour, speech, manner, dress and so forth. And using such knowledge, we all undertake work (and repair work) on managing and constructing our identities throughout our lives. In our terminology, of course, being ordinary is clearly a matter of performance – as is the matter of constructing autobiographies and biographies.

With that last claim in mind, I have attempted, in this chapter, to indicate how a large part of identity work, as performance, involves documentation. In some cases that documentation may take the form of full-length books – biographies and autobiographies. More likely it will take less notable forms – assembling and writing a curriculum vitae, or filling out a job application, a census form, an application for a driver's licence or a passport. And exactly how people use and manipulate such routine forms of documentation to do identity work is a legitimate field for research in itself.

Yet we have also noted that identities are not simply and necessarily constructed by individuals. Rather, they are assembled through networks of action. And as in the cases of Sybil and Rivière, both human and non-human agents are normally involved in such assembly work. This is so for all of us. Other humans write reports on us, they translate our wishes, desires and motives – in police reports, in hospital files, in school and welfare agency records, in social scientific studies. They also allocate us to categories – good mothers, responsible citizens, devious so and sos, or whatever.

Finally, we have noted that, as interesting as the reports of others may be, more interesting still is the manner in which documents can themselves structure identities. For, documents invariably structure their readers. They do so by offering fields into which such readers can slot themselves as moral beings, or meticulous individuals, or seriously ill people. In that sense we can view documentation as offering forms of identity that are forever open to colonization. Our specific examples drew on work relating to MPD and other illnesses, but there are of course endless types of identity awaiting colonization. Indeed in the modern world we can, perhaps, begin to talk about modern forms of identity in terms of 'cyborgs'. That is, as a hybrid of humanistic and informatic qualities, where skin and bone, PIN numbers, electronic passwords, DNA sequences and blood samples are enrolled as a single actant – text and body merged into one.

In his rather overlong and detailed account of life in a TB sanatorium (*The Magic Mountain*), Thomas Mann presented an account of the ways in which the category of 'invalid' might be created. Mann points out how documentation of all kinds plays its part in such identity construction (X-ray images, temperature charts, Gaffky scale scores and so forth), but he also notes that identity is a matter of time and place. In that sense, perhaps, Mann's novel serves to remind us that ultimately it is the role of documentation in context that should really concern us, rather than the role of documentation in the abstract. How people use documents to create and sustain identities in concert, rather than with how documents contain IDs, is the central issue for social research.

So let me sum up the key points of this chapter:

- Authorship of documents is best viewed in terms of effects rather than in terms of subjective 'identity'. How the author functions is the question that matters, rather than who he or she 'is'.
- Identity is a matter of dynamic performance rather than of inert, personal qualities. Documents have a role in that performance and, as such, should always be considered as more than mere containers of facts about identity.
- Documents structure performance (identity) – this is so for both writers and readers.
- How exactly a document structures a performance – how it is used in everyday practice – is a key question for social research.

With respect to the above, it is the anthropology of use, more than the literary study of content, that should guide the social scientist in matters of research into 'documents of life'.

RESEARCH EXERCISES

Exercise 5.1

Documentation is crucial to the presentation of self. The c.v. (and in the USA, the résumé) are key tools for the manufacture of a professional identity. Execute a web search using 'curriculum vitae' as a search term. Locate pages of rules about how to assemble a c.v. (university pages are often useful for this kind of exercise – see, for example, http://www.columbia.edu/). Note what items of information are recommended for inclusion in the c.v. and what kinds are suggested for exclusion. Then check your findings against personal details provided in a 'lonely hearts' column of a magazine. Recall that 'compare and contrast' is a useful strategy for analysing small samples of data such as are likely to be gathered here. Make an assessment as to what the results tell us about the nature of identity in the modern world.

Exercise 5.2

Constructing identity is often undertaken for fraudulent reasons, and identity theft has emerged as a growing twenty-first-century problem. Consult the US government web pages about identity theft at http://www.usdoj.gov/criminal/fraud/idtheft.html. Following that, consult some non-governmental pages on the problem. Draw up a list of documents and document content that identity fraud commonly involves. Then draw some conclusions about what the list tells us about the nature of 'doing' identity in the third millennium.

Notes

1   Hall (1972) illustrated how what he refers to as 'texts' often encode for a culturally 'preferred reading', and that acts of 'decoding' (reading) are also restrained and fashioned by the imperatives of the reader's culture.

2   One of the earliest discussions of 'accounts' was provided by Scott and Lyman (1968). They claimed that accounts were invoked when a social actor was called upon to explain untoward behaviour. In this book, however, it is argued that any call for an explanation or reasoning is a call for an account.

3   For some insights into the significance of signatures see Derrida (1977).

4   A concept borrowed from Greimas (1987), though used somewhat differently here. An actant is a construct to which we can attribute functions and effects. One and the same actant can be composed from various actors – so the author-subject (actant) is, for example, built up out of many individual actors and their actions. Greimas (1987: 107) suggests that the converse – one actor being composed of numerous actants – should also be considered.

5   Nowadays, of course, there are numerous other media that can hold and structure confessions, statements, details and judgements. Indeed, for the first time in history the twentieth century witnessed the human voice unhinged from the human body, and lodged on mechanical and electronic tapes and discs. And so audiotape or disc, as well as film, may serve as a 'dossier' on events, and thereby enter into fields of action as actants – to function as accusers, witnesses, confessors, creators of narrative and recorders of events.

6   The confessional form adopted by Rivière is often referred to these days as 'testimonio' (Beverley, 2000). The status of such testimonio as first-hand accounts is often complicated by the fact that – as with Rivière's statement – they have to be edited and/or translated by professional others. They subsequently raise a whole series of fundamental questions about the nature of authorship.

7   Hardman (2000), for example, indicates the emphasis that is placed on relational properties of identity as against the individual and personal in at least one non-western culture.

8   Ethnography and autobiography are sometimes interlinked into what is sometimes referred to as 'autoethnography' (Ellis and Bochner, 2000).

9   Hacking (1995: 5) suggests that the first person recognized as a multiple appeared in Charcot's Paris clinic in 1885.

10 http://www.bbc.co.uk/horizon/mpd_script.shtml
11 Such recontextualization of client language is a common feature of professional discourse and, among other things, serves to underpin the power of professionals – see, for example, Sarangi (1998).
12 On the relationship between MPD and schizophrenia in the history of psychiatry, see Hacking (1995).
13 For a report on a study of drug users as lay experts and the manner in which chemical compounds are talked about in everyday life see Monaghan (2001).

6

Content, Meaning and Reference

Mind, meaning and interpretation

In the summer of 1880 a 21-year-old resident of Vienna – later referred to by the pseudonym 'Anna O' – began to exhibit a range of physical and psychological symptoms of a quite stunning variety. When he reflected on the case, Ernest Jones (1964: 202) rather aptly described her as presenting a 'museum of symptoms'. The museum included headaches, squints, vision problems, paralysis of the limbs and neck muscles, hallucinations, marked swings of mood and self-starvation. Anna would variously refuse to speak in her native (German) language (using English instead), indulge in self-hypnosis, threaten suicide, and exhibit bizarre patterns of behaviour. By December of 1880, she had become so ill that she 'took to her bed', permanently, and one of the doctors who became involved in her treatment was a certain Dr Breuer. The latter was a colleague of Freud, and the two men eventually wrote up the case of Anna O (together with case material relating to four other women) in a publication entitled *Studies on Hysteria* (1895).

Our interest in *Studies* is multiple. For a start it is a book that is often recognized as the very first psychoanalytic treatise. Secondly, it is a book in which a number of key Freudian terms make their initial appearance. For example, the first psychoanalytic use of the *unconscious* occurs in *Studies* (see Breuer and Freud, 1974: 100). The terms abreaction, catharsis (1974: 59) and repression (1974: 61) also see their debut. Thirdly – and closely related to our last point – *Studies* redraws the geography of the mind so as to include among its elements not simply conscious, but also subconscious thoughts and beliefs. And in the theoretical prolegomena of Freud and Breuer's *Studies*, it is argued that subconscious tensions, left unresolved, become capable of producing symptoms of anxiety and hysteria in individuals. In short, it is argued that deep within the individual human psyche are repressed energies that can, under certain conditions, manifest themselves as physical illnesses. The paralysis, vision problems and generalized anxiety of Anna O were, for example, deemed to be traceable to mental operations. In the Freudian universe, therefore, the task of the psychoanalyst became one of unravelling the associations between inner thoughts and external symptoms – of *interpreting* the meaning of signs and symbols so as to effect a cure. Indeed, some years after writing *Studies*, Freud was to remark that the patient's or (analysand's) weapon against neurosis was talk, whilst the analyst's weapon was interpretation (Gay, 1988: 298).

We have here, then, a whole series of terms and corresponding issues to unravel. Interpretation is one such. Understanding other minds is another. The practices of reading and referencing in general also necessarily figure. In fact this vignette of Anna O's problems and their therapy ties up in one bundle almost all of the essential issues that accompany those who seek to study the meaning of texts and human actions. (For our purposes, Anna O's symptoms can, for the time being, be viewed as a text.) In that light we can ask certain questions about the narrative that I have just constructed, such as questions about the 'meaning' of Anna O's squints, headaches and other symptoms; questions about where such meaning might be found (is it to be found inside Anna's head or in Freud's head?); questions about how we are to interpret such meaning (is there, for example, a rule-book that links symptoms to mental problems?); and questions about whether there is, in any case, a fixed meaning to symptoms and signs, or whether meaning is necessarily fluid and flexible. Above all, perhaps, we can ask questions about whether we should bother with meaning at all.

Formal questions relating to the meaning of text and how it is to be known have been regarded as fundamental for some centuries. Such questions are commonly associated with the science of hermeneutics.[1] Unfortunately, the answers to hermeneutic problems are by no means easy to formulate. Nor, from the point of view of the empirical researcher, are the answers that useful once they have been located. In some circles, of course, it has been argued that a focus on the meaning of text should be ignored in favour of some other characteristic. Thus, Wittgenstein (1958: 69), for example, always argued (in relation to words) that rather than ask for the meaning of a word we ought, rather, to ask how it is used in ordinary language. That, as we have seen, is a productive principle to adopt, and I shall return to it below. In the structuralist corner, of course, writers such as Lévi-Strauss (1969: 84) consistently argued that the focus ought always to be on how what is said is arranged, rather than what it means. (Though structuralists, in general, remained as beguiled by the notion of meaning as were the interpretationists[2] – see Dosse, 1997a, 1997b.) Nevertheless, both of these alternatives have useful and practical implications for social scientific research on documents. Hermeneutics, by contrast, offers little in the way of practical guidance. Given the significance of hermeneutics to the study of text, however, it would be amiss of us not to consider some of the basic implications that the study of meaning has for the social sciences. To that end, in the section that follows I shall sketch out the various ways in which the problem of meaning has been approached in social scientific discourse.

Meaning and modernism

Let us begin by considering two quotations. The first is taken from F. Scott Fitzgerald's *The Great Gatsby* (1925), the second from Leo Tolstoy's *War and Peace* (1889).

> Daisy began to sing with the music in a husky, rhythmic whisper, bringing out a meaning in each word that it had never had before and would never have again.

> 'The road to Warsaw perhaps', Prince Ippolit said loudly … Everybody looked at him, at a loss to guess what he meant … He had no more notion than other people what he meant by his words. In the course of his diplomatic career he had more than once noticed that words suddenly uttered in that way were accepted as highly diverting, and on every occasion he uttered in that way the first words that chanced to come to his tongue. 'May be it will come out alright', he thought, 'and if it doesn't they will know how to give some turn to it'.

The two quotations emphasize the importance of meaning in human affairs, but they do so in different ways. Thus, the first provides a succinct example of the modernist stance – the notion that meaning is an inner psychological property of the author/speaker, and of subjects in general. The quote is also suggestive of a somewhat uni-dimensional image of meaning, uni-dimensional in the sense that it hints at but one true source and interpretation of meaning – Daisy's. The second quotation – written over half a century before the first – implies, on the other hand, that meaning is something bestowed on words (and actions) by a variety of others, and that the endowment of such meaning is variable or multi-dimensional. (In that respect it is characteristically 'postmodern'.) Indeed, we can begin to see by means of Tolstoy's example how 'meaning' (like text, in general) is a situated product.

The tension expressed through these examples, between the author/subject as the source of meaning and the situated 'other' as a source of meaning, has formed the battleground for numerous debates within the social sciences. This is not an appropriate point to deal with such debates in great detail. However, we may as well note immediately that since the beginning of the twentieth century it is, generally speaking, the situated 'other' – as reader and interpreter – that has gained the upper hand. Thus de Certeau (1984: 170), for example, states, 'Whether it is a question of newspapers or Proust, the text has a meaning only through its readers; it changes along with them; it is ordered in accordance with codes of perception that it does not control'. Tracing the routes through which the reader came to displace the author as the fount of meaning is an issue of some considerable interest – though one for cultural historians rather than ourselves. We have, of course, already noted the claim of Barthes (1977) that the 'birth of the reader must be at the cost of the death of the author'. It is a distinctly late twentieth-century claim, and is one that is echoed in the work of many other thinkers – Foucault, Derrida and Kristeva among them (see Dosse, 1997a, 1997b). Indeed, the ambiguity of meaning formed a critical point of focus for the latter. Derrida, for example, argued that since all texts contain ambiguities they can be read in different ways (*la différence*), and since this is so, any ultimate interpretation of a text must forever be deferred (*la différance*). In a similar manner the literary theorist Iser (1989) has referred to the 'indeterminacy of meaning' – an indeterminacy that allows space for the reader to interpolate him- or herself into the text. (Unfortunately, as other commentators have pointed out, the claim that language cannot make unambiguous claims contains a fatal and damning paradox.)

Rather than base our discussions in the work of literary theorists, such as the above, it would be more appropriate for us to ground our thinking in social scientific debates. To that end I shall, in the paragraphs that follow, highlight some markers that have been left behind in the long trek to get to grips with the nature of 'meaning' in social scientific contexts. The aim, of course, is not to provide an exhaustive analysis of the issues, but rather to provide a sketch of the journey to date.

One of the most appropriate of all possible starting points is with the ideas of Wilhelm Dilthey (1833–1911). Dilthey was among the very first of modern philosophers to argue that there was a fundamental difference between what he called the cultural and the natural (physical) sciences. The latter dealt with an exploration of facts and the causal laws that explained such facts. The former dealt with meaning. Meaning necessitated understanding (*Verstehen*) rather than 'explanation'. Indeed, argued Dilthey, since the subject matter of the two sciences differed then their methodologies must differ likewise.[3] Like many who were to follow this path, Dilthey took the presence of meaning to be self-evident.

Dilthey's arguments, together with many others, were later picked up by Max Weber (1864–1920) and developed during the earlier part of the twentieth century. Weber also held meaning to be at the core of social scientific investigation, and, like Dilthey, he claimed that such meaning had to be 'understood'. Social science therefore needed a method of *Verstehen* in order to grasp the significance of an action to the actor. For Weber, as with Dilthey, meaning was believed to reside in the minds (or intentions) of acting subjects. In that respect they both subscribed to a form of what we might call mentalism – the notion that entities reside in individual minds. Naturally, there were important differences between the ways in which the two enquirers conceptualized meaning, and they had very different ideas about how meaning was to be accessed, Dilthey arguing for a form of empathetic understanding and Weber for a more distanced, structured approach that involved the construction of typical ways of acting in given circumstances. Both authors were, however, thoroughly modernist in their desire to locate meaning as a property of subjects – as a feature of human psychology (see Outhwaite, 1975). Some of the problems faced by Weber's theory of meaning have, of course, already been touched upon in Chapter 1. Here we need only note the significance that Weber attached to the search for meaning through the method of *Verstehen*.

It is a matter for historians to decide how Weber influenced twentieth-century American sociology. What is clear is that the concern with the meaning of social action figured largely in such sociology. This was especially true of work executed in the symbolic interactionist tradition. The symbolic interactionists, however, added a new twist to the theory of meaning. They sociologized it. Thus, G.H. Mead (1863–1931), for example, argued that the meaning of objects, symbols, gestures and so forth were not so much contained in thoughts, but forged in and through human action. In stating that claim he divorced meaning from mentalism. ('Meaning is not to be conceived as a state of consciousness' (Mead, 1934: 78).) He located meaning, instead, in fields of social action. It was a critical shift, and it freed the concept of meaning from the strictures of folk psychology.

This sociologized theory of meaning was further developed in the work of the phenomenologist Alfred Schutz. Schutz argued that interpretation of meaning is the fundamental activity of social life. In that sense *Verstehen* is not some special method of the social sciences but the method by which the everyday, intersubjective world (*Lebenswelt*) is constituted. So, determining how people interpret and objectify the world is the central problem for social theory. Thus Schutz was interested, for example, in how people categorized the world into recognizable and meaningful events. (They do so, claimed Schutz, through the use of typifications.) Moreover, and as with Mead, Schutz saw meaning as specific to contexts of action. In that sense he claimed that meaning is 'indexical' and 'reflexive'. That is to say, meaning is both situated in and (at the same time) constitutes the setting in which social action occurs. Ethnomethodologists such as Garfinkel and Cicourel, of course, followed through on these insights from the late 1960s onward.

Studying the meaning of a text is not, of course, the same as studying the meaning of action. In the case of action and interaction the 'author' and the act are bound together in time and place, and so it is possible to talk in terms of a situated analysis. With text, however, author and product are forever divorced. Text is always autonomous in that respect, and the 'author' is necessarily absent. And it is for such reasons that hermeneutics is faced with problems that are somewhat different from those that confront the student of social interaction. Indeed, by facing such problems, hermeneutics has been forced to introduce various subtleties into the study and analysis of 'meaning'.

In this last respect an important figure on our quest to get to grips with meaning is Hans-Georg Gadamer. In fact, we might say that the problem of understanding was in many ways turned on its head by the work of Gadamer (1975). For, unlike Dilthey, Gadamer argued that understanding formed the basis not only for enquiry in the social sciences, but of human life and enquiry in general. Understanding for Gadamer, however, 'is not based on "getting inside" another person' (1975: 345). Instead, he suggests, we would be far better considering understanding as a form of translation. So, for example, when a person translates a text from one language to another language they do not seek to reproduce every wish and whim of the original author in a one-to-one correspondence of original and copy. More likely, the translator decodes the original from a declared culturally formed platform, and then recodes the document in his or her own style, and with his or her own words. The translation is in that sense a fusion of two parties – the meaning embodied in the original text is reproduced through a meaning interpreted by the translator.[4] It is, in the language of Gadamer, a 'hermeneutical conversation' (1975: 349). What is more, it is clear that the culture in terms of which the interpreter interprets is every bit as important in this process as is the culture in which the original text was first produced. So interpretation demands a 'fusion of horizons'. (In this regard, states Gadamer, the example of translating a text is an ideal one because we can see that psychological processes are not in any way involved in 'understanding'.) It further follows that 'meaning' is not something to be discovered, it is something to be produced. Indeed, there can never be a final, once-and-for-all interpretation of anything. To understand is to understand differently.[5] The latter point, of course, raises problems about the nature of truth in social scientific enquiry. Oddly, given the title of Gadamer's book, how we come to distinguish the true from the false is not an issue that he deals with.

A further attempt to locate understanding in terms of text is also available in the work of Ricoeur (1981). Ricoeur is of interest for several reasons. Above all, perhaps, he sees in text the ideal case in which meaning is divorced from context. There is a 'distanciation' between text and author. That is to say, that once text is sent out into the world its meaning is necessarily divorced from authorial intention. So meaning cannot be equated with the indexical or the situated. Nor, on the other hand, is it possible to fill the void of the absent author with the meanings of the reader – as, say, Iser or Derrida seem to suggest. In that respect Ricoeur is at one with Gadamer. He therefore recognizes that some kind of fusion of horizons between the text and the reader must take place. The manner in which he conceptualizes the fusion is, however, somewhat different. For what Ricoeur suggests is that although the reader necessarily appropriates the text in terms of his or her own lifeworld, the text also constrains and produces. That is to say, the text – by virtue of its content – has a creative potential that acts upon the reader, and, by its very nature, develops and broadens the reader in new ways of thought and action. There is a sense, therefore, in which a text structures its reader, and that, of course, is a point that has been illustrated in Chapter 5.

Now, it is not my aim to elaborate on these various claims, and still less to adjudicate between them. Interested readers are better referred to the texts of the cited authors (above). I have sought only to pinpoint some of the central issues. Three points, above all, need to be grasped. First, all of those who are concerned with text take it for granted that text (and action) has meaning. Secondly, they believe that meaning needs to be grasped or understood. Thirdly, they argue that in order to 'understand' some degree of interpretation is necessary. How that interpretation is to be carried out differs according to each author. And, I might add, none of them specify how interpretation should proceed in any concrete instance. In that respect they are more often concerned with issues of ontology (of existence) than of epistemology (of knowing). So I shall end this section by pointing towards a route that does carry with it some practical implications for the analysis of text. It is a route that has been signposted by the philosophers V.W. Quine (1953) and Hilary Putnam among others. Putnam (1988) has argued that meaning talk invokes a form of mentalism – or psychologism. So as with Mead and Gadamer he would argue that 'Meanings aren't "in the head"' (1988: 73), but he also considers the possibility that we can do without meaning talk altogether. In a similar way Quine argues that talk about meanings can be safely 'abandoned' (1953: 22). For, what is more important than meaning is the process of 'reference'. Reference is socially grounded. Indeed, what Putnam argues is that we ought to focus on how words, sentences and ideas are used in social practice, always keeping in mind that 'use is holistic'. That is to say, keeping in mind that there is always a body of statements to consider in which the individual words and sentences merely slumber. The social scientific focus needs, therefore, to be on the whole as well as the parts – on the corporate body of statements rather than the single claims. (Discourse is not a word that Putnam and Quine use in this context, but that does not of course prevent us from referring to it at this exact point.) In this view, then, what is important about the case of Anna O is not what she meant or thought, nor even what Breuer or Freud meant or thought, but how the parties involved variously referenced things (about the mind and body) in the framework of Freudian discourse. One advantage of this manner of approaching things is that, as we shall see, 'reference', unlike meaning, can be made tractable by the social scientific researcher.[6] As ever, in order to see how this might be so, we need to consider examples.

Referencing death

Let me begin with a relatively simple example and move outwards. In a study of death in the city of Belfast undertaken during the 1980s I looked at what I called the social distribution of sentiments. The basis of the idea came from some observations made by Durkheim (1915) and his associate Robert Hertz (1960) during the early twentieth century. Both writers claimed that what was significant about grief and mourning was not the inner psychological states of the bereaved, but outward manifestations of sorrow. Sorrow was socially structured. For example, in many societies the deaths of infants hardly pass for comment, whilst the death of a powerful man is often the occasion for considerable social disruption. Even in contemporary western societies the deaths of the stillborn, for example, are not considered to be an occasion for formal or ritualized mourning and burial, and this is in marked contrast to our responses to the death of, say, children. It follows therefore that we can gather an awful lot of information about reactions to death by observing, in detail, what people do at times of bereavement. Indeed, studying what people do is as instructive (possibly more so) than speculation about what they 'feel' or 'think' or 'believe'.

In the city of Belfast it is common (in fact, it is more or less required) for people to announce the death of a relative in the 'Deaths' announcements of one of the major regional newspapers. This textual declaration informs the world not only of a death, but also about the nature of burial or other arrangements. More importantly, such notices offer an opportunity for people to make comment on their feelings and thoughts and hopes for the deceased. Such public declarations of sentiment are used in many different ways by different kinds of contributor. For example, they are often used by friends and second-degree relatives of the deceased's family to express solidarity with the bereaved. At other times they are used to underline a claim to kinship. In some cases they are used to underline the importance and significance of the person who has died. And in yet other cases they are used to express religious or political affiliations in general. Consequently, such death notices offer a rich seam for study. Yet in mining that seam, we have no need to call upon the concept of meaning, or, indeed, of any other psychological concepts.

For example, one way in which we might study the use of such material is to undertake an analysis of the number of such notices that each person receives, as well as the origin (in terms of kin and friendship relations) of the notices, and the references that are contained within them. In short, to execute a simple content analysis (Weber, 1990) of the relevant newspaper columns. That is just what I did, and the results are reported more fully in Prior (1989). Here, I pick up on only a few of the emergent themes, most of which are contained in Table 6.1.

We can see from a simple analysis of the results contained in that table that the mean number of notices that each person gets alters according to occupational background, age and marital status of the deceased. Manual workers get more notices than non-manual workers, people under the age of 60 get far more notices than do older people, the married tend to get more than the unmarried. There is also a variation in the number of citations by gender of the deceased, but it is not 'significant' in a statistical sense.

There is no need to go into the statistical background of the examples (but do note how such manipulations can have their uses in such exercises). My purpose here is simply to indicate the fact that 'reference' can in itself serve as

TABLE 6.1   *The distribution of death notices in Belfast newspapers in a 10% sample of deaths, 1981*

Variable	Number of cases in category	Mean number of notices per person in category	Standard deviation from the mean
Occupation of deceased at death			
Non-manual	106	4.0*	3.6
Manual	270	8.6	9.1
Gender			
Male	200	6.4	6.8
Female	176	8.3	9.4
Age by category			
01–59	65	12.4*	14.5
60+	311	6.2	5.6
Marital status			
Married	159	9.2*	10.0
Single/divorced/widowed	190	6.0	6.5

*t-test indicates a significant difference $p > 0.001$.

a key point for the social researcher. Hence, the simple act of inserting a notice in a newspaper tells us things about the referencing of death in a western city and how it is related to key social variables. We could, of course, go further and look at referencing in more detail. Thus, we might ask, for example, what is it that is contained in such notices? What, for example, are the religious and political sentiments expressed in the notices and how do they vary according to the social characteristics of the deceased? That would also serve as a valuable research exercise – though it is not one that I wish to follow through at this point. Were we to do that, however, we would then be drawn into a discussion and analysis as to how the language of death notices is related to or expresses a discourse (Potter, 1996) on death. Note, however, that even at the stage of discourse the focus would be on how references are interlinked in the text rather than with what they mean in this, that, or some other person's mind. But rather than develop the death notice material any further it will serve us better to use a new example.

Referencing metaphors

It has long been observed that metaphor is central to the representation of illness. Indeed, in a rather famous literary analysis of this theme Susan Sontag produced her *Illness As Metaphor* (1978). This was a study of the ways in which metaphors were used to describe life-threatening illnesses such as TB and cancer. For example, Sontag pointed out how war metaphors were prominent in discussions of cancer as an illness. People fought cancer – to win. People shore up their defences against the threat of cancer; they demand the latest weapons against the disease; they display immense courage and bravery in their final struggle – and so forth. This use of war-related metaphor in discussions of cancer is, of course, very widely used by politicians, scientists and, indeed, authors. Proctor (1995) provides an intelligent narrative of the ways in which the metaphor was used in the USA during the 1980s and 1990s.

More recently, Seale (2001) has taken up a similar theme and examined the use of what he calls struggle language in media accounts of people with cancer. Both his findings and his methods are of interest to us. Broadly speaking his methods of study were as follows. Using an on-line database of English language newspapers he looked at the ways in which people with cancer were represented in such documents during the first week of October 1999. Almost 2,500 articles relating to cancer were identified and these were then read in order to select the 358 that provided a story about a person with cancer. Content analysis of the 358 stories was then used to map basic reference points such as the types of cancer mentioned, the types of people represented (young, old, male, female, black, white and so on), and the words that were used in the articles to describe cancer. As you might guess, struggle language – as referenced by such terms as fight, battle, survive, beat, struggle, victory, defeat – was uppermost in the content. Such struggle language was not, however, necessarily related to war images in a simple and straightforward way, but more frequently filtered through a further set of metaphors that concerned sport and sporting activity. Seale concludes by indicating how images of sport are closely tied into images of fighting and war and how sporting activity is frequently viewed 'as standing for a life and death struggle' (2001: 325).

A number of useful points arise from this analysis. The first is that, as with the death notices example, counting what is referenced in text (straightforward content analysis) can itself be of benefit in highlighting the concerns of a social group. Secondly, content counts on their own are, however, rather limiting. In order to exploit those counts one has to move into a realm beyond the mere words on the page and into some form of discourse analysis. That is to say, one has to begin to ask questions – and obtain answers – about how the various terms and concepts that are counted are interlocked one into the other so as to form a stance or position or 'weltanshauung'. Once again, however, one need not call upon mentalist ideas in order to follow through with such an analysis – as is evident from the next example.

Accounting for fatigue

Throughout this book I have suggested that to resort to inner mental properties of subjects is problematic for social science. Consequently a desire to study the 'meaning' of a document is potentially misguided. Instead, we ought to study what it is that is referenced in a document, and we have seen how that might be done by use of the two examples above. However, we have also seen how simple counting of content items has its limitations. For, we often wish to go beyond noting that something is referenced and to ask questions about how specific items are integrated into 'accounts' about this, that, or some other matter.

The concept of an account is a useful one for our purposes (see Scott and Lyman, 1968). Accounts are ubiquitous. They are usually offered in relation to questions. For example, if you were to ask me why I became a sociologist, then I would respond to you citing reasons, events, people, and possibly things that were relevant to my becoming a sociologist. All of these items would be wrapped up in an account – probably an account in narrative form. In most cases accounts are tailored for a specific audience. So, my account as to why I became a sociologist would be structured in such a way as to sound rational, persuasive and coherent to the audience that I was addressing. I would include within it only those items and relationships that I wished that audience to hear about and that I considered to be culturally appropriate. I would probably ignore things that I considered not to 'fit' with the requirements of the audience in question. For example, I may decide that a response to the question that referred to a 'calling' would be regarded as somewhat bizarre in the modern world. Consequently, I might prefer to structure my account by reference to a series of influences upon me – books that I read, people that I knew, problems that puzzled me. I might do this even if I felt that I was unsure why I became a sociologist in the first instance. After all, saying 'I don't really know' is not as impressive a response as one that contains a reasoned narrative that refers to, say, a career plan. In addition, the central question might not be one that I had ever considered, and so I might, perhaps, merely invent a response for the sake of dealing with the question posed to me. This latter is always a danger inherent in asking people for their motives, reasons and opinions, any one of which may be invented for the purpose at hand.

In what follows I am going to look at accounts of illness. When people fall ill, they often provide accounts about how the illness was caused, how it developed, and how it might be best managed and treated. Psychologists sometimes refer to 'health beliefs' in such contexts. As you might guess, however, reference to belief (as an inner mental state) is neither necessary nor particularly useful – as the following details indicate.

As far as illness is concerned, we know that different people in different parts of the world tend to construct accounts of illness that reflect their own histories and traditions and practices (see, for example, Lewis, 1975; Prior et al., 2000). What people put into an account and how they connect the things so referenced is a worthy topic of investigation in itself. All that is needed is that we study how the account hangs together and what it contains.

Just to indicate how this might be done, I am going to look at some accounts about fatigue. Feeling fatigued is a common problem (Meltzer et al., 1995). Estimates of the proportion of people who feel totally exhausted at the end of a working day sometimes reach as high as one-third of the adult population.

For most people the experience is temporary and short-lived. In a small percentage of cases, however, the feelings of fatigue persist for long periods. Sometimes there are clear reasons as to why this is so – perhaps the person is suffering from some known physical malady or working overlong hours. In other cases, where clear explanations for the fatigue are absent, medical practitioners and their patients are faced with a puzzle. How they seek to answer that puzzle is the focus of this section.

Chronic fatigue (fatigue experienced for more than six months) is a relatively rare occurrence. It is often referred to as a syndrome – that is, as chronic fatigue syndrome (CFS). In the USA it is known as CFIDS (chronic fatigue and immune deficiency syndrome). The causes of CFS are usually difficult to pin down. Nor is it always clear how such fatigue might be overcome. As you might expect, to ask 'what do you mean?' of someone who experiences CFS is usually not very helpful. Indeed, CFS sufferers often argue that no one can know what it 'means' to be fatigued unless they experience the condition. In fact, CFS sufferers normally place a heavy emphasis on their experiential knowledge of the condition as against the scientific stance that is adopted towards CFS by physicians. In line with the tenets of this chapter, then, perhaps we should ask different questions, such as, what do people who experience CFS reference in accounts of their suffering? What kinds of entities do they recruit into such accounts? And how are such references and entities interlinked?

One way of getting an account is to access patient support group literature on the WWW. CFS sufferers are very active in patient support groups and consequently they publish considerable amounts of literature on the nature of the disease, its causes, its consequences, and its treatment and management. For the purpose of this exercise I accessed just one patient support document on the WWW. Table. 6.2 provides the results of a simple counting exercise executed on that document. The table contains word counts for selected terms used in the WWW leaflet.

As we can see, even a simple counting exercise – basic indexing – can help with matters of reference,[7] though it is not of course surprising that the word 'fatigue' looms large in the table. In this leaflet it occurred 55 times in the 2,315-word text. Omitting prepositions, conjunctions and so forth (words such as to, the, and, or, but), there are in fact only five words that get 50+ mentions in the entire text. (The two words omitted from Table 6.2 are 'subject' and 'patient'.) And it seems fair to assume that the word frequency order is in some way related to the weight of concerns that sufferers have.

At the top tier of citation (50+ uses) there is comparatively little problem in identifying the key concerns. As we move down the word frequency list, however, it becomes evident that counting on its own has severe limitations. For example, the table also suggests that research is important to CFS sufferers as are viruses and virology, fibromyalgia (a related condition to CFS) and disease. Depression, psychology, psychiatry, immunology, neurology, genetics, and an

TABLE 6.2 *Occurrence of selected words in a 2,315-word patient support group leaflet on chronic fatigue syndrome*

Fatigue	55
Chronic	51
Illness	50
Syndrome	46
Research	29
Virus/viral/virology	23
Disease	19
Fibromyalgia	18
Depression	14
Immune/immune-related/immunology	9
Genetic	4
Psychology/psychological	4
Neurology/neurological	4
Psychoneuroimmunology	2
Psychiatric/psychiatrists	2
Mental	1
Mind	1

unusual hybrid referred to as psychoneuroimmunology, also get mentioned – along with hundreds of other words. However, it is not clear how these referenced items connect one to the other and how they are combined into a coherent account of what CFS might be.

Indeed, to follow through on the relationships between words we need to look at context, and using a simple concordance program this too is possible. All that is required is that we call up the context in which a given word is used. To illustrate some relevant issues I reproduce below the line contexts in which 'genetic' was referred to.

Extract 6.5.1

Is CFS genetic?

The cause of the illness is not yet known. Current theories are looking at the possibilities of neuroendocrine dysfunction, viruses, environmental toxins, genetic predisposition, or a combination of these. For a time it was thought that Epstein–Barr Virus (EBV), the cause of mononucleosis, might cause CFS but recent research has discounted this idea. The illness seems to prompt a chronic immune reaction in the body, however it is not clear that this is in response to any actual infection – this may only be a dysfunction of the immune system itself.

Extract 6.5.2

Some current research continues to investigate possible viral causes including HHV-6, other herpes viruses, enteroviruses, and retroviruses. Additionally, co-factors (such as genetic predisposition, stress, environment, gender, age, and prior illness) appear to play an important role in the development and course of the illness.

Extract 6.5.3

Is CFS genetic?

Several studies suggest that there may be a genetic component to CFS. This is not surprising since CFS seems to involve immune dysfunction to some degree, and immune-related illnesses often have a genetic component. The evidence on this point is not clear. And the fact that there seem to be cluster outbreaks of this illness seems to argue against genetics as being the sole factor.

These three extracts are instructive for a number of reasons. First, they suggest that CFS sufferers tend to focus attention on the physical causes of illness. As one can see, the presence of viruses and immune responses loom large within the selected text. Such concerns are partly reflected in the word frequency table above. In the case of 'genetic and genetics', however, it hardly ranks any higher than reference to psychiatry and psychology. So we might be drawn into arguing that psychiatry and psychology are as significant to CFS sufferers as are genetics and immune responses. In a sense they are. However, the way in which psychology and psychological factors are integrated into the text suggests that they are evaluated in a somewhat different way from the physical or somatic causes of disease. Look at the following extracts.

Extract 6.5.4

Emerging illnesses such as CFS typically go through a period of many years before they are accepted by the medical community, and during that interim time patients who have these new, unproven illnesses are all too often dismissed as being 'psychiatric cases'. This has been the experience with CFS as well.

Extract 6.5.5

[CFS] is not depression, nor does depression cause [CFS].

These extracts suggest, then, that where psychiatric factors are referenced, they are referenced in what we might call negative contexts. They suggest that CFS is not a condition in which psychiatry has any major role to play, though they also hint that someone might have suggested a link between psychological factors and CFS – a link that is to be flatly rejected.

The relationship between psychological factors and the symptoms of CFS is a contentious and complicated one. It often forms the nub of debates concerning CFS. For example, in the UK, members of the medical profession produced a report on the syndrome in 1996 (Royal Colleges, 1996). The report covered many aspects of CFS – including an overview of the role of viruses, immunology and psychological states in CFS. Their conclusions suggested that CFS was not likely to be caused by either viruses or immunological disorders. On the other hand they did suggest that psychological factors were likely to be implicated in the syndrome and that one of the most effective forms of management for CFS seemed to be a psychological therapy known as cognitive behaviour therapy Thus, the report stated that 'Depression and/or anxiety represent the strongest risk factors so far identified for CFS' (1996: 15), but cautioned against any 'simple equation of CFS with psychiatric disorder' (1996: 15). As we have seen, the first claim is quite at variance with what many sufferers argue to be the case.

Concentrating on how entities are linked and integrated into accounts is always more productive than a simple focus on what is referenced. And this is so with patient and professional accounts of CFS. In the paragraphs above I have focused, ever so briefly, on how psychological conditions are integrated into accounts. Broadly speaking, when CFS patients refer to psychological symptoms they usually interpret them as the consequences of illness rather than as a cause, and therefore as quite marginal to their real illness. Medical professionals on the other hand tend to argue in the opposite direction, and to suggest that psychological problems often lay at the base of a patient's difficulties and physical experiences. Naturally, an enquiry into how such disagreements are resolved in practice requires an analysis of doctor–patient interactions. (We certainly cannot discover how things are resolved (in practice) by using documents alone.) Nevertheless, a study of documentation is often useful as a precursor to the study of interactive episodes. For documentation often lays out the basis of practical reasoning and behaviour – as it does in the case of CFS. Thus, in a study of CFS doctor–patient interactions undertaken recently I was interested in whether debates in the literature were reflected in what CFS sufferers spoke about in a clinic. The results of the initial research are described in Banks and Prior (2001). Here I shall focus on only one extract from one patient. The patient is discussing a visit to a medical specialist (lines 75). Of particular interest is the way in which the speaker references the link between his illness and his psychological problems (lines 78–9). As you can read for yourselves, the causal link between depression and physical illness is attended to, but in such a way that the symptoms of depression are seen as a result of some other illness rather than a cause of the illness itself. In lines 75–6 the patient refers to a private consultation with a CFS specialist. In line 77 a mention is made of ME which is an alternative expression for CFS often used by patients in the UK. (ME is an abbreviation of myalgic encephalomyelitis – a physical disorder of the skeleto-muscular system.) In lines 78–9 the patient, crucially, reverses the causal direction that is suggested in the Report of the Royal Colleges (1996) mentioned above.

75 (Patient 33):	Anyway like he examined me and whatever, and um, we had a good talk and er,
76	what happened then, he wrote back to my doctor like I said, he didn't tell anything, he
77	did say to me there are symptoms of ME, the rapid fatigue you've got and whatever.
78	I told him, I said I know I was depressed at the time, but it's not depression it's the
79	fact that it's the rapid weakness is getting me down.
80 (Doctor):	Yes.

Conclusions

Documents have content and content requires analysis. Indeed, document content is usually thought to contain insight into people's thoughts, ideas and beliefs. These are often considered the meat and drink of the social scientist as well as of the literary theorist.

One obvious question to ask with respect to the content of any document is 'what does it mean?' And the analysis of the meaning of text is, as we have seen, one with a long and tortuous history (one that involves the history of hermeneutics). We have also glimpsed at how the study of meaning can entice us into a methodological minefield. For whose meaning are we to study and whose meaning is at stake? Are we to study meaning as a quality of writing authors or meaning as an interpretation of readers? Following Gadamer and Ricoeur, of course, we would have to conclude that the study of meaning requires a dialogue between interpreter and interpreted in the manner outlined. But, do we need to focus on meaning at all?

I have suggested (following Quine and Putnam) that we can safely abandon questions about meaning and, instead, look at reference. Better to ask such questions as, 'what is it that is referenced within documents?' than to ask, 'what does this mean?' For, if nothing else, references can be indexed, and then counted in the manner described above. However, we also need to be aware that the problem with straightforward content analysis is that the same words and terms can be used to reference different entities. Thus, the term 'ME' might be used by physicians and patients equally but, in the light of what I have said above, it is most likely that they would be referring to markedly different things. Consequently, in order to appreciate the force of textual discourse one has to do more than count. One has to attempt to get a picture of the ways in which the network of references interlock. It is, perhaps, what we might call a matter of intertextuality.[8]

So let us sum up the suggested strategy for dealing with content:

- Documents have content, and content requires analysis.
- Rather than focus on the 'meaning' of a word, sentence, paragraph or document, it is far more fruitful to ask about what is referenced within the document.
- In studying patterns of reference, simple content analysis has its place.
- Content analysis on its own, however, will be insufficient to highlight the full pattern of referencing between objects cited in the text. Reference therefore needs to be studied in context.
- As well as examining the words and terms that are recruited and connected within a text, we need also to look at who enrols and who attacks the text in everyday projects. Above all, we need to study how people use text in action.

In the following chapter we will look at some examples of how people use words to picture the world and to place actors within that world. The examples are drawn from two fields of human endeavour – science and anthropology. Our task, as ever, will be to unravel what it is that people are doing with words rather than with what they are intending – or 'meaning'.

RESEARCH EXERCISE

Exercise 6.1

As we have noted in Chapter 3, people with psychiatric disorders tend to be portrayed somewhat negatively in the mass media. For example, serious psychiatric disorder is often associated with violence and extreme violence is, in turn, often interpreted as 'madness'. Using electronic search facilities examine how mental illness and the mentally ill are referenced in newspapers. Make sure to select a variety of such papers and confine the text search to specific dates – say 1 January 2000 up to and including 31 July 2000. Compare the reference terms used in the different papers. Pay particular attention to any associations between psychiatric disorder and violence, and psychiatric disorder and genetics. Some helpful leads on the problems can be found in Philo (1996).

Notes

1 Hermeneut – an interpreter, especially of scripture.
2 In terms of the linguistics of Saussure (1983) the meaning of a term is given by its position in a chain. Meaning can therefore change if and when position in a system changes. The metaphor of a linguistic chain was extended beyond language and into other systems of symbolic meaning – myths, clothing – by a later generation of structuralists such as Barthes (1985) and Lévi-Strauss (1969).
3 Dilthey's desire to differentiate the human sciences (or *Geisteswissenschaften*) from the natural sciences (or *Naturwissenschaften*) stimulated debates that lasted throughout the twentieth century. A good overview of these debates and their broad methodological implications for social researchers is provided by Giddens (1978).
4 For example, the English translator of Freud's work – Lytton Strachey – translated simple German terms that were used by Freud, such as *das Ich* and *das Es*, into 'Ego' and 'Id', thereby adding a guise of scientific and technical precision to plain, everyday, words.
5 A fellow traveller in this regard is Charles Taylor (1987).
6 In what might be regarded as a parallel manner, Silverman (1993) has argued that talk ought to be scrutinized so as to uncover strategies of practical reasoning rather than meaning.

7 Many search engines currently in use on the WWW find relevant 'pages' using a similar, word counting, technique.
8 'Intertextuality' is a 'gadget' invented by the French literary critic/philosopher Julia Kristeva (1980). The term refers, in part, to the notion that the meaning of a single text is always bound up in its relations with others that are contemporary to it. The concept also implies that texts are never singular or unique but comprise bits and pieces of other texts written at other times and in other places.

7

Doing Things with Words

Traveller's tales

During the period 1911–12 Apsley Cherry-Garrard travelled with Captain Scott to the Antarctic. He was not included in Scott's team for the final leg of the journey to the South Pole, and consequently he managed to survive the rigours of Polar life whilst Captain Scott and his companions perished. On his return to England, Cherry-Garrard reports that he was asked, by the Antarctic Committee, to write the 'Official Narrative' of the 1911–12 Polar expedition. The narrative was to take the form of a scientific report on a scientific expedition. Cherry-Garrard wrote the report, but he tells us in the introduction to his 1922 book, *The Worst Journey in the World*, that he felt that he was unable to publish it under the auspices of the Official Committee, because, 'I could not reconcile a sincere personal confession with decorous obliquity of an Official Narrative' (Cherry-Garrard, 1994: lii). In short, Cherry-Garrard sensed that there was an important difference between the nature of a scientific narrative and a personal narrative. Yet, his book is full of scientific observations – about the Emperor and other species of penguin, about seal life and the behaviour of whales and birds. He uses, at times, quite extensive footnotes in his report, and makes reference to a number of scientific journals and books. Many of his observations are cross-referenced with observations recorded in Scott's diary and other sources – validated as it were. Nevertheless, *The Worst Journey in the World* is not regarded in any way as a science text. Instead it is commonly regarded as a 'travel' book – albeit one that is often described as the very best twentieth-century example of that genre.[1]

The travel book is, of course, a distinctive form of literality that, under other circumstances, might provide us with an instructive site of enquiry. (And so too, the travel writer as a variant of the author-function.) In this chapter, however, our interests are to be restricted to two other sites of writing. The first is the scientific paper, and the second is the ethnographic report. In both cases we will be interested to focus on how people can 'do' science with words. In particular we will examine the manner in which the relationship between the author/discoverer and the (natural and the social) worlds that they investigate are modulated through text. How, for example, the different types of 'author' report on the world; how they represent that world in their reports; and how they inscribe themselves and their discoveries in the reporting process. As we shall see, scientific (and anthropological) authors are normally keen to represent text as a neutral conduit for the transmission of observations and discoveries. The scientific text, in that sense, is seen as a means by which the scientist can communicate with a readership in a manner that avoids contaminating the data. Consequently, text is not seen as having any role in the constitution of the various 'facts' that it reports upon. The extent to which that claim is supportable will, however, become evident as this particular report unfolds.

Now, the analysis of documents of the kind referred to above is often undertaken in a frame of what is called discourse analysis. Unfortunately, and as we have noted before, 'discourse' and 'discourse analysis' are rather fuzzy terms. As with all other words, their meaning can only be derived from their use. In reviewing the multiple interpretations of such terms, van Dijk (1977, I: 3) argues that discourse analysis deals with 'talk and text in context' – that is, with linguistic activity – but he also points out that the word 'discourse' can refer to a much wider array of phenomena, such as styles of thought and analysis. This wider vision of discourse – as, say, a set of closely integrated ideas and practices about the nature of the world – was one favoured by Foucault (1972). The latter was keen to indicate how the world comes to be known and understood through discursive practices, and how a change in discursive regime can change the world (and social relationships within it) itself. In short, how reality is constituted through discourse.

This broader (Foucauldian) use of the term has its uses – especially in so far as it encourages us to look at the manner in which discourse structures what we might call the furniture of the world (that is, objects, 'facts' and 'things').[2] We shall defer to it in our examination of the two realms of discursive practice that have been selected. In relation to the realm of 'science', however, we shall primarily follow in the wake of a group of late twentieth-century writers – such as Gilbert and Mulkay (1984), Knorr-Cetina (1983), Latour and Woolgar (1979), Lynch (1985) and Woolgar (1981; 1988) – all of whom look at the ways in which science is created in and through discourse. That is, we shall adopt the argument that 'science' is not a body of knowledge or practices independent of scientists (such as, say, a true and correct explanation of the mechanics of 'nature'), but rather constituted in what scientists say and do. And we shall call upon a similar argument in our investigation of anthropological reports. In the latter case, however, we can supplement our claims with references to the work of those troubled by the possibility that anthropological writing might, after all, not to be too distant from forms of travel writing. So 'ethnography', in particular, might be regarded as a form of fiction rather than a form of scientific fact gathering (see Atkinson 1990; 1992b; Geertz, 1988; van Maanen, 1988). Some writers, of course, have made the claim that all forms of writing are forms of fiction (see, for example, Derrida, 1991), but that – for various reasons – is an awkward position to hold with any consistency. What we can say, however, is that there are different forms of writing in the world and that they each claim a different relationship to external reality. How that relationship is represented in text is, in large part, the subject of this chapter.

Just to narrow down our concerns a little further it might be useful to add that the specific focus of the chapter will be on the rhetoric of science and of anthropology. That is, on the ways in which authors of anthropological and scientific texts *use* words so as to persuade us of the veracity of their reports and of their status as objective observers. We need also to remain aware that rhetoric is normally regarded as only one feature of discourse. Thus, semantics (or the study of meaning), narrative, argumentation, semiotics, pragmatics and much more can also form the foundation for discourse analysis, and interested readers will find some excellent pointers to those various modes of analysis in van Dijk's (1997) text. However, some writers (such as, for example, Bazerman, 1988) argue that the study of rhetoric can encompass most of these latter forms. In so far as that may be so, then our concern with scholarly rhetoric will serve us well.

The scientific report

In 1961 Ernest Nagel opened his book on *The Structure of Science* with a chapter in which he drew contrasts between common sense and scientific thinking. Science, he claimed, organizes its knowledge and its findings in a systematic manner; common sense does not. Science provides rigorous explanations for events in the world; common sense does not. Science subjects its arguments and findings to consistent criticism and analysis; common sense does otherwise. In drawing such contrasts, Nagel developed a representation of science that firmly belonged to what is generally referred to as the 'positivist' camp (see also Chapter 8). Such positivistic pronouncements (Giddens, 1978) on what science 'is' were frequently developed and published during the nineteenth and twentieth centuries. In all such pronouncements 'science' was seen as something set apart from other ways of thinking. In particular it was viewed as a means of obtaining objective knowledge about the external world, knowledge that could be rigorously tested and retested until the truth of any matter became plain to see. In short, science was viewed as a mirror to nature.

How science is to be demarcated from other forms of thought is a matter for philosophy and philosophers, and there have been various detailed attempts to draw the required line (see Gillies, 1993). Such attempts are not of any concern to us at the moment. What we seek to examine is exactly how scientists manage (in practice) to convince us of their special status as knowing subjects. What, for example, are the textual and other strategies that they use to get their ideas across – both to the likes of lay persons such as ourselves and other scientists? Answers to that question require something other than philosophical analysis. Indeed, it requires close examination of what scientists do, and that becomes possible only when we adopt an anthropological or sociological approach to the problem.

Anthropological studies of scientists are a comparatively recent phenomenon. In the main such studies have focused on the laboratory as a site of anthropological fieldwork – see, for example, Barley and Bechky (1994). Charlesworth et al. (1989), Knorr-Cetina (1983), Latour and Woolgar (1979) and Lynch (1985). Most of this work has been executed in the realm of the biological sciences. One of the key findings of such work is that text and documents are fundamental to the very nature of laboratory work. (For where are 'ideas', 'thoughts', hypotheses, rules of procedure, results, findings and so forth if they are not contained in documentation?) Indeed, Woolgar (1988: 68) sees documents as resting at the base of the scientific discovery process. This certainly makes sense in so far as things (objects) and processes are only made visible through drawings, photographs, pencil and ink traces, scribbles on black- and whiteboards, memos, and scientific papers and books. Indeed, it may be said that scientific objects are constituted in and through the use of such documents; that texts produce scientific knowledge. Thus Latour and Woolgar, in their study of the La Jolla Laboratory, argue, for example, that scientists are 'manic writers' (1979: 48), and are constantly generating scientific facts through the use of written and other traces. Other traces – temperature charts, for example – are routinely derived from what Latour (1983) calls inscription devices. That is to say, devices that turn material substances into documentary form. So one of Latour's injunctions for any research project is to 'look at the inscription devices' (1983: 161):

> No matter if people talk about quasars, gross national products, statistics or anthrax epizootic microbes, DNA or subparticle physics; the only way they can talk and not be undermined by counter-arguments as plausible as their own statements is if, and only if, they can make the things they say they are talking about easily readable.

In the positivist world of philosophers such as that of Nagel (mentioned above), such devices would have been viewed as mere technical instruments that aid the scientist in his or her assessment of the true and real properties of an object. That is to say, they would have been treated as a mirror on nature. In the world of the 'constructivists' (Knorr-Cetina, 1983), however, inscription devices are not merely adjuncts to scientific work, but central to the construction of scientific objects themselves. What the object 'is' is in large part constituted by its trace. Indeed, for Latour (1983) and Latour and Woolgar (1979), the laboratory as a whole is viewed as a productive force – a force that manufactures the world so that 'scientific activity is not "about nature", it is a fierce fight to construct reality' (1979: 243). A similar idea is expressed by Charlesworth et al. (1989: 151) who regard laboratories as 'data-generation systems' – systems in which documentation (photographs and charts as much as writing) plays a major role. (See also Rapp (2000) on the laboratory manipulation of chromosomes.)

We have already examined the role of documents in scientific action in Chapter 4. Here, we shall concentrate on how documents (in the form of research grant applications, journal papers, textbooks and autobiographical accounts of scientific discovery) also construct an image or representation of science itself. In particular, on how documents generate an image of science as a set of activities that interrogates 'nature', and subsequently produces true and useful knowledge about how the natural world works.

In order to achieve the latter, scientists may be said to adopt a special way of 'writing science' (Myers, 1990). For example, the use of first-person pronouns (that is, 'I' and 'me') is usually considered unsuitable in scientific prose. (Perhaps this was one reason why Cherry-Garrard regarded his 'personal' account of the Antarctic expedition as unscientific.) The use of the passive, rather than the active, voice is also preferred. For example, a report in a medical journal might state that 'patients were injected with x, y and z', rather than 'we injected the patients with x, y and z', still less, 'I injected patients with x, y and z'. (Lynch (1985) also provides an interesting example of what he calls the 'missing agent' feature of scientific writing in relation to his study of rat brains). This kind of writing has the effect of distancing the scientist from the activities being reported upon, so that they are more likely to be seen as exterior to the world that they investigate and manipulate. This is sometimes all the more important when animals are being discussed in experimental reports. For animals are very often killed. Yet, one is unlikely to read in a scientific report a statement to the effect that 'we killed 80 animals and dissected their brains' (see, for example, Birke and Smith, 1995). More likely, one would read something to the effect that '80 rat brains were harvested over a 48 hour period and assayed in the laboratory using [XYZ techniques]' – or, 'n animals were sacrificed under nembutal anethesia' (Lynch, 1985), and so forth. A sentence of the latter type has many advantages. It does not mention killing, and no human agent is apparently involved in the harvesting/sacrificing process. Harvesting, in any case, is a word normally applied to the gathering up of grain, fruit and vegetables, and so the use of the word serves, perhaps, to obscure the difference between vegetable and other forms of life. Finally, only the rat brains were harvested – the fact that the brains were attached to the rats is – shall we say – subtly elided.

Woolgar (1981; 1988), in particular, has devoted some time to analysing the rhetorical techniques that scientists use in their reports to manufacture good 'science'. It would serve us well to review some of his claims here. For example, he points out the importance of the scientific paper's overall setting. Thus, a good paper ought to be published in a 'good' journal. The authors should have sound institutional affiliations ('good' universities or research institutes), and, ideally, there should be a number of authors (a team, perhaps). Clearly, a lone, amateur, scholar publishing his or her work in a local or regional newspaper is unlikely to be taken seriously. In fact, Latour (1987) points out that the adjective scientific is never attributed to isolated texts. On the contrary, it is an adjective attributed to a document only when that document is produced through a dense network of collaborators. The network will include 'researchers', reviewers of scientific papers, editors, members of scientific committees and so on – most of whom work in teams. This attention to setting is important, and we shall see in Chapter 8 that whether a scientific finding is or is not published and widely quoted seems, on the face of things, to be related to whether the findings are positive rather than negative or neutral. In academic life, of course, journals are sometimes placed in a hierarchy of influence and significance and so scientists ought not simply to get their work published, but to get their work published in 'first-class' refereed journals. So the *New England Journal of Medicine* or *The Lancet* or *Nature* are seen and regarded as prestigious publications. A published book chapter, on the other hand, would be seen as less prestigious. Indeed, by drawing attention to the 'setting' of a text in this manner we can begin to see how discourse is invariably structured by things outside of the text. Thus, Charlesworth et al. (1989: 171) argue that scientific papers are designed first and foremost so as to be published rather than read. In other words, the scientific paper is commonly regarded as an output device – a device by means of which the productivity of authors and institutes can be judged. Indeed, and as we have already seen, there are many things beyond the text[3] (and language) per se that need to be addressed in any study of a scientific paper. Discourse, in other words, always involves extra-linguistic processes. Bazerman (1988), for example, in his study of the scientific paper as a genre, makes reference to the importance of various gatekeepers in maintaining firm boundaries between what is and what is not to be regarded as scientific discourse. Such gatekeepers (journal editors and reviewers) are as significant to the structure of a rhetoric – to the fabrication of the scientific voice – as are the writers themselves. For now, however, we need to look within rather than without the text for an image of how scientific papers 'work'.

To persuade, scientific papers need references, lots of them. Latour (1987) argues that scientific authors use references in the same way as builders use cement – to bind the structure together in such a way that each little bit of the paper has to be attacked before the overall structure can collapse. Thus scientific text, it is argued, is highly stratified with technical details and their associated references. The text, as it were, recruits allies – in other texts – so as to overwhelm with a sheer weight of numbers. In his examination of citation practices and their role in the development of scientific practices, Bazerman (1988) uses the concept of 'intertextuality' to refer to the wider web of textual relations that a scientific paper is required to display. Latour argues that the use of citations ensures that weak rhetoric becomes stronger as time passes, and as more and more papers by the author (and that includes the laboratory as an author) are published (Latour, 1987: 103). References in bibliographies and footnotes are important.[4] So too is an examination of the networks and alliances in terms of which references are cited (Baldi, 1998). Yet, the rhetorical force of any scientific paper is dependent on much more than references alone. Thus, Woolgar, for example, indicates that the 'textual opening' of any paper is significant in so far as it structures the reader in his or her approach to the reading. That is to say, openings funnel the reader's attention onto specific issues and inform the reader as to how the paper is going to develop and conclude. Textual entrées are usually achieved by the use of an 'Abstract' and 'key' words – both functioning so as to mark out an audience to which the paper is believed to be relevant. Paper titles can also be used so as to exclude certain kinds of readers – and, by implication, to circumscribe an elite few who would really 'know' what the paper is about. (One is reminded here of Goody's (1968) observations on the manner in which script can be used to structure an elite of experts.) The use of 'headings' in the paper may also function to structure the reader and the reading of the text. For example, in some scientific journals there might be a formal way of proceeding through the paper – from an outline of the problem, through to the 'method' used to investigate it, an account of the 'findings' and a 'discussion' of the implications of those findings.

Woolgar also makes reference to the use of 'pathing' and 'sequencing' devices. These devices are used to indicate how the scientific results being discussed were arrived at. They often involve the use of a narrative of discovery – pointing out precursors of the work, or how the work is the latest in a long line of scientific developments, plugging gaps in the existing narrative. Pathing, then, provides a trail to be read and locates the scientific results in a context of cumulative scientific discovery. Sequencing provides a narrative in terms of which conclusions have been arrived at – and the sequence is invariably presented as inevitable. Thus, in terms of the sequence, alternative readings of the facts are closed down in the light of 'what happened next', and the focus is increasingly placed on 'relevant' (rather than background and irrelevant) events. Clearly, de Certeau's claim (1984: 186) that, 'Narrations have the power of transforming seeing into believing and of fabricating realities out of appearances' has much resonance in scientific texts. Finally Woolgar refers to 'logic', the process by which a whole series of events are necessarily connected so that other ways of seeing the world are gradually occluded (Lynch (1985) also makes reference to similar techniques).

More important from our standpoint, however, is the use of what Woolgar refers to as 'externalizing devices' in scientific discourse. Externalizing devices operate so as to distance the natural world from the social world of the scientists. For example, the very use of the word 'findings' – as referred to above – is suggestive of things already in the world, but found and discovered by investigators. This distancing effect can also be maintained by the use of carefully structured sentences. Thus one might read a scientific report to the effect, say, that 'we were able to measure for the first time X, Y and Z'. Such a statement naturally implies that the object or objects being measured exist (in the external world) long before the scientist discovers them, and that measurement of such objects had proved problematic to other scientists. (Naturally, a constructivist reading would highlight how the very act of 'measuring', in part, serves to constitute the object being studied.)

A focus on dimensions as a property of the object, rather than on measurement as a product of the scientists, is usually most evident in cases of scientific controversy. Thus Collins and Pinch (1993), for example, provide an excellent case study of measurement problems in their examination of the cold fusion debate that arose during the 1990s, a debate in which various teams of scientists argued about whether observable traces were a product of a new physical process or an artefact of the laboratory set-up. Latour (1983; 1987) contends that these kinds of problems are never resolved by appeal to superior forms of evidence or 'fact', but simply through techno-political manoeuvring. In Latour's world it is simply the weight of the laboratory that matters. Strong laboratories struggle against weaker ones. They are able to carry out more and more complex experiments, they are able to define the nature of reality, and when they do so they are able – by sheer weight of personnel – to overwhelm the opposition with more and more scientific papers.

This vision of science as a contest between heavyweights is an interesting one. Yet, it does not help us to avoid the fact that heavyweights still need to persuade in terms of the strategies referred to above. Indeed, both Latour (1987) and Woolgar (1988) have, at different times, drawn attention to the ways in which the status of scientific facts is also underpinned by the use of what they refer to as 'modalizers'. Modalizers comment on the factual status of scientific claims, and can be systematically used so as to bolster one's own facts and to cast suspicion on the facts of others. Consider the following examples.

> Newton's second law of motion asserts that force is equal to mass multiplied by acceleration ($F = ma$).
> Newton thought that his equation $F = ma$ took the form of a universal law.
> Newton believed that $F = ma$ held for all time and for all place. It was left to Einstein to correct this misapprehension.

We can see here that the factual status of the claim $F = ma$ is gradually eroded. Interestingly it is eroded by associating the claim with human agency. That is to say, the gradual implication of Newton's beliefs and thoughts underwrites the eventual claim that the universality of the physical law was somehow in error. Latour and Woolgar (1979) argue that these kinds of modalizers are readily found in scientific papers and that the factual status of claims can be alternately bolstered and undermined by their use. The use of modalizers can undoubtedly be observed in various forms of scientific discourse, though one suspects that they are much more likely to be found in spoken rather than in written discourse.

Some years ago Gilbert and Mulkay (1984) analysed how scientists' discourse changed according to context. The two contexts that they focused upon were the scientific paper and the semi-structured interview. Gilbert and Mulkay noted a variety of differences in the linguistic registers of the two discourses. For example, in the interviews scientists were more likely to interject references to 'I', 'me', 'we' and 'they' and to account for scientific discoveries in serendipitous ways. For example, in recounting the moment at which a given discovery was made, a scientist might refer to 'X' having run into the canteen with a 'what if?' statement – a statement that within 30 seconds made everything 'fall into place' or hit them like a 'bolt from the blue', whereas in the scientific paper all discovery processes are presented as a result of measured and deliberate manipulations. Sudden bolts from the blue in coffee shops are simply never mentioned.

The use of what Gilbert and Mulkay called the 'empiricist repertoire' enabled scientists to portray actions and beliefs as flowing naturally from their systematic interrogation of nature. In our terms we might refer to it as 'mirror talk'. In informal conversation, however, scientists tended to eschew this kind of talk for talk that made frequent reference to networks of workers, personal characteristics of specific scientists, to hunches and guesswork. Gilbert and Mulkay refer to the latter as forming the 'contingent' repertoire. In the contingent repertoire clashes between personalities, competition for resources, political intrigue and the like are all mentioned as an intrinsic part of the scientific process. And the two, contrasting, forms of discourse are in many ways represented in talk about the success and failure of scientific work. So scientific discovery that is subsequently validated is seen as a result of following rigorous scientific method, whilst scientific discovery that is subsequently rejected or placed in limbo is seen as a product of personal and contingent factors – as the work of bad scientists.

The contingent, situated or occasioned character of scientific discovery is also emphasized in the work of Knorr-Cetina (1983), though her work draws as much attention to the role of talk in the laboratory as it does to the role of text. Thus, she points out that 'the occasioned character of scientific work first manifests itself in the role played by that which visibly stands around at the research site, that is by facilities and measurement devices, materials which are in stock, journals and books in situ in the library' (Knorr-Cetina, 1983: 124). Just how such material is called upon in practice has been investigated, in part, in Chapters 3 and 4 of this book.

The use of the strategies and devices and repertoires referred to in the foregoing paragraphs is not, of course, peculiar to science and scientific writing. It can be found in all other arenas of text. Thus, Potter (1996), for example, draws on examples drawn from news coverage to illustrate these same processes and procedures. More importantly, such procedures are also an integral part of social scientific reporting itself. In order to see just how that is so, we need to journey once more – not to the Antarctic, perhaps, but certainly far afield.

From Kiriwana to Inishkillane

Daniel Defoe's novel *Robinson Crusoe* (1956 – first published in 1719) is a book that provides, among other things, a masterful representation of the 'anthropological' eye in the age of reason. The main story concerns a shipwrecked Englishman who subsequently struggles to subsist on an isolated island. He finds a 'native' companion, called Friday, and, with him, marches out against cannibals and mutineers and quells both. Within the narrative we see emerge some dominant themes of a newly minted capitalist ethic. They concern the western 'civilisation' of the non-western world (indeed, the word civilisation first appears around the time of Crusoe); the subordination of 'nature' to the will of humankind; and the systematic use of tools to produce and improve the most rudimentary form of social organization. More to the point, perhaps, one can view the novel as an allegory of the writing process itself (de Certeau, 1984: 136). That is, a process in which blank spaces are colonized, a system of objects is produced by a dominant subject, and the natural and social world transformed – even created – anew.

As with many things produced by humankind, the social world of others – strangers, foreigners, outsiders, 'natives' – is and was realized in a special form of literality. Between (roughly) 1914 and (even more roughly) 1980, that form could be best found within academic anthropology, and, especially, that mode of anthropology known as ethnography. (Though it is never quite clear whether 'ethnography' refers to a textual account of anthropological fieldwork, or the practical anthropological work that supposedly underpins it – see, for example, Tedlock, 2000.) In any event, ethnography as a textual genre truly appears only after the First World War, and it is thereafter set apart from the numerous traveller's tales, fiction and journalism that surrounded it. Not until the 1980s would critics begin to question whether the line that had been drawn between ethnography and works of fiction was truly impervious.

Ethnographic reports, then, were originally offered to readers as containing objective scientific accounts of life in other cultures. They were documents produced by trained anthropologists – people who had intentionally left the comforts of London and Cambridge behind them, and planted themselves in native villages across the globe, so as to experience, analyse and describe life therein. (I shall leave aside for the moment the fact that ethnography – especially as it was developed in North America – was later used as a method for studying 'exotic' locations in the advanced industrial world.)

One of the earliest and most influential of all ethnographers was Bronislaw Malinowksi (1884–1942), who studied the inhabitants of the Trobriand

Islands – in the western Pacific – between 1914 and 1920. In many ways it was he who laid down the basic rules of ethnographic work, and his 'Introduction' to *Argonauts of the Western Pacific* (1922) provides one of the clearest accounts as to how a twentieth-century ethnographer should proceed. In that Introduction, Malinowski tells us that ethnography is a science, and he contrasts such a science with 'speculative theorising' which he refers to as ethnology. No doubt, Malinowski was here thinking of such work as that produced by E.B. Tylor in his *Primitive Culture* (1871). The latter, a two-volume work, focused on mythology, philosophy, religion, art and customs of non-western peoples. It did so in an overarching theoretical context of human evolution, and it relied for its evidential base on information gathered from missionaries, sailors, travellers and other assorted observers. None of his 'observations' were made by Tylor in person. Instead, he merely compiled, ordered and theorized the data that had been amassed by others. In place of this somewhat distanced form of investigation, Malinowski sought to ground anthropology in first-hand observation – in the science of ethnography. Thus, ethnography, he says, presents us with 'the empirical and descriptive results of the science of Man' (1922: 9). It can only be produced under strict conditions. For example, in order to produce lasting and reliable evidence about the lives of others, the scientific ethnographer needs to pitch his 'camp right in [the native's] village' (1922: 6). He or she should then aim to give a complete survey of the phenomena under study, and not confine him- or herself to a study of the singular or the peculiar or to the exotic. Lots of individual cases of events and happenings should be studied. The ethnographer should 'exhaust as far as possible all the cases within reach' (1922: 14), and Malinowski referred to this precept as a 'method of statistic documentation by concrete evidence' (1922: 17). Photographs should be taken where possible. Drawings should be made if appropriate. (Malinowski does not explicitly tell the reader to use drawings and photographs, but as he incorporates them into his work I am assuming that he is teaching us by example.) Minute, detailed observations ought to be kept, and the ethnographer ought also to compose an ethnographic diary. Characteristic narratives, statements, typical utterances should also be collected. Results should be presented in charts or synoptic tables. The final goal of the ethnographer should, however, be to 'grasp the native's point of view, *his* relation to life, to realise *his* vision of his world' (1922: 25, emphasis in the original).

Some years after writing that account, Malinowski wrote another account of Trobriand life. Here are the opening sentences from the Preface to that publication.

> Once again I have to make my appearance as a chronicler and spokesman of the Trobrianders, the Melanesian community so small and lowly as to appear almost negligible – a few thousand 'savages', practically naked, scattered over a small flat archipelago of dead coral – and yet for many reasons so important to the student of primitive humanity ...
>
> In this book we are going to meet the essential Trobriander. Whatever he might appear to others, to himself he is first and foremost a gardener. (Malinowski, 1935: ix)

Clearly, then, Malinowski's science was not as objective as he claimed (see Stocking, 1983). At the crudest level one might say that it was produced in a frame of white, European, male assumptions about advanced and primitive societies; the civilized and the primitive world; the place of the female and the essential nature of 'Man'. In retrospect (and the retrospect is important here), we need only look at Malinowski's language to recognize the absurdity of his claims to objectivity, detachment and scientific discourse. Indeed, many years later, Malinowski's Diary – written during his years in the Islands – was published (Malinowski, 1967). It indicates, among other things, that the ethnographic findings were not generated purely and simply from observational work. In fact, it appears as if many of his significant 'observations' of native life (such as those concerning the Kula system) had in fact been stimulated by discussion with other westerners who were present in the Islands. (We might say that such westerners were hidden auteurs of the ethnographic report.) And it is certainly the case that the complete erasure of westerners from his published accounts of 1922 and 1935 enabled Malinowski to present himself as a detached, isolated, scientific observer of native life. The Diary also reveals that he actually hated the 'lousy villages' (1967: 129) of the Trobrianders and thought comparatively little of the natives – often describing them in blatantly racist terms. The Eurocentric and distinctly 'malestream' terminology called upon by Malinowski was, however, just one of many ways in which the anthropologist was able to construct an exotic 'other' on which the entire academic discipline of social and cultural anthropology depended.

During the period in question (1914–22) the 'other' that was observed was invariably non-western and non-white. In the next and the following decades, however, the mysterious and exotic 'other' was to be found in almost any setting. The immigrant 'zone' of downtown Chicago (Zorbaugh, 1929), Chicago's gangland (Thrasher, 1927), the conservative setting of a mid-west town (Lynd and Lynd, 1929), and the street corner of a Boston neighbourhood (Whyte, 1955), were all suitable subjects for ethnographic study – though in the latter cases in the frame of academic sociology rather than anthropology. But whatever the setting, the key task of the ethnographer was to underscore that notion of 'otherness'. For whether it be of the inhabitants of the slum, or the gang, or the box-car, or of darkest colonial Africa, the theme that the ethnographer wished to emphasize above all was the contrast between a puzzling 'they' and a familiar 'us'. Here, for example, is an extract from the Foreword to an anthropological study of Middle America as represented by the residents of Muncie, Indiana.

Whatever may be the deficiencies of anthropology, it achieves a large measure of objectivity because anthropologists are by the nature of the case 'outsiders'. To study ourselves as through the eye of an outsider is the basic difficulty in social science, and may be insurmountable, but the authors of this volume have made a serious attempt, by approaching an American community as an anthropologist does a primitive tribe. (Lynd and Lynd, 1929: Foreword)

One task of the ethnographer, then, is to position him- or herself as a neutral (but participant) outsider reporting upon the activities and beliefs of strange and puzzling 'others'. It necessitates a precarious, perhaps impossible, point of balance. For on the one hand the ethnographer has to present him- or herself as a mere conduit for the processing of scientific information and, on the other, as someone who is intimately and deeply involved with 'the native's point of view'. Indeed, one might ask why, if all that is needed is the native's point of view, do we not simply ask a 'native' to write up the study? Or, if the ethnographer is merely acting as a conduit for scientific observations, then why doesn't the ethnographer simply publish the field notes? The answers to such questions are, of course, clear. The ethnographer is much more than a mere conduit or a crystal through which the worlds of others are refracted. He or she is a teller of tales (van Maanen, 1988) – someone who has to create his or her community and represent it in writing.[5] In that respect, the scientific volumes that the anthropologist creates have been closely allied to the traveller's tales recruited by Tylor, and even the literary imaginings of a Daniel Defoe (see Geertz, 1988).

Now, it is undoubtedly the case that the very act of recording the lived worlds of others in writing changes, in the most fundamental of ways, the nature of human culture. Thus Goody (1977) and Ong (1982), for example, indicate how the translation of the symbols and thoughts of people from oral cultures into writing cannot but fail to alter the very nature of the thought system that is being discussed. Malinowski's synoptic charts and tables, for example, put into written form what was only spoken of in Trobriand society and it is quite clear that the systematization belongs to the Polish-born observer rather than the western Pacific Islanders. Even Malinowski, of course, recognized that ethnography involved construction. Thus, in his post-fieldwork *Coral Gardens*, he pointed out that:

> The main achievement in field-work consists, not in a passive registering of facts, but in the constructive drafting of what might be called the charters of native institutions. The observer should function not as a mere automaton; a sort of combined camera and phonographic or shorthand recorder of native statements. While making his observations the field-worker must constantly construct. (Malinowski, 1935: 317)

Similarly, in the *Argonauts*, whilst discussing the features of the Kula (see Chapter 9), Malinowski (1922: 84) had pointed out how the Trobriand Islanders had no outline of their social structure and that, consequently, 'the Ethnographer has to *construct* the picture of the big institution', (emphasis in original).

All ethnographies are constructions. Indeed, ethnographic field notes may be said to construct the very circumstances they claim to describe (Clifford and Marcus, 1986). For, in many cases, what is represented in the text appears there and there alone. Often, such acts of creation are blatant. Thus, Haddon's family trees – mentioned in Chapter 1 – were not in any sense visible within Torres Straits society. In the same manner, Lienhardt's (1961) description of Dinka cosmology – executed through a constant comparison with 'western' ideas – is a product of Lienhardt's thinking rather than of the Dinka. And the same might be said of Evans-Pritchard's (1937) view of the Zande. Put simply, then, '[T]exts do not simply and transparently report on an independent order of reality. Rather, the texts themselves are implicated in the work of reality-construction' (Atkinson, 1990: 7). How the text puts that reality together is something that Atkinson (1990) and van Maanen (1988) have reported on in detail. Indeed Atkinson, as with van Maanen, suggests that scientific ethnographies should more correctly be seen as 'persuasive fictions' (1990: 26). The ethnographer merely uses various rhetorical tricks to persuade us that the descriptions being offered are 'real', 'true', 'accurate', 'telling it like it is'. For example, one such trick Atkinson refers to as 'hypotyposis' (1990: 71) – the use of highly graphic passages of descriptive writing to portray some scene or other in a vivid manner. Here, for example, is an illustrative extract from an anthropological account of the west of Ireland, penned during the 1960s. The ethnographer is talking of his meeting with Joseph – a middle-aged man who had problems with his 'nerves'.

> In 1968 came another breakdown. I was present for the first three days of Joseph's dis-
> tress. At seven o'clock one morning he began forcing himself to vomit. Straining every
> muscle in his diaphragm he sank to his knees by the chair in which he had spent a sleep-
> less night. He pulled an old newspaper from the range side, placed it to catch a few gobs
> of mucus and bile which ran off his chin. The effort forced tears to his eyes. The crisis had
> been precipitated by local opposition to Joseph's intention of selling part of his land to
> strangers. (Brody, 1974: 105)

We can see here how Brody positions himself as a direct, first-hand, observer of Joseph's distress, not only by use of the phrase 'I was present', but also by moving into a 'thick description' of Joseph's behaviour, and of the setting in which he found himself (the range, the chair, the newspaper, the gobs of mucus). The eyewitness status of the account is, of course, designed to under-line the authenticity of Brody's description of life in Inishkillane. He knows of village life intimately, and this intimate, experiential knowledge of Joseph's distress is further linked to something bigger – knowledge concerning the ownership of land in a small community. Indeed, the two issues go hand in hand, and serve as evidence for a broad and general thesis that Brody is attempting to establish. Namely, that far from being an integrated and cohe-sive community, Inishkillane was a community riven by divisions and factions. There were divisions between the enterprising and the traditional members of the community, and between the married and the single and isolated. Joseph, of course, belongs to the latter group. His only friend, apparently, is the ethnographer.

This interpolation of the eyewitness (or what Geertz (1988) refers to as 'I-witness') account is a staple of any ethnographer. For, in manufacturing an ethnographic study the first and foremost task of any author is to establish his or her 'being there' – on the spot – in the native's camp. Various devices can be used to underpin such 'being thereness'. Some involve the positioning of the author – as in the Brody case, above. More usually, they focus on underlying the 'otherness' of the subjects, such as may be achieved, for example, by the use and display of photographs and sketches. (One of the earliest attempts to make systematic use of photographs in ethnographic study was that of Bateson and Mead – see, Sullivan (1999) – though, as we have already noted, photographs appear in much earlier works than theirs.) Indeed, ethnographic accounts of both western and non-western societies are normally peppered with (black and white) photographs to varying effect (see Becker, 1986). But photographs without eyewitness accounts are usually insufficient to convey the sense of first-hand knowledge. This is perhaps why, in many of the North American (sociological) ethnographies, the first-handed nature of accounts is bolstered by the use of documents written by the subjects of study themselves. Thus Thrasher's *The Gang* (1927) – a study of gang life in early twentieth-century Chicago – often makes reference in its footnotes to such things as a 'gang boy's own story', or a manuscript 'prepared by a former gang member' and so forth. Whyte's *Street Corner Society* (1955), on the other hand, uses verbatim conversation of 'Doc' and others as data, and this is these days the most common ploy of the ethnographer. Producing such realist tales, as van Maanen (1988) calls them, requires the ethnographer to call upon his or her subjects as 'informants' rather than mere tellers of tales. Indeed, we have already noted in Chapter 5 how social scientists attempted to get the 'native' to speak directly to an academic audience through the construction of an autobiographical narrative – a narrative that supposedly avoided the confounding and contaminating effects of the ethnographer.

The ethnographic text is, then, a form of literality that enrols various rhetorical devices, all designed so as to persuade readers of the text that they are dealing with scientific, objective or factual accounts of first-hand observers, rather than created images and representations. The anthropologist is thereby positioned as a mirror on society in the same way that the lab scientist is positioned to serve as a mirror on nature. Ethnography is presented, so to speak, as a form of 'factology'. Yet the extent to which the supposedly objective findings of ethnographers can be replicated by other observers has, on occasion, been a subject of some dispute. Thus, in Chapter 1, for example, we made reference to the manner in which Haddon and his colleagues seem to have completely misunderstood the nature of 'adoption' in the Torres Straits. It is a worrying finding for realists and positivists, because it suggests that the in-depth analysis of anthropologists may be at variance with the truth. In this respect, possibly the most instructive debate relates to Freeman's (1983) study of Samoa, though similar concerns have arisen in relation to anthropological work in other regions of the world.

Anthropological texts about the nature of Samoan society had been widely published by Margaret Mead during the 1920s and 1930s (see Mead, 1928). Her focus had been mainly on the processes associated with adolescent development. The broad sweep of her argument was that adolescence in Samoa was relatively free from parent–child conflict and the kinds of sexual repression that she had observed in her own (North American) society. Freeman, however, on the basis of his observations – executed during the 1940s and 1960s – disputed this portrait. In place of it, he substituted a picture of unduly repressive parent–child relationships and of a closely monitored adolescence. It is a conflict of interpretation that is in large part paralleled in anthropological studies of other areas of the world – such as those made in the west of Ireland. In the latter case, the likes of Arensberg (1937) had witnessed friendship, co-operation and mutual respect as key features of Atlantic coast culture. Yet, Brody's (1974) interpretation of the same setting emphasized (as we have seen above) conflict, antagonism and social isolation. Both of these examples, then, throw doubt on the role of the ethnographer as one who can offer a transparent window on the world. And it is interesting to note how such conflicting interpretations can be reconciled in the context of anthropology as a whole. Thus the realist or positivist route to reconciliation emphasizes the time differences involved in the respective fieldwork (suggesting that had the various anthropologists been present in the same society at the same time, then they would have 'seen' the same things), whilst the post-modern turn in anthropology uses alternative interpretations as evidence for constructivist claims. Our interest in this chapter, of course, is not in the relationship between an anthropological account and the external, independent world that it claims to report upon, but in how that anthropological account is assembled in text.

Naturally, in the pre-1980 world – a world in which ethnography was widely regarded as a 'scientific' exercise – it was possible to find reference to a number of 'how to do it' texts and statements (as, for example, in Whyte's (1955) methodological appendix, or that of Radcliffe-Brown, 1958). Such how-to-do-it texts provided rules that could be, and often were, enrolled by later authors to justify the status of new work as rigorous and systematic, and to show how such work belonged to that corpus of scientific observation that was ethnography. At times, the how-to-do-it accounts plunged into detailed confessional tales in which the author related his or her innermost feelings about the field to the reader. Geertz (1988) reviews a number of examples. Such confessional forms (van Maanen, 1988) invariably sought to blur the line between objective accounts and subjective impressions and may well have contributed to the demise of scientific ethnography as a whole. In any event, and for whatever reasons, after the 1980s, fieldworkers tended to turn away from describing how ethnography was done 'in the field', and towards an examination of how it was manufactured on the page – that is, to the study of rhetoric.

To recognize that an anthropological account is dressed in rhetoric does not mean, however, that it is contaminated and ought not to be. Rhetoric is simply unavoidable in an academic or any other form of text. The task is to discover and note the rhetorical devices that are used to produce reports. (Such as the use of distancing styles, the mechanisms that draw an abrupt division between the author of the ethnography and the informant through the use of quotations, the use of photographs and so forth.) Anthropological narratives, of course, are themselves composed out of field notes. Yet there are relatively few accounts as to how field notes and the narrative of an ethnography relate to each other (Atkinson, 1992a; Burgess, 1982; 1984). Certainly, field notes often contain their own narratives, and may well be written with an eye as to how they will ultimately relate to the final (published) text (Atkinson, 1992b). In most cases, however, such narratives will be routinely fractured, fragmented and decontextualized in accordance with the methodological precepts of fieldwork manuals. These days such fragmentation is fashioned as much by machines as by humans – for example, through the use of such data processing programs as NUD•IST or NVivo (see Richards, 1999), programs that tend to be built around the all-encompassing rhetoric of 'grounded theory' (Glaser and Strauss, 1967). Grounded theory, of course, supposedly allows theoretical insight to emerge out of the data themselves, the researcher merely rearranging and making explicit that which is implicit in the data. Yet, the fracturing of observational or conversational data into 'nodal' points – based on themes and concepts selected by the researcher – and the rearrangement of data via the use of 'memos' and research reports fundamentally alter the data that have been assiduously collected. In that respect, the social scientific researcher invariably and inevitably imposes a new order on the world as reported by his or her informants (for some examples see Charmaz, 2000). As Goody (1977) suggests, the act of writing is never a neutral process.

Conclusions

In their *Official Discourse* Burton and Carlen (1979) focused on the discourse contained in official (UK) government reports on various law and order problems – many relating to street disturbances in Northern Ireland during the late 1960s and early 1970s. They were interested, for example, in how such things as 'common sense', 'natural reason' and the like were recruited by the writers of such reports so as to explain and account for the events under scrutiny. Yet, Burton and Carlen's analysis very naturally operates within another form of discourse (no writer can escape the iron cage). In this instance it was a social scientific discourse of a special kind. In particular the authors composed their book in a conceptual grid drawn from the work of the French structuralists and especially those of a Marxist bent. And from this distance it is interesting to ask why they felt it necessary to recruit, so fervently, the likes of Althusser and Lacan (see Dosse, 1997a and 1997b) into their work. One reason must have been that French structuralists formed a powerful intellectual group in the Europe of the 1960s and 1970s. A serious intellectual work in the social sciences had therefore to recognize and acknowledge that power, and to engage with the debates of its members. One wrote sociology by referring to the convoluted language of the Parisians in the same way that, during the late 1950s and 1960s, one wrote sociology by engaging with the convoluted language of Talcott Parsons. But who now reads Parsons? (Parsons had once posed the question, 'who now reads Spencer?' – given that Spencer had been one of the most influential and powerful of figures in nineteenth-century biology, geology and sociology.)

The recruitment and abandonment of authors and networks of authors forms an interesting field for investigation in itself. How authors circulate and are picked up and set aside can tell us much about the natural history of a discourse. An investigation of citation networks (Baldi, 1998) in scientific papers, for example, could well tell us about the various 'core-groups' (Collins and Pinch, 1993) that are actively engaged in a scientific controversy. Such a task lies well beyond the aims of the present chapter, however. For here I have elected to concentrate on what is in the text rather than on how the text is recruited by networks of authors. In particular, we have looked at the ways in which authors structure specific forms of literality, and how they locate themselves within such forms. More specifically, it has been suggested that the following questions constitute useful entrées into the analysis of the resources that social scientists use in the research process.

How is the author-function played out in the document? Exactly who authorized the document, and how were they positioned in the production process? How are authors made visible or invisible? Are we dealing with the work of absent and unmentioned actors – such as coding clerks, an 'office', or hidden Europeans? Or are we dealing with one of d'Hémery's identifiable 'auteurs'? Is the work offered to us as the product of a team or of a committee – as is the case with DSM-IV (see DSM-IV 'Acknowledgements') – or as the work of a lone scholar?

How does the rhetor position him- or herself in the creative process and to what desired effect? As a first-hand observer (an 'I-witness')? An impartial observer? A collector of tales? Or as a mere conduit (a 'mirror') for the transmission of scientific data and information? Indeed, at what points does the rhetor turn him- or herself from observer into participant, and at what points does he or she appear as an absent and invisible cipher? For it is clear that ethnographers in particular have often sought to present themselves in text in a dual role – as an intimate of 'others' and, at the very same time, as distanced and objective observers of exotic life. (Social scientific interviewers usually position themselves similarly.)

What resources were exploited in the process of production? In particular, what papers and books were recruited by the author(s) to underpin their rhetoric? What kind of network does the citation and recruitment process inscribe? These, of course, are questions that relate to issues of intertextuality – see Chapter 6, note 7.

How do the documents structure their readers? That is to say, what specific audience is structured by the title of the document, its place and manner of publication? Thus Cherry-Garrard, with whom we opened this chapter, structured his narrative to appeal to a 'general' audience and eschewed an appeal to the scientific community of his day. The very title of his work, *The Worst Journey in the World*, was markedly different from that which might have been expected to symbolize a scientific report. In exactly the same way, a paper entitled, say, 'The arthropods Mimetaster and Vachonisia from the Devonian Hunsrück Shale', in *Paläontologische Zeitschrift* 1978 (cited in Gould, 1989), structures its readers in a radically different mode from a book or paper entitled 'Looking for fossils'. (We can only wonder about what Malinowski intended by entitling one of his books *The sexual life of savages*.)

Finally, one needs to ask how, through the use of textual devices, the document structures the world. In this respect, we should also be aware that it is not simply ethnographers who have shaped the worlds that they claim to have experienced in objective and distanced measure, but also interviewers in general. The analysis of interview data as manufactured text, however, lays well beyond the remit of this chapter. With that in mind I shall draw attention to one further limitation of our analysis so far – namely, that we have focused almost entirely on literary stratagems, and somewhat ignored the role of diagrams and illustrations. Yet, we know that scientific and other texts often use illustrations and other images (see Bastide, 1990; Lynch, 1985; 1990) to convey a notion of frozen factuality about the objects being discussed. Just how they achieve that goal is a subject worthy of enquiry in itself – as we have seen in Chapter 4.

RESEARCH EXERCISES

Exercise 7.1

In the light of the discussion above, examine ways in which the social scientific interview has been represented in some key methods texts since the 1960s. Pay particular attention to the manner in which the interviewer is 'positioned' vis-à-vis the interviewee. A useful starting point for such an exercise might be Fontana and Frey (2000).

Exercise 7.2

More specifically, and using the work of feminist writers and writers on feminist methodology, examine how the interviewer has been repositioned with respect to the interviewee. Some useful starting points may be found in DeVault (1987; 1990), Oakley (1981) and Reinharz (1992).

Notes

1   The notion of genre is itself worthy of investigation, see Dubrow (1982).
2   An interesting philosophical position on the manufacture of facts and things – especially in relation to 'science' – is provided by Heidegger (1967), in what must be one of his more readable works.
3   For the likes of Derrida (1976; 1988), of course, this position is untenable since a text references only itself and, by the nature of language, can have no referents to some objective ('real') world beyond the text.
4   On the function of the footnote in scientific discourse, see Grafton (1997).
5   We must not overlook the possibility that the ethnographer's informants have also to construct his or her community and culture in order to represent them. So the act of construction becomes a multi-voiced process – see, for example, Rabinow (1977). The role of informants in the construction process has, however, been little researched.

8

Documents as Evidence.
Researching the Inert Text

Conjectures and refutations[1]

A belief in the existence of a single, common source of civilization has been a persistent one in human history. It is held even today, at the commencement of the twenty-first century, where it often takes on fantastical forms – sometimes involving references to the existence of lost civilizations such as that of Atlantis. Atlantis appears in ancient Greek myth as a vast and important land situated somewhere 'beyond the Pillars of Heracles'. Its people and rulers were defeated by the Athenians. The land was drowned by an act of the gods. In modern mythology it is often taken to symbolize a sophisticated and mysterious civilization that served as a key source of human knowledge – knowledge about the domestication of cattle and the cultivation of seed, the smelting of metals, the skills of navigation and astronomy, and much else beside. Among the 'much else' we might include building techniques, techniques and effects that often appear to be similar in different parts of the ancient world, such as is the case, for example, with the construction of pyramids.

Pyramids can be found in ancient world sites of Asia, Africa and the Americas. On the basis that building structures are similar in different regions of the ancient world, a number of amateur historians and archaeologists have sometimes erected entire theories. Thus, Graham Hancock for example, in his *Heaven's Mirror: Quest for the Lost Civilisation* (1999), has argued that human knowledge about building technique and the heavens was passed down from the members of a once-mighty civilization that had reached its zenith around

10,500 years before the Christian era (BCE). At one point he surmised that the single, central civilization was buried under the Antarctic ice, and so he does not actually refer to Atlantis per se. However, he does claim that the members of the lost civilization were great astronomers. They held detailed knowledge of the stars and the constellations, and they left a legacy of information that was later spread throughout the ancient world. We can see evidence of their handy work even today. For example, the Great Pyramids at Giza are exactly aligned so as to mimic the position of the stars in Orion's belt, whilst the temples of Angkor Wat, in Cambodia, trace out on the ground the pattern that the constellation of Draco forms in the northern sky (or, more precisely, as Draco would have appeared to a human eye 10,500 years BCE). The strange city of Tiwanaku near Lake Titicaca in Bolivia has similar (though, as yet, unfathomed) astronomical properties. The evidence is present for all to see. Unfortunately, according to Hancock, academic archaeologists are blinded by prejudice and outdated theory, and unable to recognize the larger patterns that these observations point towards.[2]

The Great Pyramids at Giza (there are three particularly close together) are indeed arranged in a rough line, where a smaller pyramid is offset from the other two by some 40 degrees. In that respect they do appear to mimic the three stars that lie in Orion's belt (one star offset from the other two by about 50 degrees to the north). What is more, we know that the fourth-dynasty Egyptians, who built the pyramids, were particularly interested in the cosmos and oriented their tombs to reflect some of its features – especially the cardinal points of the compass. They certainly knew where the direction of north was, and they would have been well able to mimic the stars in Orion's belt exactly – had they so wished. It is something of a puzzle, therefore, as to why the smaller of the Giza pyramids is offset to the south and not to the north. In other words, the layout on the ground, and the stars in Orion's belt, only match exactly if we turn Egypt upside down, or if we turn the sky upside down and leave Egypt as it is – whichever is the easier.

So our first piece of evidence only fits with the theory if we ignore the cardinal points. Unsurprisingly, it is not an issue that is addressed in Hancock's book. But let us proceed further. We know that there are at least 16 stars in Orion and some 80 pyramids in Egypt. Yet it is only a (very bad) fit of three stars and three pyramids that are selected for inclusion in the evidential base. And the same problem arises with Angkor Wat and Draco. Again the constellation of Draco is simply not matched by the temple pattern, and Hancock uses only 10 out of more than 60 temples to support his case. More importantly, perhaps, from our understanding of Khmer society we remain unaware that Draco (the dragon) had any place in Khmer culture whatsoever. For neither dragons nor the constellation seem to have figured in Khmer religious or political life. So, in the language of social science, the evidence just does not 'triangulate' (Denzin, 1978).

So here we have a book that is classified by the publisher as 'non-fiction'. The author presents his case in an academic, authoritative rhetoric. He cites the work of archaeological experts and authorities. He talks of conjecture, evidence and proof. To all appearances we have a thesis, and reference to substantiating evidence. In that respect the book conforms, superficially at least, to a traditional (positivist) scientific model. Yet the bits of evidence that we have so far examined have already thrown up a number of problems. The evidence is highly selective. We are not provided with good reasons why confirming instances (of matches between stars and buildings) are chosen whilst others are ignored. Furthermore, we would expect the evidence to be consistent over many sources. For example, if the constellation of Draco were so central to Khmer builders then we would expect to find references to its significance in various symbols systems and drawings from the relevant period – but we do not.

What is worrying about Hancock's claims, then, is that they seem to be supported by the flimsiest kinds of evidence. And that raises issues about what 'good', reliable evidence might look like. Unfortunately, that is not an easy question to answer. One of the reasons for difficulty lies in the fact that – as we know from sociological studies of scientific controversy – what counts as good, reliable and well-validated evidence is always open to social negotiation. Thus, in their analysis of specific controversies (such as the cold fusion debate, for example) Collins and Pinch (1993) point out how what counts as evidence to one party of scientists often serves as no more than mere conjecture to another.

Our interest in debates about evidence, of course, relates only to the use of documents as sources of evidence. The topic is an important one because, as I have indicated previously, in matters of social research, documents usually appear only in so far as they serve as receptacles of evidence for some claim or other. Indeed, as I have been keen to emphasize throughout the book, social researchers are far more interested in asking questions about what documents contain than with what people do with documents and how they manipulate them in organizational contexts. Consequently, as researchers of the inert text it would undoubtedly be of considerable help to us if we could appeal to a set of generally accepted rules about evidence to demonstrate that our scrutiny of document content was done 'in the right way' and to the highest standards – rules that would help establish that our ultimate claims are valid and reliable. Unfortunately, no such body of rules exists. That is not to say that there are no rules (see, for example, Platt, 1981a; 1981b; Seale, 1999), only that their status is always contested.

In what follows I am going to make reference to a rhetoric that relates to evidence. It is a rhetoric that concentrates on distinguishing 'good' from 'bad' evidence and it is one that is widely called upon in contemporary medical research. In many respects it is a rhetoric that fits rather badly with the demands of qualitative research. Nevertheless its key concerns serve to highlight some issues that are central to persuading readers that one's research results are robust, reliable and valid – good enough, in fact, to stake one's health and well-being on them.

Evidence, evidence, evidence

Social scientific debates concerning the use of suitable evidential foundations for the acceptance of theories and hypotheses are at least as old as the sciences themselves. John Stuart Mill's (1843) attempt to 'systematize' the rules of scientific evidence and scientific method is among the earliest of such strategies – and it still has an impact (see Lieberson, 1992). Mill, of course, wrote in the shadow of the Enlightenment, an age where trust and faith in reason and truth (especially as exemplified in a codified scientific method) was commonplace. It seems a long way from Mill's *System of logic* to a late modern age where as far as methodology and much else are concerned, 'anything goes', and where science is regarded as 'much closer to myth than scientific philosophy is prepared to admit' (Feyerabend, 1975: 295). Indeed, we might characterize our own world as a world in which all claims are regarded as provisional and tentative, and even equivalent; story writing every bit as good as traditional ethnography (Denzin, 1988).

Now, one of the most powerful and persuasive rhetorics of science ever developed emerged out of what is often referred to as the 'positivist' movement. What positivism is, how it is expressed and how it came to dominate western scientific discourse is a complex field of study in its own right (Giddens, 1978; Gillies, 1993). At this point we need focus on only a few of its central tenets – in particular those that concern the application of what is sometimes called the hypothetico-deductive method of scientific discovery. The latter was developed in large part by post-positivist philosophers such as Karl Popper (1959; 1963) and Ernest Nagel (1961) during the first half of the twentieth century. The method has many intricate features, but included among them are the suggestions that science proceeds not on the basis of making lots of unconnected observations, but rather on the basis of advancing theoretically informed hypotheses – hypotheses that, ideally, incorporate law-like statements. That is, statements of the type advanced by, say, Sir Isaac Newton to the effect that 'force' equals 'mass' multiplied by 'acceleration' ($F = Ma$). Or the even more famous Einstein equation that energy equals mass multiplied by a constant squared ($e = mc^2$), where the constant c is the speed of light. In the rhetoric of positivism, however, such laws and hypotheses are always provisional. In other words, we should hold to them only as long as there is evidence to support them, and all and any evidence should be collected and analysed in an objective and dispassionate manner. ('Experimentation' is, of course, the preferred strategy for collecting evidence.) Disconfirming instances of evidence should carry special weight. In other words, evidence that does not fit a hypothesis should carry more weight than any number of pieces of evidence that do. Unfortunately, we know from empirical studies of what scientists actually do that there is invariably a divergence between the theory as outlined above and what happens in practice – see, again, Collins and Pinch (1993).[3]

During the 1950s–1970s there were many who argued that the hypothetico-deductive method of enquiry should be applied every bit as much to social scientific research as to research in the natural sciences (see Brodbeck, 1968). It was not, however, an argument that persisted quite so strongly beyond the 1970s. Yet social scientists have been and are always concerned with rules of good practice and with amassing reliable and valid data sources. In fact, social scientists often make use of the twin concepts of reliability and validity to distinguish between good and bad forms of evidence. The concept of 'reliability' in social research refers to the requirement that the 'findings' of any research programme are independent of the particular circumstances in which the research was carried out. In other words, any researcher in similar circumstances and adopting the same research strategy should get more or less the same results as the original researcher. The concept of validity relates to the issue as to whether the research findings are actually providing appropriate and valid evidence for the claims being made by the researcher. With respect to the Graham Hancock example above, of course, the suggestion is being made that his findings are neither reliable nor valid.

Naturally, most commentators on research practice usually fragment the demands that results should be reliable and valid into a series of issues about data collection and analysis. And so it is with people who comment on research with documents. Thus, Burgess (1984), for example, insists that matters of authenticity (of the documents) and distortion should be taken into account. Platt (1981a) states that the researcher should pay attention to issues of authenticity, the availability of documents, sampling of the documents and what inferences can be made from the documentation that is studied. Scott (1990) lists authenticity, credibility, representativeness and meaning as matters to be attended by the researcher. Such lists of criteria are commonplace and Seale (1999) provides an excellent overview of the various criteria that have been applied in judgements about the virtues of qualitative research in general.

Rather than review lists of criteria, however, it will be much more useful for us to refer to an existing template of what is regarded in a scientific community as good practice. The template that I am about to refer to is commonly drawn upon in the framework of what is called evidence-based medicine (Sackett, 2000). The latter is part of a strategy that was adopted in western medical practice during the closing decades of the twentieth century. Its aim is to determine what is and what is not 'effective' – in the way of drugs, therapies and medical interventions of all kinds. Crucially, from our point of view, it achieves results through the review and analysis of document content.[4] Though the documents reviewed are invariably restricted to those that contain specific kinds of research findings. Nevertheless, it is argued that by examining document content in terms of a strictly defined set of procedures, researchers can produce robust and reliable conclusions about the effectiveness of professional practice. The procedures add up to what is sometimes called systematic review methodology. It is a methodology that may be looked upon as a form of modern medical technology, a form of technology that recruits into its frame information processing techniques, statistics, mathematics and social science.

In what follows I am going to deal with what are often regarded as three central issues of systematic review procedures. They concern (1) the selection of evidence, (2) the scope and robustness of data, and (3) data extraction. As we shall see, it is simply not possible to lift the systematic review template off the shelf and apply it to qualitative work without important modifications – even if we limit ourselves to just three areas of interest. Nevertheless, the general stance of the review techniques has a virtue that extends far beyond the realm of medicine.

The selection of evidence

In terms of the rhetoric of good research practice, one of the problems with the Hancock example, provided above, is that the stars and buildings that he matched together were selected on a highly idiosyncratic basis. That is to say, not all stars and not all buildings were selected for the analysis. Sampling of populations – whether of people, things or events – is, of course, a legitimate procedure. But as we have stated above, where it does occur, then the selection process needs to be justified. Ideally, and according to systematic review techniques, the reasons for including and excluding cases ought to be defined in advance of any study. It is simply not good enough to select cases that fit an hypothesis, and to ignore those that do not. In quantitative research the central requirements for the selection of items from any population are usually twofold. First, once the criteria for including or excluding documents in a study are set, the subsequent selection of documents should result in a representative sample of the sum total. Second, the selection should be unbiased or random. In qualitative research, of course, the selection of 'cases' can be justified on numerous grounds, and it is not always possible to define in advance what is to be studied (see, for example, Charmaz, 2000).

Representativeness and randomness usually go hand in hand in quantitative research practice. Even in qualitative research – with or without documents – randomness can have its virtues. Thus a study of letters, wills, contracts, certificates or whatever that is based on a random selection from a wider population of such documents will be regarded as producing more reliable conclusions than a study that is 'biased' and restricted only to those that fit the arguments being advanced. Random selection may also have other benefits. For example, in the absence of random principles, the temptation to focus on the strange, the exotic and the unusual at the cost of the uneventful and boringly normal might be difficult to resist. Perhaps that is why Malinowski (1922) always took care to warn his followers to aim for complete coverage of the phenomena under study and not to focus on the abnormal and exotic. I found this to be a valuable principle in my own work on death certification (Prior, 1989). It was work in which I found complicated sequences of cause of death far more interesting than straightforward sequences. Without adopting the principle of random selection (I opted for a simple random sample of 10 per cent of all cases in a twelve-month period), I might easily have weighted the sample unfairly towards the inclusion of 'difficult' and atypical medical narratives of death.

An essential first step to random case selection, then, must involve identification of all of the members of a given population. This, in turn, should lead to the construction of a sampling frame (de Vaus, 1996). When we are dealing with people we can normally call upon lists or registers – such as a list of death certificates – from which to sample. No register ever made is without its problems, but most of the widely used types of register (such as electoral rolls, school registers and so forth) have a good coverage of their populations. Such frames are easy to identify and sometimes easy to get hold of. With documents, however, life is rather more difficult. For example, there are many e-mail letter writers in the world, but we have no rational way of finding out who they are or what they are writing about. Nor do we know how what is saved in the way of documentation differs from what is lost. Hence, without a reasonably complete list of e-mail letter writers or letters written, any study of letter writing would risk the possibility of focusing on only a small and highly unusual selection of cases.

In their fascinating work on 'correspondence' Chartier et al. (1997) provide some interesting insights into the above problem. In the course of their various research programmes into styles of letter writing from the Middle Ages to the nineteenth century, for example, they focused on 'secrétaires' or manuals devoted to instructing their readers as to how a letter ought to be written. One of the great virtues of the 'secrétaires' is that they were published, and we know that published documents are always listed (somewhere). Furthermore published documents have a considerable chance of survival across the centuries. So by focusing on the manuals rather than individual letters, it is possible (if not desirable) to obtain a complete listing of relevant items. It might also be the case that by focusing on the letter templates, rather than letters first hand, the researchers could be reasonably certain that a complete range of letter styles were available for study. In the nineteenth-century case it was possible to check the influence of the 'secrétaires' on actual letters written by studying a pragmatic sample of over 600 letters written between 1830 and 1865 and lodged in the Paris Postal Museum. In addition, Chartier et al., also encountered data from a French postal survey of 1847 that listed almost every letter posted in France from almost every postal box during the month of November of that year. The latter were used to provide a picture of communication in France during the mid nineteenth century. (Note how, in this example, the

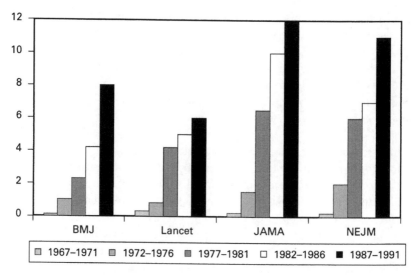

FIGURE 8.1   *The growth of risk as a focus for medicine: percentage of articles with 'risk' in title or abstract (after Skolbekken, 1995)*

circulation of letters (documents) serves to map out the skeletal nature of a social network.)

In a similar manner, of course, one could use travel manuals, recipe books and other types of document as templates for other everyday activities, though whether people travelled or cooked in accordance with the manuals is forever a matter of empirical enquiry. Social scientists who focus on aspects of contemporary life can, of course, always ask their subjects to produce documents anew. This is often the case when people are asked to produce diaries and other accounts specifically for the research process. It is a well-established strategy, and Plummer (2001) lists numerous examples of it.

Another possibility is for the social scientists to request documentation that people might ordinarily produce or use in their everyday lives. Such 'naturally occurring' forms of documentation were called upon in one of the most famous of all twentieth-century American sociological studies – *The Polish Peasant in Europe and America*. In that study, the authors, Thomas and Zaniecki (1958), obtained their letters (754 in total) by advertising for them in a Polish émigré journal. They offered letter holders 10 to 20 cents for each letter. Unfortunately, the sociologists were not entirely clear about the process of acquisition. Their acquisition strategy became known only many years after the publication of the original study (Madge, 1963). And although the collection contained letters from almost every strata of Polish society, it could by no means be regarded as a systematic sample of available letters. That is to say, it was not random.

Information technology can of course assist in document sample strategies – though the sheer weight of results can often overwhelm the novice researcher. Thus, by using computerized search devices it is not too difficult to come up with a volume of results for documents that are listed on some database or other. Thus, a search for, say, a full list of scientific papers on 'suicide' can easily be obtained from a database such as *Medline*[5] or *Sociological Abstracts*[6]. The difficulty, of course, is not so much to get results but to limit the results to a manageable size. Figure 8.1 (adapted from Skolbekken, 1995) illustrates the potential use of such searches. In this case the searcher was seeking evidence for the claim that, as far as medical publications were concerned, an interest in 'risk' grew substantially and significantly during the last quarter of the twentieth century – that, in fact, there had been a risk epidemic in the realm of journal publications. (The four medical journals included in the figure are *The British Medical Journal* (BMJ), *The Lancet*, the *Journal of the American Medical Association* (JAMA) and the *New England Journal of Medicine* (NEJM).) As is evident from the chart, a simple search of appropriate databases using 'risk' as the only key word produces a quite stunning and persuasive result on the general thesis.

Unfortunately, and as we shall note shortly, not all research results find their way into mainstream journals. Some research documents can be particularly difficult to trace and to list. For example, certain kinds of hard-to-trace items are sometimes referred to as the 'grey literature'. Fortunately, there is a database (known as SIGLE)[7] for such literature, and it often throws up otherwise neglected items of documentation. But why some literature is 'grey' and remains 'grey' is an interesting issue in itself.

As I have already suggested, calls for random and representative samples of data are to be heard mainly from the mouths of survey and quantitative researchers. With qualitative research, however, it is often the case that there are sound reasons for side-stepping such requirements. For example, there might be good reasons for selecting only certain kinds of document or certain kinds of event where documents come into play. Thus, in his study of laboratory life, Lynch (1985) focused specifically on 'agreement' and instances of interaction where agreements and disagreements arose – some of which involved disagreements about the use of documents. Platt (1996; 1981a; 1981b) has argued that, in the history of both psychology and sociology, the (highly selective) 'case study' method has played a major role in social research. As far as research with documents is concerned, the bulk of case studies involved the use of life histories (see Chapter 5), though case studies have also been used to study organizations and events as well as people. (A good modern example of a case study is provided by Vaughan, 1996). Naturally, case studies by their very nature cannot be representative. However, they can be indispensable for developing theoretical insight, and for examining the fine detail of social life. (For a justification of the method, see Yin 1994.)

We should also recall that in qualitative work the use of sampling to refine ideas rather than to satisfy the demands of calculation is a well-established principle. Thus, qualitative researchers often develop sample strategies that are deliberately aimed at gathering cases that are not in any sense representative of the general population. Instead the sampling is devised so as to gain a particular insight into social processes (see, for example, Charmaz, 2000). Thus, in work with documentation, the use of such principles as purposive, pragmatic sampling and 'theoretical' sampling could easily be justified. The notion of theoretical sampling was, of course, popularized by Glaser and Strauss (1967: 45) in their discussions of grounded theory. According to their principles researchers should select cases for study on an individual basis – seeking at all times to expand the scope of their data and variations in the social practices being studied. Furthermore, a researcher ought always to be on the look-out for cases that disconfirm any current hypotheses. Indeed Glaser and Strauss argue that sampling ought to proceed up to that point where no new data – and no disconfirming instances – seem to be emerging. It is a stage that they refer to as 'theoretical saturation' (1967: 61). The practical application of the methodology was best illustrated in studies relating to dying trajectories – see, for example, Glaser and Strauss (1965).

What matters above all, of course, is that the researcher should specify in detail why it is that the cases selected for study have been so selected, and what the limits of the selection process might be (see Seale, 1999). With the Hancock example that opened this chapter, it is not at all clear why disconfirming instances of the general hypothesis (about stars and building layout) were ignored and one is left wondering whether it was merely because the data failed to fit the author's generalizations.

The scope and robustness of data

The technology of the systematic review depends, in part, upon the classification of evidence into a hierarchy of reliability and 'strength' (see, for example, http://www.york.ac.uk/inst/crd/report4.htm). At the top of the hierarchy are research studies that concern experimental designs, in particular, designs in which the allocation of cases to experimental and control groups has been randomized. Such studies are often known as randomized controlled trials (RCTs). The growth, development and influence of RCTs in medical practice is a worthy topic of investigation in itself, though one that falls far outside the remit of this book (see, for example, Matthews, 1995).

Following the RCT in the contemporary hierarchy of evidence are other trials where random allocation of individuals to experimental and control groups has not been possible for some (good) reason. After that come what are called cohort studies. These commonly rest on the analysis of existing groups in society (say, age and gender groups) that can be compared in some systematic manner one to the other. The aim is to determine what kinds of factors in two or more groups might lead to differences in outcome with respect to a health intervention. For example, one might compare rates of lung cancer among groups of people who smoke cigarettes and those who do not. At the bottom of the knowledge hierarchy come 'opinions of respected authorities', descriptive studies and reports of expert committees. Qualitative research would probably be slotted in at this point – were it to figure at all.

So, in terms of qualitative research, the hierarchy of evidence outlined above has little relevance. I have drawn attention to it, however, so as to emphasize the fact that judgements about the reliability and robustness of evidence are socially (in this case professionally) based. Nevertheless, and irrespective as to whether one is engaged in quantitative or qualitative research, such judgements have always to be attended to.

In the realm of documents, and with respect to reliability, it is clear, for example, that evidence can often be forged. In Chapter 1, I mentioned the issue of forgery with reference to *Ann Frank's Diary* and *The Diary of a Nobody*.[8] Scott (1990), in his analysis of research with records, pays considerable attention to the issue of forgery in available documentation. Forgery and fakery can, of course, be a problem in all fields of human endeavour. And in some contexts it could be just as interesting to study forged as to study genuine documents. 'Scientific' forgery or forgery of scientific findings is especially instructive as it highlights the nature of problems relating to evidence.[9] A more pressing problem in qualitative research, however, is more likely to arise from the fact that what is studied is carefully selected, rather than forged or faked. And biased selection might not be intentional – as it seems to have been with Hancock's selection of stars and pyramids. To illustrate how this might be so we need to examine Figure 8.2.

Figure 8.2 is called a funnel plot. In this particular case it is derived from a study of 'risk communication' in the context of patients and medical practitioners (Edwards et al., 2000). Medical practitioners often have to communicate information about, say, the attendant risks and benefits of different kinds of treatment. For example, hormone replacement therapy that is provided to older women has benefits for such women as far as the onset of certain types of arthritis are concerned, but also carries a measure of risk as far as other matters are concerned (as with, say, risk of thrombosis). But how can such information be best communicated? For example, when practitioners communicate information about risk it is not always clear whether they should use only words (such as high, moderate and low risk) or whether they should use numbers (percentages), whether they should use diagrams or whether they use only language and so forth. The Edwards et al., study was concerned to review the literature on such matters and to see what conclusions might be reached with respect to advice on risk communication.

As was hinted at earlier, systematic reviews normally concentrate on the 'effect sizes' of various interventions. For example, we might want to know whether a discussion between a doctor and a patient that involved the use of diagrams was rated as more effective than one that used just words and numbers.

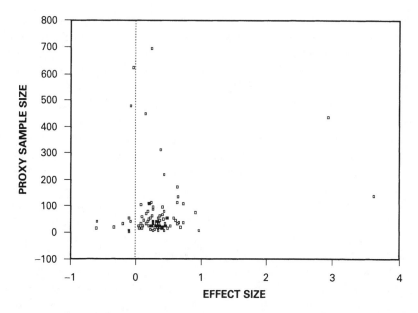

FIGURE 8.2   *Funnel plot demonstrating the presence of 'invisible' knowledge: plot of effect sizes in literature dealing with risk communication (Edwards et al., 2000)*

Studies that test and report on such effect sizes are normally published in academic journals and it is these papers that are usually collected together in a review.

When effects, such as the above, are studied, they are usually studied for a population of people. And the key figure that is gathered from such studies is the average or mean difference in response between those people who experienced one kind of intervention (say, they were given drug, or intervention, 'A') from another (who were, perhaps, given drug, or intervention, 'B'). Maybe the people given intervention 'A' recovered earlier, or lived longer and so forth. A focus on the average or mean time for recovery or the average number of years lived after intervention should show up differences in effect. In the risk communication study the 'effects' were often reports of improved understanding or improved compliance with medical advice.

A funnel plot extracts the information about such 'effects' – from all known studies – and plots them on a graph in the shape of an inverted funnel. In Figure 8.2 these effect sizes have been rescaled so that most of the data points fall between +1 and −1 on the horizontal scale. We have no need to delve into the manner of the rescaling here. What is important to note is that most of the data points lay on the positive side of zero, while hardly any data points lay on the negative side of an imaginary vertical line running through zero. In short, part of the funnel is missing. It is an interesting shape. And what it suggests is that 'negative' findings are absent from the published literature.

Could that be because researchers only find positive things? Well, perhaps that is so, but it is unlikely. In fact we know from the manner in which things are generally distributed in the world that the funnel plot should look symmetrical. In other words, in the case of Figure 8.2, there should be far more negative data points than are available in the graph. Or to put it another way, the left hand side of the graph should be fuller than it is. Indeed, it seems likely that what has happened here is that negative and inconclusive research results have not appeared in published outlets, whilst positive results have.

The reasons as to why some research results are published whilst others are not raises important questions about pathways to publication and the manipulation of knowledge in general. The factors structuring such pathways remain open to speculation, but one set of influences that affects publication is that papers that report on effects that are relatively unequivocal and likely to 'make a difference' are generally favoured over findings that are ambiguous or contradict prevailing assumptions. The funnel plot provides an image of this tendency in action.

With qualitative research of course the luxury of numbers is not available, but the significance of the negative remains important. So it is often argued that qualitative researchers should always pay special attention to cases that seemingly fail to fit the pattern that has been observed by the researcher (Seale, 1999; Silverman, 1993). This emphasis on the disconfirming case is sometimes known as 'deviant case analysis' and it has a special function in qualitative research. I shall return to deviant case analysis shortly. Before I do that, I need to turn to broader matters of indexing and coding data.

Data extraction: indexing and coding

Systematic review procedure requires the use of data extraction protocols or forms. In the case of a systematic review the form would require that details be collected of where a study is published, authors, sample sizes, 'effect sizes', conclusions and so forth. Naturally in qualitative work one is unlikely to have access to or to be interested in details of quantitative data sources. Nevertheless, the notion of having a standardized form that is applied to all 'cases' is a useful one, otherwise there might be a tendency to select only data that fit a preconceived notion or theory and to ignore the negative cases. (For an example of a standardized data extraction form see Yin, 1994.)

Extracting data by means of a standardized procedure has its uses. However, it is often easier said than done. Thus we know, for example, that different individuals can often see different things in the same data set and read different messages from one and the same document. In terms of extraction procedure, therefore, systematic review procedure requires that it should be performed independently by at least two people. In such cases, disagreements between data coders are bound to arise and procedures need to be established for dealing with the problem. When it comes to the coding of qualitative data other kinds of issues can also emerge (see Ryan and Bernard, 2000). In order to illustrate such problems I am going to refer to some interview data that were collected on a research project concerned with traumatic brain injury (TBI).

TBI can arise as a result of vehicle accidents or accidents in the home or violent assault. When it occurs the individuals affected usually experience impairment of cognitive and physical functions. Memory, speech, bodily movements and social functioning can all be severely affected. Medical professionals assess the outcome of TBI according to many dimensions. How injured people assess such outcomes, however, is not at all clear. In what follows I am going to refer to some work that I undertook with some colleagues on how injured people assessed the impact of their injuries on their daily life.

The research team initially decided to gather the data by asking injured people about (1) how they acquired their injuries and (2) how such injuries had affected them in the intervening years between the traumatic event and the interview. Interviews were translated into written transcripts. It was the transcripts (as documents) that were subsequently analysed.

In a case such as this it is difficult in advance to design a template for data extraction. This is partly because the injured as individuals talk about different events and different experiences. At the same time it is easy to see how someone seeking to code interview data might be seen to have a free hand about deciding what was most and least important in the transcripts. So how might we avoid falling into such a trap? One method of overcoming this problem is to use a concordance program to index each interview. A concordance program – as was stated in Chapter 6 – provides a complete list of words used in an interview together with a count of the number of times that a word is used. It also provides a context for word use – that is, a sentence or phrase in which a given word use is embedded.

In the case of interviews it is inevitable that some words will be those used by an interviewer and some by a subject. So the first task of the researcher is to exclude interviewer talk from the results. What remains is then the vocabulary of the interviewee. At this early stage, of course, one must always keep uppermost in mind that words taken out of context can provide a severely misleading picture of what the talk is about. Nevertheless, there is no doubt that the words that people use – in letters, written confessions, interviews or whatever – relate directly to the issues that concern them. In semi-structured interviews that are being used as an example here, it will become clear that interview subjects talk about what is relevant to them in words of their own choosing. Indexing that talk provides an essential first-base image of what is and what is not considered relevant in the framework of the interview.

Table 8.1 contains data from 12 interviewees, all of whom had experienced head injury as a result of a road traffic accident or a violent attack on them by others. The 12 interviews being used here were merely the first of 60. The table indexes a selected series of words that were used in the interview together

TABLE 8.1 Occurrence of key words in 12 interview transcripts

Words	Case 1	Case 2	Case 3	Case 4	Case 5	Case 6	Case 7	Case 8	Case 9	Case 10	Case 11	Case 12
accident	14	3	6	7	0	3	4	4	0	15	2	2
aggression	0	1	0	0	0	0	0	0	1	0	3	6
anxiety	2	0	0	0	0	0	0	0	0	1	0	0
before	11	12	6	6	0	6	18	3	15	0	3	16
change	9	4	2	0	1	4	3	2	9	0	0	6
concentrate	5	1	2	1	0	6	2	7	1	7	2	4
confidence	0	0	0	0	0	0	7	1	1	1	0	0
depressed	2	1	0	0	0	6	2	1	8	4	2	0
different	3	2	2	3	1	2	7	0	8	5	3	3
disable	0	0	1	4	1	0	0	6	0	0	0	0
forget	7	9	1	3	1	2	0	0	1	2	2	2
friend	1	7	1	1	1	2	10	0	0	2	3	10
girl/boys	0	2	1	4	2	3	0	8	7	0	3	1
head	1	14	4	12	2	17	7	8	0	5	5	7
headache	0	1	0	0	0	5	1	2	0	2	0	3
injury	1	4	0	2	0	7	5	4	18	1	7	13
loss	2	1	1	2	1	2	4	1	4	4	0	3
lucky	3	1	3	2	0	1	0	1	1	0	0	2
memory	13	19	11	18	1	11	7	1	10	10	0	9
moods	0	0	0	1	0	1	0	0	0	0	0	1
personality	0	0	0	0	0	0	0	2	0	2	0	2
physical	0	1	2	0	1	1	4	5	1	1	1	4
since	7	4	0	2	0	0	1	1	11	3	0	3
sleep	14	4	0	1	1	4	0	0	0	9	2	11
speech	4	11	1	1	0	3	1	7	4	0	2	0
talk	9	5	2	5	1	14	5	4	4	7	10	4
walk	4	10	5	11	0	2	6	11	1	12	5	3
work	53	25	4	6	0	4	5	11	23	18	17	8
worry	1	0	1	0	0	3	0	1	5	5	1	5

with a word count. It is evident from the table that 'accident', 'head' and 'injury' figure prominently in the table. This is of course nothing less than what we would expect given knowledge of the context of the research interview. Beyond that, however, we can see that interview subjects also mentioned specific symptoms of disorder (concentration, depression, memory, sleep and so forth). They also failed to mention with any frequency other supposedly 'common' symptoms of TBI – such as aggression and personality changes. (This could be because only familiar others would notice these changes and that the injured themselves are oblivious to such features.) Interestingly, subjects also referenced the importance of such things as walking and work (as employment) to their everyday lives.

None of this, however, can tell us how these words are actually tied together and woven within the narrative of the interviews. More importantly, this kind of analysis can only produce an analysis of words used. It cannot throw light on the underlying concepts that relate to the use of such words. Let us consider some examples.

TBI involves traumatic life events. A life as lived before injury cannot be regained and this loss is often central to those who experience TBI. The loss involves loss of physical control, loss of many ordinary everyday experiences such as the ability to follow a television narrative for more than a few seconds, and loss or impairment of cognitive function (such as memory). Again, as one might deduce from elements in Table 8.1, many of these issues emerge through the index. For example, 'loss' is specifically mentioned. Of all the elements of life that are lost, however, one of the most important is a set of social relationships. In particular injured people can become dependent on others. Dominant husbands might become as childlike dependants. Adult children might return home in a state of dependence very much as was experienced several decades previously. In fact, intimate family relationships of dependence can often be quickly reversed. Equally, friendships that existed before injury rarely carry on after injury. Girlfriends and old friends disappear. The injured become relatively isolated and lose social contacts beyond their immediate carers.

Now, we might refer to these kinds of issues as issues of 'dependency', or 'social disruption', or 'bereavement', or we might use some other concept. The point is that such terms will not appear in the transcript. And it is at this point that we begin to move over from indexing to coding. For what we do when we code data is to arrange and organize the data according to social scientific perspectives and interests. Coding terms are terms that have to be read into the interview by the researcher. And as we move from indexing to coding we begin as researchers to add things to the data. We interpret – but hopefully we do so on good grounds.

The upshot of this discussion, then, is that coding data begins to move us beyond the language and terminology of the 'text' and into a realm of social scientific analysis. This, of course, is just what is needed, but it moves the researcher into the realm of speculation. As a result it is all the more important that coding is undertaken in a rigorous manner. And in the light of our previous discussion it is also essential that special attention is given to negative or deviant cases. Let us consider one or two examples.

The research interviews referred to above were structured as narratives. Narratives are a particularly useful form of discourse to social researchers (see Mattingly and Garro, 2000; Plummer, 2001), and their analysis never fails to yield insight into the manner in which people organize accounts of their lives. In the case of the head injury interviews the dominant narrative seemed to be one of abrupt change and a certain kind of yearning for the old way of life. On some occasions the narrative of loss was emphasized repeatedly. This is for example partly evident in Case 9 (Table 8.1), whose reference to 'before' to 'change' and 'loss' and 'work' added up to a doleful narrative of a fundamentally altered world – and this was so for both the subject and his carer. Yet not all respondents apparently emphasized loss and change.

For example, in Table 8.1, we see few references from Case 5. However, this is where contextual information comes to the fore. This person had lost the facility for speaking. He communicated via a voice box linked to a computer. Not surprisingly, he reported getting easily tired, and the interview was abbreviated in its questioning and in its answering. In that light one might consider the words used by Case 5 as being of particular value. It is of special note therefore that of the few words that are used those relating to loss and change are present. Case 11, on the other hand, makes no reference to change and loss. Does this hint at a narrative that was different from others? Checking the full transcript reveals that Case 11 had structured almost the entire interview in terms of change and difference, but he spoke of what he 'used to' do, say, act like, take an interest in and so on. In short he merely used a slightly different lexicon from most other people. The basis of the narrative was not in its fundamentals different from those of other respondents, and it seems justifiable, therefore, to argue that the narrative produced by Case 11 also expressed a sense of irreversible change. The larger point, of course, is that by examining apparently deviant cases such as the above, generalizations or hypotheses about expected outcomes can be tested robustly and rigorously – and are therefore more likely to be accepted as 'evidence'. As such, our comments here have implications for the issues raised in the previous section on the robustness of data.

Conclusions: conjectural history

Conjectural history – as with conjectural social science generally – was, and is, capable of producing any number of narratives of human development, though all such narratives are derived from 'theoretical' rather than empirical considerations. Undoubtedly the most powerful narrative frame to emerge during the infancy of the social sciences was that of evolutionary theory. During the nineteenth and early twentieth centuries, evolutionary thought pervaded not only biology, but archaeology, anthropology, psychology, sociology and much else besides (Burrow, 1966). It is not, of course, our fate to investigate the emergence and development of such ideas, but it will prove useful for us to focus, ever so briefly, on one particular thesis that was associated with evolutionary social theory. It was a thesis nestled in the study of human origins, and particularly in the work of speculative archaeology. Put simply, it was a thesis to the effect that human civilization originated in one particular region (usually located as the Mesopotamian plains) and then spread outward to the remainder of the world. During the earlier part of the twentieth century, this thesis concerning the diffusion of civilization served as a kind of spine on to which many detailed archaeological observations were hooked. Indeed, grand and not so grand hypotheses were attached to the diffusionist skeleton. Thus, Gordon Childe (1936), for example, developed his synthesis of early pre-history around a diffusionist thesis that was embellished with ideas drawn from a Marxist materialist history. Childe's theses, as well as those of many others, could, however, only flourish in a world where scholars could be cavalier with chronology – in particular, in a world where the dating of objects was a somewhat speculative affair. In short, in a world where, as Childe (1936) put it, 'Dates in years before 3000 B.C. are just guesses.'

Some 10 years after Childe published his book, carbon-14 (C14) dating techniques were adopted in his science. Such techniques enabled, for the first time, reasonably accurate dates to be established for the creation of almost any human artefact – pottery, clothing, seed remnants, bones or whatever. And once it became possible to establish a detailed chronology of activity, the evidence for the diffusionist thesis mentioned above appeared increasingly fragile. Indeed, little by little it became clear that the chronology of early human activity was more consistent with a thesis that argued for a multi-centred origin to human productive processes rather than a single, central origin. What is more, the time span of human history was greatly expanded. Indeed, the rise of C14 dating techniques implied a consequent collapse of the rather simple diffusionist theory outlined herein, and it held profound consequences for archaeologists generally. Their adoption certainly had a deep personal effect on Childe, who was subsequently reported to have considered much, if not most, of his life's work to have been in error.

Whatever his feelings, Childe at least recognized that theoretical speculation must always be restrained by and checked against what counts as 'good' evidence in a professional domain. Thus, during the 1940s and 1950s the physics of radioactive decay (C14 dating) had to be taken into account, and generalizations and hypotheses about chronology had to fit with findings derived from the new technology. Childe very properly recognized this, as well as other rules and conventions relating to evidence and proof.

Rules and conventions about good and bad practice clearly differ in one realm to another. Thus 'evidence' as presented in courts of law clearly differs from what is taken to be evidence in ordinary, everyday discourse. Proof in mathematics is a radically different thing from proof in forensic science. Robust conclusions reached via quantitative investigation depend on quite different judgements from those used in qualitative enquiry. In all cases, however, there should be a transparency about what is to count as valid and reliable evidence. That is to say, a clarity about what was done in the research process, and how conclusions were arrived at. For, one can always argue about the validity of the rules of the game, but if the rules remain opaque then it is very difficult to distinguish between the conscientious and rigorous player and the cheat. In this chapter I hope that I have indicated how one can play to reliable standards.

In summary, the following key points emerge:

- Researching the inert text requires one to attend to issues of reliability and validity.
- Issues of reliability and validity in turn require that we state at the outset of the research project what, exactly, we are seeking to achieve, and what is to be included in the field of study.
- Selection (and exclusion) of documentary materials should be in accordance with the principles established in the preceding point.
- In those instances where documentary materials have to be sampled, a thorough justification for the sampling procedures needs to be provided.
- Indexing and coding of data need to be executed in a rigorous and unbiased manner.
- Whilst drawing conclusions from data, always pay special attention to data that apparently fail to confirm one's claims and generalizations.

RESEARCH EXERCISES

Exercise 8.1

Some of the most puzzling events of the last quarter of the twentieth century concern the appearance and spread of a new kind of disease in cattle, humans and other mammals such as domestic cats. The disease has various names – for example, it is known as both 'mad cow disease' and variant CJD. The UK government instigated a full investigation into the origins and consequences of the disease. The report is available in full at (http://www.bse.org.uk/index.htm) Included in the report are volumes of 'evidence'.

1. Read the 'Executive Summary' of the report to get a feel for the issues and problems that were examined by the investigative committee.
2. Draw up a list of things that the inquirers counted as 'evidence'. (Make sure to include the 'Materials' volume in your overview.)

3. Draw some conclusions about the way in which the written evidence that was offered to the committee members differed from oral evidence in its variety, structure and function.
4. Scrutinize Volume 2 of the report entitled 'Science' and note how 'evidence' is used in that volume. Pay particular attention to the relationships between hypotheses and conclusions, and the grounds on which hypotheses are rejected.
5. By using Volume 2 or any other volume of the report draw some conclusions about the way in which text and 'evidence' are related in the report as a whole.
6. Finally, offer some suggestions as to how the report functions in relation to its terms of reference. (The latter are listed in the 'Introduction' to the report.)

Notes

1 The title of a book by Karl Popper (1963), a book in which he laid down principles for the acceptance and rejection of scientific assertions.
2 These issues were taken up in a BBC *Horizon* programme (go to http://www.bbc.co.uk/science/horizon, and search for 'Atlantis').
3 One reason for failure to accept disconfirming experimental results is that it is quite normal for different runs of the 'same' experiment to produce different and divergent results. Systematic review methodology overcomes this problem by accepting all results and analysing the bigger picture that is produced by the sum total.
4 See http://www.york.ac.uk/inst/crd/report4.htm and http://www.cebm.net/
5 http://www.nlm.nih.gov/
6 http://www.csa.com/detailsV3/socioabs.html
7 http://www.cas.org/ONLINE/DBSS/sigless.html
8 In this respect the case of the so-called Hitler Diaries is rather interesting, see Harris (1996).
9 A useful example for study concerns the 'missing link' forgery – known as the forgery of the Piltdown man. Extensive documentation of the case and surrounding issues can be found at http://www.clarku.edu/~piltdown/pp_map.html

9

Production, Consumption and Exchange

Lessons from southern Sudan

> Documents? There never were any. There are no written orders, no ordnance maps, cryptographs, leaflets, proclamations, newspapers, letters. The custom of writing memoirs and diaries does not exist (most frequently there is simply no paper). There is no tradition of writing histories. Most importantly – who would do this? (Kapuściński, 2001: 4)

Kapuściński is speaking of life in southern Sudan in the last decade of the twentieth century; of life in a war zone; of life among peoples such as the Dinka and the Nuer, peoples who had been closely studied during the middle part of the last century by anthropologists such as Evans-Pritchard (1940) and Lienhardt (1961). He is also speaking of a world that is lost – precisely because there is no documentation to hold it in place. Without documents there are no traces. Things remain invisible and events remain unrecorded. The only resource is word of mouth accounts. It was in such worlds that anthropology was developed. So it is, perhaps, understandable that the research act of the anthropologist turned on matters of observation, and the recording of speech and behaviours. How could one use documents in the absence of paper? Naturally, in the modern affluent world – the world in which we live – documentation is central. The written order forms a cornerstone of modern life, a point emphasized by Max Weber in his account of that quintessential organizational form of the twentieth century – bureaucracy. Yet, in modern social science, the written trace continues to be neglected. There are few studies concerned directly, and not just tangentially, with the use of documentation in contemporary life and even fewer texts devoted to the problem of research on

forms of documentation. For analysis of speech, on the other hand, the range
of materials is expansive. This is so even though the analysis of speech has,
necessarily, to be mediated through text; that is, via a transcription (see, for
example, Silverman, 1996: 254). In that light it would be an interesting research
exercise in itself to look at the emergence of the various social scientific tools
and techniques that have been used to translate talk into text.

There is, of course, no obvious way to account for the differing fortunes of
speech and writing in social scientific research. Perhaps the neglect of the role of
writing in contemporary life serves as something of a pointer towards a fundamental blind spot in western culture. Such an undervaluing of the written, as
opposed to the spoken word, has of course been remarked upon elsewhere.
Thus, the anthropologist Jack Goody (1968; 1977) has frequently referred to
writing as a rich, yet neglected, field for research studies. More fundamentally,
the philosopher Jacques Derrida (see Howells, 1998) has underlined, on a
number of occasions, how the written word has always been considered subsidiary and secondary to the spoken word in the philosophical corpus of the
west. Yet the subordinate role of writing to speech is far from deserved, and I
hope that I have demonstrated just how that is so throughout this book.

One of the key claims embedded in previous chapters is that documents, and
especially written documents, can be taken as a field of research in their own
right. In particular, the study of the processes of production and consumption
(or use) of written materials provides two sturdy pillars around which interesting and essential research programmes can be built and developed. Naturally,
in the hurly-burly of ordinary everyday activity issues of production and consumption become entwined, and it is not always easy, as we have seen, to distinguish clearly between the one process and the other. To end our analysis
therefore let us consider some final examples. This, not merely so as to underline the central issues, but also in order to push our analysis in one last – and
rather important – direction.

Circuits of production and consumption

Consider a map – a road map, perhaps. We commonly think of maps and charts
as providing true and accurate reflections of the world out there. If they did
not, then how else would we find our way across the countryside? Yet clearly,
a map can never depict with precision the terrain it claims to represent otherwise it would be useless. It is an issue well taken up, for example, in a short
story by Jorge Luis Borges entitled 'Of exactitude in science' (Borges, 1975).
The story concerns a map of an entire empire 'that coincided with it point for
point', but being too cumbersome to use, it was abandoned – tattered fragments of the map later being found in the western deserts where it was used
to shelter 'an occasional beast or beggar'. Not surprising you may think, for a
useful map obviously has to involve abbreviation and abstraction – as well as

scaling. A map, moreover, must contain identifiable items and patterns – features that we can recognize and group together.

Abbreviation, abstraction, scaling, grouping, pattern identification; these are essential human activities, and they are necessarily implicated in the manufacture of maps and numerous other documents. In Chapters 2 and 4, in particular, we examined such processes in detail and in a variety of contexts. We also noted in Chapter 2 how documents are not simply produced and manufactured and consumed, but often used to produce new facts and new things. In that respect it was suggested that documents can often become enmeshed in a circuit of production. And there are many documents such as the DSM and the ICD (see Chapter 2) that may be looked upon in that light as machine tools. That is, tools used to produce other manufactured goods. Such documents are, by their very nature, implicated in endless circuits of production.

However, documents are not simply an adjunct to fact-producing activities – mere tools to be used. Rather, fact production lies at the heart of their very being. Indeed, most of the things that we commonly consider to be 'facts of nature', or facts about society, can be said to exist only in documents. This, despite claims to the effect that the materials contained within this or that document merely reflect or represent some external reality beyond the document. As has been pointed out in earlier chapters, the social science researcher should therefore never be tempted to think of the descriptions, images and explanations that are contained in documents as mere representations of the world as it 'really is'. Instead the researcher should consider the possibility that the world is actually constituted in and through documentation. The materials referred to in Chapters 3 and 4 provided some first-class examples of how this can be so, and here I offer a further example.

Norton's Star Atlas (Ridpath, 1989) is commonly referred to as the amateur astronomer's 'bible'. It is a book of star maps. As with all maps, we find within evidence of abbreviation, scaling, abstraction and fact production in abundance. Evidently, then, the starry firmament as presented in a star map is a humanly created phenomenon. Naturally, the matter of which stars and nebulae are composed exists independently of human intervention and creation, but the moment we categorize the stars into constellations and galaxies we divorce ourselves from a self-sustaining and independent world and begin to engage with a universe constructed by feeble humanity. In fact the map (document) mediates the relationship between human beings and the universe. Thus, it is, after all, only earthpersons who 'see' Orion and trace its 'movements' through the northern sky in winter, and it is only earthpersons who view the blue–white stars that make up Cassiopeia's 'W' as somehow belonging together. Indeed, neither Orion, nor Cassiopeia, nor Pisces, nor any other feature of the constellations appears outside of human documents, and without the texts they would fail to exist at all.

Stars and star maps are a long way from social science perhaps. Yet, as with the natural world, many features of the social world are also created with the aid of documents. Thus, we saw in Chapter 1 how the anthropological documents of the Torres Straits anthropologists served to create kinship. And we noted in Chapter 4 how a family tree (pedigree) as drawn up in a genetics clinic can act so as to manufacture both families and genetic disorders. Indeed, borrowing our terminology from the sociology of science, we described the machine that draws human pedigrees as an 'inscription device' (Latour and Woolgar, 1979: 51). In the work of the latter, such a device is an apparatus that turns matter into documentation – as, say, with the graphical trace of temperature changes in a living body. In this book we have broadened the meaning to refer to any device – a questionnaire, a statistical device, a table or chart – that is capable of translating social concepts (such as the family, or social class) into visible facts.

Documents, then, represent and make things visible. They also construct. They construct and stabilize objects and things (Chapters 2, 4 and 7), identities (Chapter 5) and processes (Chapter 3). Yet in researching documentation we must forever remain aware that representation, construction, stabilization are carried out in concert – in concert with other agents. So it is the production and consumption of documents in their social settings that are important – how the document fits into the entire network of activities and agents of which it forms a part. That is the key to the research process.

In this light it is instructive to consider a further essay on maps, one written by George Psathas (1979) some years ago. In that essay, Psathas looked at how maps were used in context. His specific focus was on the kind of maps that people draw and dispense for and to others so as to find the forthcoming party at 'our house' or some such. His sociological interest was on the reasoning that was implicated in the drawing of such maps. For example, he pointed out how direction maps are always drawn with reference to a destination rather than, say, to the topography of a given neighbourhood. Indeed, the use of such maps clearly implicates readers as well as writers (or in this case amateur cartographers). For readers of such maps are invariably inveigled into following the sequences drawn on the map. They are obliged, as it were, to perform the route. Thus, in reading and using the map, the map-reader moves him- or herself from point A to point B in a manner dictated above all by the map-maker. Such use provides a good example of a process referred to as action-at-a-distance. It also serves to demonstrate how documents in use can structure and pattern their readers (a process expanded upon in Chapter 5). This is precisely why I have argued that documents can often be considered as agents in, rather than mere adjuncts to, networks of action. And, as was stated in the introductory chapter, documents in action often take on qualities of the broom set in motion by Goethe's Sorcerer's Apprentice, or the monster unleashed on the world by Mary Shelley's Frankenstein. That is, qualities that are independent of the creator. Perhaps it is not so surprising, then, as Wheeler (1969) indicated, that records and dossiers necessarily have a career independent of the human subjects that they supposedly report upon. But rather than refer back to issues that have already been dealt with, it will prove more fruitful for us to consider one final feature of the map-making example. Maps are constructed, and maps are used or consumed in practical activities.[1] Maps are also exchanged. Yet, of this latter process we have so far said little.

The sociology of the Kula

In modern cultural studies there exists a concept of the cultural circuit (du Gay et al., 1997). The circuit supposedly incorporates 'moments' of production and consumption as well as of representation, regulation and identity. The image of a circuit is, in part, chosen to illustrate the dynamic and interlinked nature of the ways in which cultural products are appropriated and produced in the modern world.[2] Documents can be considered likewise. Yet, somewhat oddly, there is one important theme that is entirely absent from the 'circuit' that is discussed and analysed by the cultural studies cohort. It is the theme of circulation itself.

The circulation and exchange of goods and services has often formed a major topic of investigation by anthropologists. It was in that context, for example, that Malinowski, in his *Argonauts of the Western Pacific*, examined the sociology of the Kula. As Malinowski pointed out, 'The Kula is a form of exchange' (1922: 81). It was a form of exchange carried on by peoples among a ring of islands in Melanesia. The islands may be imagined as belonging to a circle. Malinowski noted that in the clockwise direction of the islands flowed long necklaces of red shell (called *soulva*), whilst in the anti-clockwise direction flowed bracelets of white shell (called *mwali*). Each type of article was constantly being exchanged for the other. (The necklaces and bracelets were never kept as private property.) Further, the act of exchange was normally accompanied by extensive ritual, and associated with the Kula were many other activities – such as commerce and boat building.

In writing about the Kula, Malinowski was developing insights about social life in general. Thus, he noted that the Kula system was not primary to economic life, but rather to social life. In so doing, he was emphasizing the fact that the exchange process cemented social partnerships, rather than economic relations. His insights were built upon throughout the twentieth century, and were later developed into what has been called social exchange theory (Ekeh, 1974). Our interest in Malinowski's analysis is that we can consider documents and their exchange and circulation in much the same way as Malinowski considered necklaces and shells. For, documents can also be used to trace out patterns of social exchange and thereby the social networks that lay behind them.

For example, in the modern world the exchange of greeting cards is a commonplace event. Birthdays, weddings and even deaths form occasions where people send cards to oneanother. People also buy and send cards to those who are ill – 'Get well soon cards'. But to whom, exactly, do people send such cards? And what do the patterns tell us about social life? In a rather fascinating study

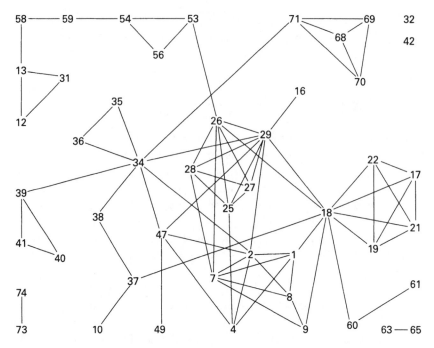

FIGURE 9.1   *Information contacts among professionals in South Wales, 1999*

Weiner et al. (1999) looked at the distribution of such cards among hospital patients suffering from two different types of disorder. The first were medical disorders (for example, heart diseases and diabetes) and the second were serious psychiatric disorders. What they noted was that although both sets of patients were hospitalized (for more than three days), the medical patients were far more likely to get visits, gifts and 'Get well soon cards' than were the psychiatric patients. Such a pattern of gift exchange, suggested the authors, tells us something fundamental about how we view psychiatric illness and psychiatric patients in our society. (Psychiatric patients are commonly regarded as not being 'really' ill and even when they are so regarded it is often thought to be their own fault – so sympathy is in short supply.) Although it was not part of the planned investigation, the hospital researchers could have gone further, and used the cards to do something more. They could have used the exchange of cards to trace patterns of a social network.

The exchange of communications – such as cards – between individuals not only facilitates the flow of information, but also marks out channels and boundaries of social influence. For example, Figure 9.1 is a network graph. It represents a trace of information exchange events among a small group of primary-care practitioners in Wales. The lines represent connections between people who seek 'advice and information' from one another. Thus, by viewing the graph it is possible to see clearly the existence of groups of people who seemingly consult each other a lot, possibly because they work closely together – in the same building. For instance, individuals referred to as numbers 25, 26, 27, 28 and 29 evidently belong together, as do the GPs numbered 17–22. It is also possible to see that some people are contacted considerably (numbers 29 and 34, for example) whilst others look relatively isolated (numbers 61, 32 and 42).

Such a pattern of contact and communication is traceable in other ways – say by asking people about their e-mail contacts.[3] And what the results of such questioning show is not simply evidence about who contacts whom, but also evidence of social power and social influence. In the study concerning the GP contacts, discussed here, it was possible to link the patterns in the graph to other information about the GPs, so as to understand why the patterns were as they were. Professional factors, ethnic factors and gender factors all seemingly structured the patterns of contact and communication. And although the graph in Figure 9.1 represents an image of verbal communication it could, in theory, be extended to represent an image of communication via the use of written documents.

In his conversations with Latour, Serres (1995: 161) refers to objects that trace or 'make visible the relations that constitute the group through which [the object] passes, like the token in a children's game'. The term that Serres uses to refer to such objects is 'quasi-object' – a term chosen to emphasize the fact that the world cannot be simply divided into objects and humans, for objects and people belong in an ensemble that is often difficult to unravel. For example, in the GP network just referred to one of the questions being studied related to the dissemination of innovations, in particular the dissemination of knowledge about new drugs (pharmaceuticals) such as Viagra. At a distance it might seem that it is easy to distinguish between such an object and the human influences upon it. Yet, in practice it is not. For what the drug (Viagra) is, is fashioned by what is said about it, by patterns of use, and by patterns of reception. The technology that is represented by the drug is thereby wrapped up in a whole series of relationships and networks. To understand the technology we need to follow the thing (document) through its social channels. And all the while the circulation of communications about the document will serve to mark out the boundaries of social groupings and social relationships – as in Figure 9.1.

Documents as technology

Goody (1977) and Ong (1982) point out that writing is a form of technology, and a very important one at that. They argue, for example, that the move from oral to written culture changed the technological potential of human society. Thoughts once written were able to be re-analysed and re-examined. Derrida refers to this property of writing as its iterability (see Howells, 1998). Iterability encourages the development of critical and scientific thought. Writing also bolsters the development of rational systems of accounting and monitoring, and encourages close scrutiny of the ways in which we list and classify things.

Looking at documents as technology encourages us to think about how the technology is linked into productive relationships. For example, Goody (1968) provides insight into how, in Imperial China and other traditional societies, the complexities of (Chinese) script were consciously and deliberately manipulated by the literati so as to underpin their monopoly on state activity. The development and widespread use of a phonetic alphabet (as used in the world of Latin Christianity) would clearly have undermined the exclusivity of such power groups. Not surprisingly the adoption of phonetic forms of writing were always opposed within traditional China.

By understanding how technology is used, who recruits it and allies themselves with it, how it is adopted, and adapted, and how it circulates, can form a series of key entry points into the investigation of social life. This is especially so when alternative technologies are available in the same time and place. For then it becomes possible to see how the supporters of the alternatives line up one against the other, and how the different forms of technology change social relations in which they are enmeshed. Though we must be forever mindful that technology is not merely the wires and widgets within the 'machine box' – see Mackay (1997). It is always hardware plus social relationships that count, and not simply hardware alone. It is a lesson that is well underlined in the work of Bijker et al. (1989) who provide numerous examples of technology in action.

In the case of documentation, of course, wires and widgets are usually of marginal significance, though instrumentation is not. Thus, we have seen in Chapter 4, for example, how measuring instruments of various kinds constitute a form of technology. Indeed, social researchers usually refer to their questionnaires and the like simply as 'instruments'. Quality of life instruments, health outcome instruments, survey instruments and the like constitute a particularly interesting genre of modern technology. Systematic review techniques (as referred to in Chapter 8) may be said to form another. In all cases, the technology is linked to particular kinds of professional practice and political and managerial manoeuvrings. And it is such relationships between things and their contexts that determine the shapes and appearances of the elements. Consequently, what is needed for work with documentation is a focus on relations rather than on things in isolation.

A final plea

Production, consumption and exchange are three processes that are central to the study of documentation in use. It might be objected of course that the most important feature of documentation – content – has been given too low a profile throughout the entire book. I might defend such a lack of focus by saying that there are numerous other texts that deal with aspects of content analysis, or discourse analysis, and that there would be little point in duplicating such work here. However, I offer no such defence. There is no need. Instead I offer an analogy. My analogy concerns an operatic libretto (the set of words and phrases that is sung). Taken on its own a libretto rarely adds up to much. The text as narrative is often disjointed, repetitive and lacking in depth. I cannot think of a single one that might hold a person's attention as a gripping tale. Yet, a libretto is not intended to be analysed in isolation. It demands to be analysed in action. How it is integrated into the dramatic action on stage, how it relates to the melody and rhythm of the music, how it is called upon (recruited) and manipulated by the singers, how it is *performed* – all of these are of primary importance. Its substance as displayed on the inert page is of only secondary concern.

RESEARCH EXERCISE

Exercise 9.1

Consider identifying a small sample of people (say, $N = 5$) who use text messaging services on mobile phones. Question them about how they use such messages. Pay particular attention to the following issues: (1) How the messages circulate and the extent to which they function to mark out the boundaries of a social clique. (2) How the text messages are integrated into the social activities of senders and receivers. (3) How the messaging technology functions in the everyday life of the user (Mackay's (1997) work might be useful here). (4) How the shape and form of the text can itself serve as an agent in the structuring of social interaction.

Then consider expanding the sample so as to gain coverage of additional kinds of user or to explore elementary hypotheses that may have emerged from working with the initial sample.

Notes

1 For another example of maps in use see Brody (1981).
2 In this vein, Fiske (1989) has illustrated how acts of consumption can, in turn, be viewed as 'work' or production.
3 Citation searches can also be used to map out a network of researchers or an emergent network or boundaries of research networks. See Webster (1991).

Bibliography

Abelen, E., Redeker, G. and Thompson, S.A. (1993) 'The rhetorical structure of US-American and Dutch fund-raising letters' *Text*, 13:3: 323–50.

ABPI (1996) *Compendium of patient information leaflets, 1996–97*. London: Datapharm.

American Psychiatric Association (2000) *The Diagnostic and Statistical Manual of Mental Disorders. DSM-IV-TR*. Washington, DC: American Psychiatric Association.

Arensberg, C.M. (1937) *The Irish Countryman. An Anthropological Study*. New York: Macmillan.

Ariès, P. (1981) *The Hour of Our Death*. Tr. H. Weaver. New York: Knopf.

Ariès, P. (1985) *Images of Man and Death*. Tr. J. Lloyd. Cambridge, MA: Harvard University Press.

Aristotle (1995) *Poetics*. Tr. S. Halliwell. Cambridge, MA: Harvard University Press.

Ash, T.G. (1997) *The File. A Personal History*. London: HarperCollins.

Atkinson, J.M. (1978) *Discovering Suicide*. London: Macmillan.

Atkinson, P. (1990) *The Ethnographic Imagination. Textual Constructions of Reality*. London: Routledge.

Atkinson, P. (1992a) 'The ethnography of a medical setting. Reading, writing and rhetoric', *Qualitative Health Research*, 2 (4): 451–74.

Atkinson, P. (1992b) *Understanding Ethnographic Texts*. London: Sage.

Atkinson, P. and Coffey, A. (1997) 'Analysing documentary realities', in D. Silverman (ed.), *Qualitative Research. Theory, Method, Practice*. London: Sage. pp. 44–62.

Atkinson, R. (1998) *The Life Story Interview*. London: Sage.

Austin, J.L. (1962) *How to do Things with Words*. Ed. J.O. Urmson and M. Sbisà. Oxford: Clarendon Press.

Baldi, S. (1998) 'Normative versus social constructivist processes in the allocation of citations. A network-analytic model'. *American Sociological Review*, 63: 829–46.

Banks, J. and Prior, L. (2001) 'Doing things with illness. The micro-politics of the CFS clinic', *Social Science and Medicine*, 52 (1): 11–23.

Barnouw, D. and Van Der Stroom, G. (1989) *The Diary of Anne Frank. The Critical Edition*. London: Viking.

Barrett, R. (1996) *The Psychiatric Team and the Social Definition of Schizophrenia. An Anthropological Study of Person and Illness*. Cambridge: Cambridge University Press.

Barthes, R. (1977) *Image-Music-Text*. Tr. S. Heath. London: Fontana.

Barthes, R. (1985) *The Fashion System*. Tr. M. Ward and R. Howard. London: Jonathan Cape.

Barthes, R. (1990) *S/Z*. Tr. R. Miller. Oxford: Blackwell.

Barley, S.R. and Bechky, B.A. (1994) 'In the background of science. The work of technicians in science labs'. *Work and Occupations*, 21 (1): 85–126.

Barton, D. and Hall, N. (2000) *Letter Writing as Social Practice*. Amsterdam: John Benjamins.

Bastide, F. (1990) 'The iconography of scientific texts: principles of analysis', in M. Lynch and S. Woolgar (eds), *Representation in Scientific Practice*. London: MIT Press. pp. 187–230.

Bauer, M.W. and Gaskell, G. (eds) (2000) *Qualitative Researching. With Text, Image and Sound*. London: Sage.

Bauman, Z. (1991) *Intimations of Postmodernity*. London: Routledge.

Bauman, Z. (1992) *Mortality, Immortality and Other Life Strategies*. Cambridge: Polity Press.

Baxter, R. (1673) *A Christian Directory*. Ann Arbor, MI: University Microfilms, 1970.

Bazerman, C. (1988) *Shaping Written Knowledge. The Genre and Activity of the Experimental Article in Science*. Madison, WI: University of Wisconsin Press.

Becker, H.S. (1953–4) 'Becoming a marihuana user', *American Journal of Sociology*, 59: 253–4.

Becker, H.S. (1986) *Doing Things Together*. Evanston, IL: Northwestern University Press.

Benson, D. and Hughes, J.A. (1983) *The Perspective of Ethnomethodology*. London: Longman.

Berg, M. (1996) 'Practices of reading and writing. The constitutive role of the patient record in medical work', *Sociology of Health and Illness*, 18 (4): 499–524.

Berg, M. (1997) *Rationalizing Medical Work. Decision-support techniques and medical practices*. Cambridge, MA: MIT Press.

Beverley, J. (2000) 'Testimonio, subalternity, and narrative authority', in N.K. Denzin and Y.S. Lincoln (eds), *Handbook of Qualitative Research*. 2nd edition. Thousand Oaks. CA: Sage. pp. 555–65.

Bijker, W.E., Pinch, T. and Hughes, T.P. (eds) (1987) *The Social Construction of Technological Systems*. Cambridge, MA: MIT Press.

Birke, L. and Smith, J. (1995) 'Animals in experimental reports. The rhetoric of science', *Society and Animals*, 3 (1): 23–41.

Bloch, A. and Bloch, C. (1995) *The Song of Songs. A New Translation*. New York: Random House.

Bloor, M. (1991) 'A minor office. The variable and socially constructed character of death certification in a Scottish city', *Journal of Health and Social Behaviour*, 32 (3): 273–87.

Borges, J.L. (1975) *A Universal History of Infamy*. Tr. Norman Thomas di Giovanni. Harmondsworth: Penguin.

Boswell, J. (1976) *Boswell's Life of Johnson*. London: Dent.

Bourdieu, P. (1977) *Outline of a Theory of Practice*. Tr. R. Nice. Cambridge: Cambridge University Press.

Bowker, G.C. (1994) *Science on the Run: Information Management and Industrial Geophysics at Schlumberger, 1920–40*. Cambridge, MA: MIT Press.

Bowker, G.C. and Star, S.L. (1999) *Sorting Things Out. Classification and Its Consequences*. Cambridge, MA: MIT Press.

Bowling, A. (1997) *Measuring Health. A Review of Quality of Life Measurement Scales*. 2nd edition. Buckingham: Open University Press.

Breuer, J. and Freud, S. (1974) *Studies on Hysteria. Pelican Freud Library Vol. 3*. Tr. J. Strachey and A. Strachey. Harmondsworth: Penguin.

Brodbeck, M. (ed.) (1968) *Readings in the Philosophy of the Social Sciences*. New York: Macmillan.

Brody, H. (1974) *Inishkillane. Change and Decline in the West of Ireland*. New York: Schocken Books.

Brody, H. (1981) *Maps and Dreams*. London: Jill Norman and Hobhouse.

Brown, G. (1981) 'Etiological studies and the definition of a case', in J.K. Wing, P. Bebbington and L.N. Robins (eds), *What is a case? The problem of definition in psychiatric community surveys*. London: Grant McIntyre. pp. 62–9.

Bruner, J. (1987) 'Life as narrative', *Social Research*, 54 (1): 11–32.

Bruner, J. (1993) 'The autobiographical process', in R. Folkenflik (ed.), *The Culture of Autobiography: Constructions of Self Representation*. Stanford, CA: Stanford University Press. pp. 38–56.

Bulmer, M. (1980) 'Why don't sociologists make more use of official statistics?', *Sociology*, 14 (4): 505–23.

Burgess, R.G. (ed.) (1982) *Field Research: A Sourcebook and Field Manual*. London: Allen and Unwin.

Burgess, R.G. (1984) *In the Field. An Introduction to Field Research*. London: Allen and Unwin.

Burgher, M.S. (1997) *Atlas of Mortality in Europe: Subnational Patterns, 1980/1981 and 1990/1991*. WHO European Centre for Environment and Health. WHO Regional publications. European series no. 75. Copenhagen: WHO Regional Office for Europe.

Burgos-Debray, E. (ed.) (1984) *I, Rigoberta Menchú. An Indian Woman in Guatemala*. New York: Verso.

Burrow, J.W. (1966) *Evolution and Society*. Cambridge: Cambridge University Press.

Burton, F. and Carlen, P. (1979) *Official Discourse. On Discourse Analysis, Government Publications, Ideology and the State*. London: Routledge.

Callon, M. (1989) 'Society in the making. The study of technology as a tool for socio-logical analysis', in W. E. Bijker, T. Pinch and T.P. Hughes (eds), *The Social Construction of Technological Systems*. Cambridge, MA: MIT Press. pp. 83–103.

Casagrande, J.B. (ed.) (1960) *In the Company of Man*. New York: Harper Row.

Castells, M. (1997) *The Power of Identity*. London: Blackwell.

Chapman, C.J. (1997) *Cyrillic for Pedigree Drawing*. Oxford: Cherwell Scientific Publishing.

Charlesworth, M., Farrall, L., Stokes, T. and Turnbull, D. (1989) *Life Among the Scientists. An Anthropological Study of an Australian Scientific Community*. Melbourne: Oxford University Press.

Charmaz, K. (2000) 'Grounded theory: objectivist and constructivist methods', in N.K. Denzin and Y.S. Lincoln (eds), *Handbook of Qualitative Research*. 2nd edition. Thousand Oaks, CA: Sage. pp. 509–36.

Chartier, R., Boureau, A. and Dauphin, C. (1997) *Correspondence. Models of Letter Writing from the Middle Ages to the Nineteenth Century*. Tr. C. Woodall. Princeton, NJ: Princeton University Press.

Chauvel, L. (1997) 'L'uniformisation du taux de suicide masculin selon l'âge: effet de génèration ou recomposition du cycle de vie?', *Revue française de sociologie*, XXXVIII (4): 681–734.

Cherry-Garrard, A. (1994) *The Worst Journey in the World*. London: Picador. (1st edition, 1922).

Childe, V.G. (1936) *Man Makes Himself*. London: Watts.

Cicourel, A.V. (1964) *Method and Measurement in Sociology*. New York: The Free Press.

Cicourel, A.V. (1976) *The Social Organisation of Juvenile Justice*. London: Heinemann.

Claus, E.B., Risch, N. and Thompson, W.D. (1991) 'Genetic analysis of breast cancer in the cancer and steroid hormone study', *American Journal of Human Genetics*, 48: 232–42.

Clifford, J. and Marcus, G.E. (eds) (1986) *Writing Culture: The Poetics and Politics of Ethnography*. Berkeley, CA: University of California Press.

Cobb, R. (1978) *Death in Paris. 1795–1801*. Oxford: Oxford University Press.

Coleman, C. and Moynihan, J. (1996) *Understanding Crime Data. Haunted by the Dark Figure*. Buckingham: Open University Press.

Collins, H.M. and Pinch, T. (1993) *The Golem*. Cambridge: Cambridge University Press.

Crapanzano, V. (1980) *Tuhami: Portrait of a Moroccan*. Chicago: University of Chicago Press.

Daniell, D. (1989) *Tyndale's New Testament*. New Haven, CT: Yale University Press.

Darnton, R. (1984) *The Great Cat Massacre and Other Episodes in French Cultural History*. New York: Basic Books.

Darnton, R. (2000) 'An early information society. News and the media in eighteenth-century Paris', *American Historical Review*, 105 (1): 1–35.

de Certeau, M. (1984) *The Practice of Everyday Life*. Tr. S. Rendall. London: University of California Press.

de Duve, T. (1993) *The Definitively Unfinished Marcel Duchamp*. Cambridge, MA: MIT Press.

Defoe, D. (1956) *The Adventures of Robinson Crusoe*. London: Shorter Classics.

Denzin, N.K. (1970) *The Research Act in Sociology*. 1st edition. London: Butterworth.

Denzin, N.K. (1978) *The Research Act. A Theoretical Introduction to Sociological Methods*. 2nd. edition. New York: McGraw-Hill.

Denzin, N.K. (1988) 'Qualitative analysis for social scientists', *Contemporary Sociology*, 17 (3): 430–2.

Denzin, N.K. (1989) *Interpretive Biography*, London: Sage.

Derrida, J. (1976) *Of Grammatology*. Tr. G.C. Spivak. Baltimore, MD: Johns Hopkins University Press.

Derrida, J. (1977) 'Signature, event, context', *Glyph*, 1: 172–97.

Derrida, J. (1988) *Limited Inc*. Evanston, IL: Northwestern University Press.

Derrida, J. (1991) *A Derrida Reader. Between the Blinds*. Ed. P. Kamuf. London: Harvester Wheatsheaf.

Desrosieres, A. (1994) 'Official statistics and business: history, classifications, uses', in L. Bud-Frierman (ed.), *Information Acumen. The Understanding and Use of Knowledge in Modern Business*. London: Routledge. pp.168–86.

DeVault, M.L. (1987) 'Women's talk. Feminist strategies for analyzing research interviews', *Women and Language*, 10: 33–6.

DeVault, M.L. (1990) 'Talking and listening from women's standpoint. Feminist strategies for interviewing and analysis', *Social Problems*, 37: 96–116.

De Vaus, D.A. (1996) *Surveys in Social Research*. 4th edition. London: UCL Press.

Dosse, F. (1997a) *History of Structuralism. Vol. 1. The Rising Sign. 1945–1966*. Tr. D. Glassman. Minneapolis: University of Minnesota Press.

Dosse, F. (1997b) *History of Structuralism. Vol. 2. The Sign Sets. 1967-Present*. Tr. D. Classman Minneapolis: University of Minnesota Press.

Douglas, J.D. (1967) *The Social Meanings of Suicide*. Princeton, NJ: Princeton University Press.

Douglas, M. (1966) *Purity and Danger. An Analysis of the Concepts of Pollution and Taboo.* London: Routledge & Kegan Paul.

Dubrow, H. (1982) *Genre.* London: Methuen.

du Gay, P., Hall, S., Janes, L., Mackay, H. and Negus, K. (1997) *Doing Cultural Studies. The story of the Sony Walkman.* London: Sage.

Durkheim, E. (1915) *The Elementary Forms of the Religious Life.* Tr. J.W. Swain. London: Allen and Unwin.

Durkheim, E. (1951) *Suicide. A Study in Sociology.* Tr. J.A. Spaulding and G. Simpson. London: Routledge & Kegan Paul.

Edwards, A., Hood, K., Mathews, E., Russell, D., Russell, I., Barker, J., Bloor, M., Burnard, P., Covey, J., Pill, R., Wilkinson, C. and Stott, N. (2000) 'The effectiveness of one-to-one risk-communication interventions in health care', *Medical Decision Making*, 20: 290–7.

Ekeh, P. (1974) *Social Exchange Theory.* London. Heinemann.

Ellis, C. and Bochner, P. (2000) 'Autoethnography, personal narrative, reflexivity', in N.K. Denzin and Y.S. Lincoln (eds), *Handbook of Qualitative Research.* 2nd edition. Thousand Oaks, CA: Sage. pp. 733–68.

Emmison, M. and Smith, P. (2000) *Researching the Visual.* London: Sage.

Evans-Pritchard, E.E. (1937) *Witchcraft, Oracles and Magic among the Azande.* London: Oxford University Press.

Evans-Pritchard, E.E. (1940) *The Nuer. A description of the modes of the livelihood and political institutions of a Nilotic people.* Oxford: Clarendon Press.

Evenhuis, H.M., Kengen, M. and Eurlings, H. (1992) 'Evaluation of a screening instrument for dementia in ageing mentally retarded persons', *Journal of Intellectual Disability Research*, 36: 337–47.

Fay, L.E. (2000) *Shostakovich. A Life.* Oxford: Oxford University Press.

Feyerabend, P. (1975) *Against Method.* London: New Left Books.

Finnegan, R. (1996) 'Using documents', in R. Sapsford and V. Jupp (eds), *Data Collection and Analysis.* London: Sage. pp.138–51.

Finley, M.I. (1977) *The World of Odysseus.* 2nd edition. London: Chatto and Windus.

Fiske, J. (1989) *Understanding Popular Culture.* Boston, MA: Unwin Hyman.

Fitzgerald, F. Scott (1925) *The Great Gatsby.* New York: New Directions Books.

Folstein, M.F., Folstein, S.E. and McHugh, P.R. (1975) 'Mini Mental State. A practical method for grading the cognitive state of patients for the clinician', *Journal of Psychiatric Research*, 12: 189–98.

Fontana, A. and Frey, J.H. (2000) 'The interview. From structured questions to negotiated text', in N.K. Denzin and Y.S. Lincoln (eds), *Handbook of Qualitative Research.* 2nd edition. Thousand Oaks, CA: Sage. pp. 645–72.

Foucault, M. (1970) *The Order of Things.* London: Tavistock.

Foucault, M. (1972) *The Archaeology of Knowledge.* Tr. A. Sheridan. New York: Pantheon.

Foucault, M. (1973) *The Birth of the Clinic.* Tr. A.M. Sheridan. London: Tavistock.

Foucault, M. (1977) *Language, Counter-Memory, Practice.* Oxford: Blackwell.

Foucault, M. (ed.) (1978) *I, Pierre Rivière.* London: Penguin.

Foucault, M. (1979) 'What is an author?', *Screen*, 20: 13–35.

Foucault, M. (1988) *Technologies of the Self. A Seminar with Michel Foucault.* Ed. L.H. Martin, H. Gutman and P.H. Hutton. London: Tavistock.

Foucault, M. (1991) *The Foucault Effect. Studies in Governmentality.* Ed. G. Burchill, C. Gordon and P. Miller. London: Harvester Wheatsheaf.

Freeman, C.J., Brown, A., Dunleavy, D. and Graham, F. (1996) *The Report of the Inquiry into the care and treatment of Shaun Anthony Armstrong*. Middlesborough: Tees District Health Authority.

Freeman, D. (1983) *Margaret Mead and Samoa*. Cambridge, MA: Harvard University Press.

Fujimura, J.H. (1996) *Crafting Science. A Sociohistory of the Quest for the Genetics of Cancer*. Cambridge, MA: Harvard University Press.

Gabe, J. (ed.) (1995) *Medicine, Health and Risk. Sociological Approaches*. Oxford: Blackwell.

Gadamer, H.-G. (1975) *Truth and Method*. Tr. W. Glen-Doepel, London: Sheed and Ward.

Garfinkel, H. (1967) *Studies in Ethnomethodology*. Englewood Cliffs, NJ: Prentice Hall.

Gay, P. (1988) *Freud. A Life for our Time*. New York: W.W. Norton.

Gedye, A. (1995) *Dementia Scale for Down Syndrome. Manual*. Gedye Research and Consulting, Vancouver, BC.

Geertz, C. (1988) *Works and Lives. The Anthropologist as Author*. Cambridge: Polity Press.

Geertz, C. (1993) *The Interpretation of Cultures*. London: Fontana.

Gerth, H. and Mills, C.W. (1953) *Character and Social Structure*. New York: Harcourt, Brace.

Giddens, A. (1978) 'Positivism and its critics', in T. Bottomore and R. Nisbet (eds), *A History of Sociological Analysis*. London: Heinemann. pp. 237–86.

Giddens, A. (1984) *The Constitution of Society*. Cambridge: Polity Press.

Giddens, A. (1991) *Modernity and Self-Identity. Self and Society in the Late Modern Age*. Stanford, CA: Stanford University Press.

Gilbert, G.N. and Mulkay, M. (1984) *Opening Pandora's Box. A Sociological Analysis of Scientists' Discourse*. Cambridge: Cambridge University Press.

Gill, A.M. and Whedbee, K. (1997) 'Rhetoric', in T.A. van Dijk (ed.), *Discourse as Structure and Process. Vol. 1*. London: Sage. pp. 157–84.

Gill, R. (2000) 'Discourse analysis', in M.W. Bauer and G. Gaskell (eds), *Qualitative Researching with Text, Image and Sound*. London: Sage.

Gillies, D. (1993) *Philosophy of Science in the Twentieth Century*. Oxford: Blackwell.

Glaser, B.G. and Strauss, A.L. (1965) *Awareness of Dying*. Chicago: Aldine.

Glaser, B. and Strauss, A. (1967) *The Discovery of Grounded Theory. Strategies for Qualitative Research*. Chicago: Aldine.

Goffman, E. (1959) *The Presentation of the Self in Everyday Life*. New York: Doubleday Anchor Books.

Gogol, N.V. (1996) *Dead Souls*. Tr. B. Guilbert. London: Yale University Press.

Goode, W.J. and Hatt, P.K. (1952) *Methods in Social Research*. New York: McGraw-Hill.

Goody, J. (1968) *Literacy in Traditional Societies*. Cambridge: Cambridge University Press.

Goody, J. (1977) *The Domestication of the Savage Mind*. Cambridge: Cambridge University Press.

Gould, S.J. (1989) *Wonderful Life. The Burgess Shale and the Nature of History*. New York: W.W. Norton.

Grafton, A. (1997) *The Footnote. A Curious History*. London: Faber.

Greimas, A.J. (1987) *On Meaning. Selected Writings in Semiotic Theory*. Tr. P.J. Perron and F.H. Collins. London: Francis Pinter.

Grossmith, G. and Grossmith, W. (1999) *The Diary of a Nobody*. London: Penguin.

Gubrium, J.F., Holstein, J.A. and Buckholdt, D.R. (1994) *Constructing the Life Course*. New York: General Hall.

Hacking, I. (1990) *The Taming of Chance*. Cambridge: Cambridge University Press.

Hacking, I. (1995) *Rewriting the Soul. Multiple Personality and the Sciences of Memory*. Princeton, NJ: Princeton University Press.

Haddon, A.C. (1904) *Reports of the Cambridge Anthropological Expedition to Torres Straits. Vol. VI. Society, Magic and Religion of the Western Islanders*. Cambridge: Cambridge University Press.

Hak, T. (1992) 'Psychiatric records as transformations of other texts', in G. Watson and R.M. Seiler (eds), *Text in Context. Contributions to Ethnomethodology*. London: Sage. pp. 138–55.

Hall, S. (1972) *Encoding and Decoding in the Television Discourse*. Media series SP No. 7. University of Birmingham, Centre for Contemporary Cultural Studies.

Hancock, G. (1999) *Heaven's Mirror. Quest for the Lost Civilisation*. Harmondsworth: Penguin.

Handlin, O. (1953) *The Uprooted. From the Old World to the New*. London: Watts.

Harding, N. and Palfrey, C. (1997) *The Social Construction of Dementia. Confused Professionals?*. London: Jessica Kingsley.

Hardman, C.E. (2000) *Other Worlds. Notions of Self and Emotion Among the Lohorung Rai*. Oxford: Berg.

Harper, R.H.R., O'Hara, K.P.A., Sellen, A.J. and Duthie, D.J.R. (1997) 'Towards a paperless hospital?', *British Journal of Anaesthesia*, 78: 762–7.

Harris, R. (1996) *Selling Hitler. The Story of the Hitler Diaries*. London: Arnold.

Healy, D. (1997) *The Antidepressant Era*. Cambridge, MA: Harvard University Press.

Heidegger, M. (1967) *What Is a Thing?* Tr. W.B. Barton and V. Deutsch. Chicago: Henry Regnery.

Hertz, R. (1960) *Death and the Right Hand*. Tr. R. and C. Needham. London: Cohen & West.

Hindess, B. (1973) *The Use of Official Statistics in Sociology*. London: Macmillan.

Houtkoup-Steenstra, H. (2000) *Interaction and the Standardized Survey Interview*. Cambridge: Cambridge University Press.

Howells, C. (1998) *Derrida. Deconstruction: From Phenomenology to Ethics*. Cambridge: Polity Press.

Hughes, D. and Griffiths, L. (1999) 'On penalties and the *Patient's Charter*: centralism v de-centralised governance in the NHS', *Sociology of Health and Illness*, 21 (1): 71–94.

Hughes, T.P. (1989) 'The evolution of large technological systems', in W.E. Bijker, T. Pinch and T.P. Hughes (eds), *The Social Construction of Technological Systems*. Cambridge, MA: MIT Press. pp. 51–82.

Iser, W. (1989) *Prospecting. From Reader Response to Literary Anthropology*. Baltimore, MD: Johns Hopkins University Press.

Jackson, H.J. (2001) *Marginalia. Readers Writing in Books*. New Haven, CT: Yale University Press.

Jones, E. (1964) *The Life and Work of Sigmund Freud*. Ed. L. Trilling and S. Marcus. Harmondsworth: Penguin.

Jönsson, L. and Linell, P. (1991) 'Story generations: From dialogical interviews to written reports in police interrogations'. *Text*, 11 (3): 19–40.

Jordan, M. (1995) *The Encyclopaedia of Fungi of Britain and Europe*. Newton Abbot: David and Charles.

Kapuściński, R. (2001) 'Death in Sudan'. Tr. K. Glowczewska. *New York Review of Books*, 48 (7): 4–6.

Keating, P. and Cambrosio, A. (2000) '"Real compared to what?" Diagnosing leukemias and lymphomas', in M. Lock, A. Young and A. Cambrosio (eds), *Living and Working with the New Medical Technologies. Intersections of Inquiry*. Cambridge: Cambridge University Press. pp. 103–34.

Keller, E.F. (2000) *The Century of the Gene*. Cambridge, MA: Harvard University Press.

Klockars, C.B. (1975) *The Professional Fence*. London: Tavistock.

Kluckhohn, C. (1945) 'The personal document in anthropological science', in L. Gottschalk, C. Kluckhohn and R. Angell (eds), *The Use of Personal Documents in History, Anthropology, and Sociology*. New York: Social Science Research Council Bulletin, 53: 78–173.

Knorr-Cetina, K.D. (1983) 'The ethnographic study of scientific work. Towards a constructivist interpretation of science', in K.D. Knorr-Cetina and M. Mulkay (eds), *Science Observed*. London: Sage. pp. 115–40.

Knox, B. (1990) 'Introduction', in Homer. *The Illiad*. Tr. Robert Fagles. New York: Viking Penguin.

Knox, B. (1996) 'Introduction', in Homer. *The Odyssey*. Tr. Robert Fagles. London: Viking.

Kress, G., Leite-Garcia, R. and van Leeuwen, T, (1997) 'Discourse semiotics', in T.A. van Dijk (ed.), *Discourse as Structure and Process. Vol. 1*. London: Sage. pp. 257–91.

Kristeva, J. (1980) *Desire in Language. A Semiotic Approach to Literature and Art*. New York: Columbia University Press.

Kwaśnik, B.H. (1991) 'The importance of factors that are not document attributes in the organization of personal documents'. *Journal of Documentation*, 47 (4): 389–98.

Langness, L.L. (1965) *The Life History in Anthropological Science*. New York: Holt, Rinehart and Winston.

Latour, B. (1983) 'Give me a laboratory and I will raise the world', in K.D. Knorr-Cetina and M. Mulkay (eds), *Science Observed*. London: Sage. pp. 141–70.

Latour, B. (1987) *Science in Action. How to Follow Engineers and Scientists Through Society*. Buckingham: Open University Press.

Latour, B. (1988) *The Pasteurization of France*. Tr. A. Sheridan. London: Harvard University Press.

Latour, B. and Woolgar, S. (1979) *Laboratory Life. The Social Construction of Scientific Facts*. London: Sage.

Law, J. (1994) *Organising Modernity*. Oxford: Blackwell.

Law, J. and Hassard, J. (eds) (1999) *Actor-Network Theory and After*. Oxford: Blackwell.

Lepper, G. (2000) *Categories in Text and Talk*. London: Sage.

Lévi-Strauss, C. (1969) *Totemism*. Tr. R. Needham. Harmondsworth: Penguin.

Levitas, R. and Guy, M. (eds) (1996) *Interpreting Official Statistics*. London: Routledge.

Lewis, G. (1975) *Knowledge of Illness in a Sepik Society. A study of the Gnau, New Guinea*. London: Athlone Press.

Lidchi, H. (1997) 'The poetics and politics of exhibiting other cultures', in S. Hall (ed.), *Representation. Cultural Representations and Signifying Practices*. London: Sage. pp. 151–222.

Lieberson, S. (1992) 'Small N's and big conclusions. An examination of the reasoning in comparative studies based on a small number of cases', in C.C. Ragin and H.S. Becker (eds), *What is a Case? Exploring the Foundations of Social Inquiry*. Cambridge: Cambridge University Press. pp. 10–118.

Lienhardt, G. (1961) *Divinity and Experience. The Religion of the Dinka*. Oxford: Oxford University Press.

Lincoln, Y.S. and Gubba, E.G. (1985) *Naturalistic Inquiry*. Beverly Hills, CA: Sage.

Lynch, M. (1985) *Art and Artifact in Laboratory Science. A Study of Shop Work and Shop Talk in a Research Laboratory*. London: Routledge & Kegan Paul.

Lynch, M. (1990) 'The externalized retina: Section and mathematization in the visual documentation of objects in the life sciences', in M. Lynch and S. Woolgar (eds), *Representation in Scientific Practice*. London: MIT Press. pp. 153–86.

Lynd, R.S. and Lynd, H.M. (1929) *Middletown*. New York: Harcourt, Brace.

Mächler, S. (2001) *The Wilkomirski Affair. A Study in Biographical Truth*. Tr. J.E. Woods. New York: Schocken Books.

Mackay, H. (1997) 'Consuming communication technologies at home', in H. Mackay (ed.), *Consumption and Everyday Life*. London: Sage.

Madge, J. (1963) *The Origins of Scientific Sociology*. London: Tavistock.

Malinowski, B. (1922) *Argonauts of the Western Pacific*. London: Routledge.

Malinowski, B. (1935) *Coral Gardens and their Magic*. London: George Allen and Unwin.

Malinowski, B. (1967) *A Diary in the Strict Sense of the Term*. Tr. N. Guterman. London: Routledge & Kegan Paul.

Matthews, J.R. (1995) *Quantification and the Quest for Medical Certainty*. Princeton, NJ: Princeton University Press.

Mattingly, C. and Garro, L.C. (eds) (2000) *Narrative and the Cultural Construction of Illness and Healing*. Berkeley, CA: University of California Press.

Mead, G.H. (1934) *Mind, Self and Society from the Standpoint of a Social Behaviorist*. Ed. C.W. Morris. Chicago: University of Chicago Press.

Mead, M. (1928) *Coming of Age in Samoa. A Psychological Study of Primitive Youth for Western Civilization*. New York: William Morrow.

Meltzer, H., Gill, B., Petticrew, M. and Hinds, K. (1995) *The Prevalence of Psychiatric Morbidity among Adults Living in Private Households. OPCS Surveys of Psychiatric Morbidity in Great Britain. Report 1*. London: HMSO.

Miles, C. and Irvine, J. (1979) 'The critique of official statistics', in J. Irvine, C. Miles and I. Evans (eds), *Demystifying Official Statistics*. London: Pluto.

Mill, J.S. (1843) *A System of Logic, Ratiocinative and Inductive. Being a Connected View of the Principles of Evidence, and the Methods of Scientific Investigations*. London: Parker.

Mill, J.S. (1989) *Autobiography*. London: Penguin.

Miller, N. and Morgan, D. (1993) 'Called to account: The CV as an autobiographical practice', *Sociology*, 27 (1): 133–43.

Ministry of Health (1954) *Reports on Public Health and Medical Subjects. No. 95. Mortality and Morbidity during the London Fog of December 1952*. London: HMSO.

Mol, A. (1999) 'Ontological politics. A word and some questions', in J. Law and J. Hassard (eds), *Actor Network Theory and After*. Oxford: Blackwell. pp. 75–89.

Mol, A. (2000) 'Pathology and the clinic. An ethnographic presentation of two athero-scleroses', in M. Lock, A. Young and A. Cambrosio (eds), *Living and Working with the New Medical Technologies. Intersections of Inquiry*. Cambridge: Cambridge University Press. pp. 82–102.

Monaghan, L. (2001) *Bodybuilding Drugs and Risk*. London: Routledge.

Murphy, F.A., Fauquet, C.M., Bishop, D., Ghabrial, S., Jarvis, A., Martelli, G., Mayo, M. and Summers, M. (eds) (1995) *Virus Taxonomy. Classification and Nomenclature of Viruses. Sixth Report of the International Committee on Taxonomy of Viruses. Virology Division. International Union of Microbiological Societies.* Vienna: Springer Verlag.

Myers, G. (1990) *Writing Biology. Texts in the Construction of Scientific Knowledge*. London: University of Wisconsin Press.

Nagel, E. (1961) *The Structure of Science*. London: Routledge & Kegan Paul.

NHS Executive (1994) *Guidance on the Discharge of Mentally Disordered People and their Continuing Care in the Community*. HSG(94)27/LASL(94)4. London: Department of Health.

Nukuga, Y. (2002) 'Between tradition and innovation in new genetics: The continuity of medical pedigrees and the development of combination work in the case of Huntington's disease'. *New Genetics and Society*, 21 (1): 39–64.

Nukuga, Y. and Cambrosio, A. (1997) 'Medical pedigrees and the visual production of family disease in Canadian and Japanese genetic counselling practice', *Sociology of Health and Illness*, 19 (5): 29–55.

Oakley, A. (1981) 'Interviewing women. A contradiction in terms', in H. Roberts (ed.), *Doing Feminist Research*. London: Routledge & Kegan Paul.

Ong, W.J. (1982) *Orality and Literacy. The Technologizing of the Word*. London: Methuen.

Outhwaite, W. (1975) *Understanding Social Life. The Method Called Verstehen*. London: Allen and Unwin.

Pepys, S. (1970) *The Diary of Samuel Pepys. 11 Vols*. Ed. R. Latham and W. Mathews. Berkeley, CA: University of California Press.

Phillips, T. (ed.) (1995) *Africa. The Art of a Continent*. London: Prestel Verlag.

Philo, G. (ed.) (1996) *Media and Mental Distress*. London: Longman.

Pilnick, A. (2002) *Genetics and Society. An Introduction*. Buckingham: Open University Press.

Pinch, T.J. and Bijker, W.E. (1989) 'The social construction of facts and artifacts: Or how the sociology of science and the sociology of technology might benefit each other' in W.E. Bijker, T.P. Hughes and T. Pinch, (eds), *The Social Construction of Technological Systems*. Cambridge, MA: MIT Press. pp. 17–50.

Platt, J. (1981a) 'Evidence and proof in documentary research. Some shared problems of documentary research'. *Sociological Review*, 29 (1): 31–52.

Platt, J. (1981b) 'Evidence and proof in documentary research. Some shared problems of documentary research'. *Sociological Review*, 29 (1): 53–66.

Platt, J. (1996) *A History of Sociological Research Methods in America. 1920–1960*. Cambridge: Cambridge University Press.

Plummer, K. (2001) *Documents of Life. 2. An Invitation to Critical Humanism*. London: Sage.

Poole, R. (1969) 'Introduction', in C. Lévi-Strauss. *Totemism*. Tr. R. Needham. Harmondsworth: Penguin.

Popper, K.R. (1959) *The Logic of Scientific Discovery*. London: Hutchinson.

Popper, K.R. (1963) *Conjectures and Refutations. Growth of Scientific Knowledge*. London: Routledge.

Porter, T.M. (1994) 'Information, power and the view from nowhere', in L. Bud-Frierman (ed.), *Information Acumen. The Understanding and Use of Knowledge in Modern Business*. London: Routledge. pp. 217–30.

Potter, J. (1996) *Representing Reality. Discourse, Rhetoric and Social Construction*. London: Sage.

Prior, L. (1988) 'The architecture of the hospital. A study in spatial organisation and medical knowledge', *British Journal of Sociology*. 39 (March): 86–115.

Prior, L. (1989) *The Social Organization of Death*. Basingstoke: Macmillan.

Prior, L. (1992) 'The local space of medical knowledge. Disease, illness and hospital architecture', in J. Lachmund and G. Stollberg (eds), *The Social Construction of Illness*. Stuttgart: Franz Steiner Verlag. pp. 67–84.

Prior, L. (1993) *The Social Organization of Mental Illness*. London and Newbury Park, CA: Sage.

Prior, L. (1997) 'Following in Foucault's footsteps. Text and context in qualitative research', in D. Silverman (ed.), *Qualitative Analysis. Issues of Theory and Method*. Sage. pp. 63–79.

Prior, L., Pang, L.C. and See, B.H. (2000) 'Beliefs and accounts of illness. Views from two Cantonese speaking communities in England', *Sociology of Health and Illness*, 22 (6): 815–39.

Prior, L., Wood, F., Gray, J., Pill, R. and Hughes, D. (2002) 'Making risk visible: The role of images in the assessment of (cancer) genetic risk. *Health, Risk and Society*, 4 (3).

Proctor, R.N. (1995) *Cancer Wars*. New York: Basic Books.

Psathas, G. (1979) 'Organizational features of direction maps', in G. Psathas (ed.), *Everyday Language. Studies in Ethnomethodology*. New York: Irvington. pp. 203–25.

Putnam, H. (1988) *Representation and Reality*. Cambridge, MA: MIT Press.

Quine, V.W. (1953) *From a Logical Point of View. 9 Logico-Philosophical Essays*. Cambridge, MA: Harvard University Press.

Rabinow, P. (1977) *Reflections on Fieldwork in Morocco*. London: University of California Press.

Radcliffe-Brown, A.R. (1922) *The Andaman Islanders. A Study in Social Anthropology*. Cambridge: Cambridge University Press.

Radcliffe-Brown, A.R. (1958) 'The method of ethnology and social anthropology', in M.N. Srinivas (ed.), *Method in Social Anthropology*. Chicago: Chicago University Press.

Ragin, C.C. (1992) 'Introduction', in C.C. Ragin and H.S. Becker (eds), *What is A Case?*. Cambridge: Cambridge University Press. pp. 1–17.

Rapp, R. (2000) *Testing women, Testing the Fetus. The Social Impact of Amniocentesis in America*. New York: Routledge.

Reiner, R. (1996) 'The case of the missing crimes', in R. Levitas and M. Guy (eds), *Interpreting Official Statistics*. London: Routledge.

Reinharz, S. (1992) 'Feminist interviewing', in *Feminist Methods in Social Research*. Oxford: Oxford University Press.

Reith, M. (1998) *Community Care Tragedies*. London: Venture Press.

Richards, L. (1999) *Using NVivo in Qualitative Research*. Thousand Oaks, CA: Sage.

Ricoeur, P. (1977) 'The model of the text. Meaningful action considered as a text', in F. Dallmayr and T. McCarthey (eds), *Understanding and Social Inquiry*. Notre Dame, IN: Notre Dame University Press.

Ricoeur, P. (1981) *Hermeneutics and the Human Sciences*. Ed. tr. and intro. J.B. Thompson. Cambridge: Cambridge University Press.

Ridpath, I. (ed.) (1989) *Norton's 2000.0. Star Atlas and Reference Handbook*. 18th edition. Harlow: Longman.

Ritchie, J.H., Dick, D. and Lingham, R. (1994) *The Report of the Inquiry into the Care and Treatment of Christopher Clunis*. London: HMSO.

Ritvo, H. (1997) *The Platypus and the Mermaid, and Other Figments of the Classifying Imagination*. Cambridge, MA: MIT Press.

Rousseau, J.-J. (2000) *Confessions*. Tr. A. Scholar. Oxford: Oxford University Press.

Royal College of Physicians, Royal College of Psychiatrists and Royal College of General Practitioners (1996) *Chronic Fatigue Syndrome: Report of a Joint Working Group of the Royal Colleges of Physicians, Psychiatrists and General Practitioners*. London: Royal College of Physicians.

Ryan, G.W. and Bernard, H.R. (2000) 'Data management and analysis methods', in N.K. Denzin and Y.S. Lincoln (eds), *Handbook of Qualitative Research*. 2nd edition. Thousand Oaks, CA: Sage. pp. 769–802.

Ryle, G. (1990) *The Concept of Mind*. Harmondsworth: Penguin.

Sackett, D.L. (2000) *Evidence-based Medicine. How to Practice and Teach EBM*. Edinburgh: Churchill Livingstone.

Sacks, H. (1984) 'On doing "being ordinary"', in J.M. Atkinson and J. Heritage (eds), *Structures of Social Action. Studies in Conversational Analysis*. Cambridge: Cambridge University Press.

Sacks, O. (1986) *The Man who Mistook his Wife for a Hat*. London: Picador.

Sacks, H. (1992) *Lectures of Conversation. 2 Vols*. Oxford: Blackwell.

Sarangi, S. (1998) 'Rethinking recontextualization in professional discourse studies. An epilogue', *Text*, 18: (2): 301–18.

Saussure, F. de (1983) *Course in General Linguistics*. Ed. C. Bally and A. Sechehave in collaboration with A. Riedlinger. Tr. R. Harris. London: Duckworth.

Schreiber, F.R. (1974) *Sybil*. London: Allen Lane.

Schutz, A. (1962) *Collected Papers. Vol. 1. The Problem of Social Reality*. The Hague: Martinus Nijhoff.

Scott, J. (1990) *A Matter of Record*. Cambridge: Polity Press.

Scott, M.B. and Lyman, S.M. (1968) 'Accounts', *American Sociological Review*, 33: 46–62.

Seale, C. (1998) *Constructing Death. The Sociology of Dying and Bereavement*. Cambridge: Cambridge University Press.

Seale, C. (1999) *The Quality of Qualitative Research*. London: Sage.

Seale, C. (2001) 'Sporting cancer. Struggle language in news reports of people with cancer', *Sociology of Health and Illness*, 23 (3): 308–29.

Serres, M. (1995) *Conversations on Science, Culture and Time*. With Bruno Latour. Tr. R. Lapidus. Ann Arbor, MI: The University of Michigan Press.

Sharpe, K. (2000) *Reading Revolutions. The Politics of Reading in Early Modern England*. New Haven, CT: Yale University Press.

Shaw, C.R. (1931) *The Natural History of a Delinquent Career*. Chicago. University of Chicago Press.

Shelley, M.W. (1996) *Frankenstein or the Modern Prometheus*. London: Pickering and Chatto.

Silverman, D. (1993) *Interpreting Qualitative Data. Methods for Analysing Talk, Text and Interaction*. London: Sage.

Silverman, D. (ed.) (1996) *Qualitative Research. Theory, Method and Practice*. London: Sage.

Silverman, D. (1998) *Harvey Sacks. Social Science and Conversation Analysis*. Cambridge: Polity Press.

Simmons, W. (ed.) (1942) *Sun Chief. The Autobiography of a Hopi Indian*. New Haven, CT: Yale University Institute of Human Relations.

Skolbekken, J.-A. (1995) 'The risk epidemic in medical journals', *Social Science and Medicine*, 40: 291–305.

Smith, D. (1978) 'K is mentally ill. The anatomy of a factual account', *Sociology*, 12: 23–53.

Smith, D.E. (1984) 'Textually mediated social organization', *International Journal of Social Science*, 36 (1): 59–75.

Smith, D.E. (1990) *Texts, Facts and Femininity. Exploring the Relations of Ruling*. London: Routledge.

Smith, R. (1997a) 'Authorship. Time for a paradigm shift', *British Medical Journal*. 314: 992.

Smith, R. (1997b) 'Authorship is dying. Long live contributorship', *British Medical Journal*, 315: 696.

Smith, S. and Watson, J. (eds) (1992) *De/colonizing the Subject. The Politics of Gender in Women's Autobiography*. Minneapolis: University of Minnesota Press.

Sontag, S. (1978) *Illness As Metaphor*. New York: Farrar, Strauss and Giroux.

Spiegel, H. (1997) 'Sybil – the making of a disease', *New York Review of Books*, XLIV (7): 60–4.

Spiegelman, D., Colditz, G.A., Hunter, D. and Hertzmark, E. (1994) 'Validation of the Gail et al., model for predicting individual breast cancer risk', *Journal of the National Cancer Institute*, 86: 600–8.

Stanley, L. and Morgan, D. (eds) (1993) 'Biography and autobiography in sociology', *Sociology*, 27 (1): 1–197.

Stannard, D.E. (1977) *The Puritan Way of Death*. New York: Oxford University Press.

Star, S.L. (1989) 'The structure of ill-structured solutions: Boundary objects and heterogeneous distributed problem solving', in M. Hunhs and L. Casser (eds), *Distributed Artificial Intelligence 2*. London: Pitman. pp. 37–54.

Star, S.L. and Griesemer, J.R. (1989) 'Institutional ecology "translations" and boundary objects. Amateurs and professionals in Berkeley's Museum Vertebrate Zoology, 1907–39', *Social Studies of Science*, 19: 387–420.

Stocking, G.W. (1983) 'The ethnographer's magic', in G.W. Stocking (ed.), *Observers Observed*. Madison, WI: University of Wisconsin Press. pp. 70–118.

Sullivan, G. (1999) *Margaret Mead, Gregory Bateson, and Highland Bali. Fieldwork Photographs of Bayung Gedé, 1936–1939*. Chicago: University of Chicago Press.

Sutherland, E.H. (1937) *The Professional Thief by a Professional Thief*. Chicago: University of Chicago Press.

Tambiah, S.J. (1968) 'Literacy in a Buddhist village in North-east Thailand', in J. Goody (ed.), *Literacy in Traditional Societies*. Cambridge: Cambridge University Press. pp. 86–131.

Taylor, C. (1987) 'Interpretation and the sciences of man', in P. Rabinow and M.W. Sullivan (eds), *Interpretive Social Science. A Second Look*. London: University of California Press. pp. 33–81.

Taylor, S. (1982) *Durkheim and the Study of Suicide*. London: Macmillan.

Tedlock, B. (2000) 'Ethnography and ethnographic representation', in N.K. Denzin and Y.S. Lincoln (eds), *Handbook of Qualitative Research*. 2nd edition. Thousand Oaks. CA: Sage. pp. 455–86.

Thigpen, C.H. and Cleckley, H. (1957) *The Three Faces of Eve*. New York: McGraw-Hill.

Thomas, W.I. and Znaniecki, F. (1958) *The Polish Peasant in Europe and America*. New York: Dover.

Thrasher, F.M. (1927) *The Gang. A Study of 1,313 Gangs in Chicago*. Chicago: University of Chicago Press.

Tischkowitz, M., Wheeler, D., France, E., Chapman, C., Lucassen, A., Sampson, J., Harper, P., Krawczak, M. and Gray, J. (2000) 'A comparison of methods currently used in clinical practice to estimate familial breast cancer risks', *Annals of Oncology*, 11 (4): 451–4.

Tolstoy, Leo (1889) *War and Peace*. Tr. N.H. Dole. London: Walter Scott.

Torfing, J. (1999) *New Theories of Discourse. Laclau, Mouffe and Zizek*. Oxford: Blackwell.

Tukey, J.W. (1977) *Exploratory Data Analysis*. New York: Addison-Wesley.

Tylor, E.B. (1871) *Primitive Culture. 2 Vols*. London: John Murray.

Unwin, N., Carr, S. and Leeson, J. (1997) *An Introductory Study Guide to Public Health and Epidemiology*. Buckingham: Open University Press.

van Dijk, T.A. (ed.) (1997) *Discourse as Structure and Process. 2 Vols*. London: Sage.

van Maanen, J. (1988) *Tales of the Field*. Chicago: University of Chicago Press.

Vaughan, D. (1983) *Controlling Unlawful Organizational Behavior. Social Structure and Corporate Misconduct*. Chicago: University of Chicago Press.

Vaughan, D. (1996) *The Challenger Launch Decision. Risky Technology, Culture, and Deviance at NASA*. London: University of Chicago Press.

Vaughan, D. (1999) 'The Role of the organization in the production of techno-scientific knowledge', *Social Studies of Science*, 29 (6): 913–43.

von Goethe, J.W. (1986) *Faust. Part One*. Tr. P. Wayne. Harmondsworth: Penguin.

Watson, G. and Seiler, R.M. (eds) (1992) *Text in Context. Contributions to Ethnomethodology*. London: Sage.

Watson, L.C. and Watson-Franke, M.B. (1985) *Interpreting Life Histories. An Anthropological Inquiry*. New Brunswick, NJ: Transaction Books.

Weber, M. (1930) *The Protestant Ethic and the Spirit of Capitalism*. Tr. T. Parsons. London: Unwin.

Weber, M. (1979) *Economy and Society. 2 Vols*. Ed. G. Roth and C. Wittich. Berkeley, CA: University of California Press.

Weber, R.P. (1990) *Basic Content Analysis*. Newbury Park, CA: Sage.

Webster, A. (1991) *Science, Technology and Society*. Basingstoke: Macmillan.

Weiner, A., Wessely, S. and Lewis, G. (1999) '"You don't give me flowers anymore". An analysis of gift-giving to medical and psychiatric inpatients', *Social Psychiatry and Psychiatric Epidemiology*. 34: 136–40.

Wheeler, S. (ed.) (1969) *On Record. Files and Dossiers in American Life*. New York: Russell Sage Foundation.

Whyte, W.F. (1955) *Street Corner Society*. Chicago: Chicago University Press.

Wilkomirski, B. (1996) *Fragments. Memories of a Childhood, 1939–1948*. Tr. C.B. Janeway. London: Picador.

Wittgenstein, L. (1958) *Preliminary Studies for the 'Philosophical Investigations'*. Ed. R. Rees. Oxford: Blackwell.

Woolgar, S. (1981) 'Discovery. Logic and sequence in a scientific text', in K.D. Knorr and R. Krohn (eds), *The Social Process of Scientific Investigation*. Dordrecht: D. Reidel. pp. 239–68.

Woolgar, S. (1988) *Science. The Very Idea*. London: Tavistock.

World Health Organization (1992) *International Statistical Classification of Diseases and Related Health Problems. 10th. Revision. 3 Vols*. London: HMSO.

World Health Organization (1998) *World Health Statistics Annual. 1996*. WHO: Geneva.

Yin, R.K. (1994) *Case Study Research. Design and Methods.* 2nd edition. London: Sage.

Young, A. (1995) *The Harmony of Illusions. Inventing Post-traumatic Stress Disorder.* Princeton, NJ: Princeton University Press.

Zerubavel, E. (1979) *Patterns of Time in Hospital Life. A Sociological Perspective.* London: University of Chicago Press.

Zhukov, G.K. (1971) *The Memoirs of Marshal Zhukov.* London: Cape.

Zimmerman, D.H. (1969) 'Record-keeping and the intake process in a public welfare agency', in S. Wheeler (ed.), *On Record. Files and Dossiers in American Life.* New York: Russell Sage Foundation. pp. 319–45.

Zimmerman, D.H. and Pollner, M. (1971) 'The everyday world as a phenomenon', in J.D. Douglas (ed.), *Understanding Everyday Life.* London: Routledge & Kegan Paul. pp. 80–103.

Zorbaugh, H.W. (1929) *The Gold Coast and the Slum. A Sociological Study of Chicago's Near North Side.* Chicago: University of Chicago Press.

Index